Beginning Microsoft 365 Collaboration Apps

Working in the Microsoft Cloud

Second Edition

Ralph Mercurio
Brian Merrill

Apress®

Beginning Microsoft 365 Collaboration Apps: Working in the Microsoft Cloud

Ralph Mercurio
Clayton, NC, USA

Brian Merrill
Morrisville, PA, USA

ISBN-13 (pbk): 978-1-4842-6935-0
https://doi.org/10.1007/978-1-4842-6936-7

ISBN-13 (electronic): 978-1-4842-6936-7

Managing Director, Apress Media LLC: Welmoed Spahr
Acquisitions Editor: Joan Murray
Development Editor: Laura Berendson
Coordinating Editor: Jill Balzano

Cover image designed by Freepik (www.freepik.com)

Distributed to the book trade worldwide by Springer Science+Business Media LLC, 1 New York Plaza, Suite 4600, New York, NY 10004. Phone 1-800-SPRINGER, fax (201) 348-4505, e-mail orders-ny@springer-sbm.com, or visit www.springeronline.com. Apress Media, LLC is a California LLC and the sole member (owner) is Springer Science + Business Media Finance Inc (SSBM Finance Inc). SSBM Finance Inc is a **Delaware** corporation.

For information on translations, please e-mail booktranslations@springernature.com; for reprint, paperback, or audio rights, please e-mail bookpermissions@springernature.com.

Apress titles may be purchased in bulk for academic, corporate, or promotional use. eBook versions and licenses are also available for most titles. For more information, reference our Print and eBook Bulk Sales web page at http://www.apress.com/bulk-sales.

Any source code or other supplementary material referenced by the author in this book is available to readers on GitHub via the book's product page, located at www.apress.com/9781484269350. For more detailed information, please visit http://www.apress.com/source-code.

Printed on acid-free paper

To my wife, Sarah: Thank you for always being in my corner.
I love you more and more every day.
To our children, Bobby and Julia: You have made me so proud,
and I am excited for the future for both of you. I love you.
—Ralph

To Meredith: Thank you for your love and support.
I love you more today than yesterday!
To our beautiful children, Charlotte, Bridget, Brian, and Erin:
Keep shining brightly!
—Brian

Table of Contents

About the Authors

 **Ralph Mercurio** is a Microsoft Certified Professional with 18 years of experience. He works for the City of Durham in North Carolina and focuses his efforts on providing collaborative solutions to its many departments. He has held various roles in the technology field, including as a SharePoint infrastructure architect consulting for various companies in the New York City metro area.

Ralph also has experience architecting and deploying solutions that leverage the best features of Microsoft 365 and provide real business value while solving user experience issues. He has seen many technology changes throughout the years, and he discovered a passion for helping users find ways to leverage what they need to know to learn a new technology. With Microsoft 365, he has made it his goal to help users realize the potential of this powerful platform in order to get the most out of these ever-changing applications.

Brian Merrill is a Microsoft Certified Educator (MCE) and a Microsoft Certified Trainer (MCT). He is currently the educational technology analyst for one of the largest school districts in Pennsylvania. In that role, he serves as the global administrator of the district's Microsoft 365 environment, managing Microsoft Teams and SharePoint and training faculty and staff on new technologies and systems. Brian is also adjunct faculty at the Harrisburg University of Science and Technology, where he teaches courses in the Learning Technology and Media Studies program. He also teaches courses on learning technologies and solutions as well as Microsoft tools. Brian is a Microsoft Innovative Educator Expert and a member of the Minecraft for Education Advisory Board.

About the Technical Reviewer

 **Jesse Roos** has worked in numerous information technology roles since the year 2001. Jesse has a lifelong passion for technology that started with building computers at the age of 8 and building websites by age 10.

He has served in many roles from data processing, technical support, and telecommunications to network and server administration. For the last 15 years, Jesse has worked for the Central Bucks School District in Pennsylvania, where he currently serves as Senior Network Administrator.

He has been administering Microsoft 365 since the beginning when it was called Live@edu. Jesse now specializes in administering all aspects of Microsoft's cloud platforms including Microsoft 365, Azure, and Intune.

Acknowledgments

I would like to extend a thank you to Jill Balzano, Joan Murray, and the rest of the team at Apress for your patience and guidance in writing the second edition of this book.
I thought the first time writing this book was daunting, but the second time seemed just as hard.

I would also like to acknowledge Brian Merrill, my co-author on this book. I appreciate his persistence and help in writing the content for this book. I truly believe he added value and hope you will find it valuable as well.

Finally, I would also like to thank the technical reviewer, Jesse Roos, for his work reviewing the chapters quickly to ensure their technical accuracy.

—Ralph Mercurio

Introduction

Microsoft 365 is Microsoft's SaaS (Software as a Service) platform. It offers Outlook, SharePoint, OneDrive, Office, and other collaboration applications to help businesses and other entities use the cloud to provide these applications to their users.

By utilizing Microsoft 365, entities can offer low-cost access and reduce the administrative and IT overhead associated with providing these services. By doing so, end users gain access to updated applications without having to wait and can utilize these new features or applications once Microsoft releases them. However, many users are not adequately trained in using these applications, and without a foundational understanding of them, these applications can be overwhelming. Because of this ever-increasing issue, this book attempts to bridge the gap for end users new to the Microsoft 365 platform as well as for more advanced users by providing a functional understanding of each application in the Microsoft 365 suite.

As Microsoft 365 evolves and Microsoft releases new features or applications, feel free to reach out to me via LinkedIn or by contacting me at `ralph@capelesssolutions.com` or visit my website, `capelesssolutions.com`.

Who This Book Is For

The goal and purpose of this book is to provide the knowledge to use Microsoft 365, particularly around the collaboration apps described in the following. These applications form the foundation of Microsoft 365, and each chapter guides you through the basics of them via text and images.

This book also serves as a resource to users who have been introduced to Microsoft 365 but are still unfamiliar with many of the applications. This book does not require a subscription to Microsoft 365, but having one will allow you to follow along as we dive into each collaboration application.

If you are a reader of the previous edition of this book, then perhaps seeing Microsoft 365 in the title might seem a little strange. In the not too distant past, "Microsoft 365" was referred to as "Office 365," a name a lot of us got pretty used to and the name many users still reference. However, to keep current and stay in tune with Microsoft's latest naming conventions, we will use "Microsoft 365" throughout the book.

How This Book Is Structured

This book is organized by chapters, with each chapter introducing a particular collaboration app in Microsoft 365. This was done on purpose because it will allow you to read the chapters that interest you most or that cover the application you are currently using – without the need to read the entire book cover to cover. This book includes step-by-step instructions, images, tables, and examples detailing the features of each application.

Chapter 1: Welcome to Microsoft 365

This chapter introduces you to the concept of Microsoft 365 and SaaS. It also guides you through creating a Microsoft 365 trial account, if needed.

Chapter 2: SharePoint Online

This chapter provides an overview of creating lists, libraries, and sites. It also introduces some of the basic principles such as list/library columns, metadata, views, and the available templates to use.

Chapter 3: OneDrive

This chapter covers OneDrive and how to navigate around OneDrive and use it effectively to manage your files. This chapter also shows how to create Office files within OneDrive and how to share files with users.

Chapter 4: Microsoft 365 Groups

This chapter discusses the components of a Microsoft 365 group as well as how to create and maintain a group. It also shows you how to manage users and invite external users.

Chapter 5: Teams

This chapter introduces Teams and provides a functional understanding of the application. You learn how to navigate within Teams and understand the interface. This chapter also discusses creating teams and channels and using some of the basic functions included in Teams.

Chapter 6: Yammer

This chapter details using Yammer within an enterprise environment. It discusses the Yammer interface and creating posts that can be shared with users.

Chapter 7: Office

This chapter introduces Office and Office Online. It discusses some of the similarities and differences between the versions. It also demonstrates some of the advanced capabilities of the platform including real-time co-authoring.

Chapter 8: Planner

This chapter introduces Microsoft Planner and is concerned with task management. It covers the basics of Planner, including creating tasks, editing tasks, deleting tasks, and reporting on task statuses.

Chapter 9: Stream

This chapter introduces Microsoft Stream, an enterprise-capable video platform, and some of the basic functions within Stream. This chapter also discusses some of the advanced features of Stream and how to access them.

Chapter 10: Forms

This chapter introduces Microsoft Forms, an application to create a variety of browser- and mobile-ready forms. You can create forms, surveys, and quizzes. You also learn about some of the features within the application, such as data types, reporting, and grading.

Chapter 11: Power Automate

This chapter demonstrates how to utilize Microsoft Power Automate, from a simple flow to a complex flow. It will guide you through creating a flow. You will create an approval flow and a flow that incorporates a third-party service for electronic signatures.

Chapter 12: Power BI

This chapter serves as an introduction to Microsoft Power BI, the data analytics platform of Microsoft 365. Power BI is a very powerful application that can use multiple data sources and pull the data into convenient dashboards to be consumed.

Chapter 13: Power Apps

In this chapter, we will introduce Microsoft Power Apps and walk through two examples: creating a PowerApp and editing a SharePoint list form.

Chapter 14: Making Sense of It All

This chapter serves as a summary chapter, highlighting each application and its intended purpose within Microsoft 365.

PART I

Getting Started

CHAPTER 1

Welcome to Microsoft 365

Welcome to *Beginning Microsoft 365 Collaboration Apps*. My intention with this book is to introduce the concepts behind Microsoft 365, how it works, and what it can offer you regarding functionality, collaboration, and ease of use. There are many applications within Microsoft 365, and I will focus on the specific applications that foster collaboration, dedicating a chapter to each.

In this book, I will discuss SharePoint, OneDrive, Teams, Office, and a few other applications that make up Microsoft 365. I will also introduce two relatively new applications from Microsoft: Stream and Power Automate. Microsoft Stream is a video sharing and collaboration application; Power Automate connects workflow actions across most of Microsoft 365 and external applications.

In this chapter, I will approach Microsoft 365 from a very high level, including a perspective on collaboration and how it has evolved throughout the years. It is important to understand and acknowledge the past and present as Microsoft 365 lays the foundation for workplace collaboration in the future. I will also discuss how to set up a Microsoft 365 account so that you can experiment and follow along. I am a firm believer in doing as opposed to reading because it reinforces the content and allows you to become familiar with and confident in the interface and nuances of Microsoft 365.

As we navigate through the various chapters of this book, please be aware that Microsoft has changed the name of the product from Office 365 to Microsoft 365. This change aligns the platform with its use and eases some of the confusion of the old name. Due to this change, some parts of the platform have not been fully updated by Microsoft with regard to the name change, but for our purposes we will refer to the platform as Microsoft 365.

© Ralph Mercurio and Brian Merrill 2021
R. Mercurio and B. Merrill, *Beginning Microsoft 365 Collaboration Apps*,
https://doi.org/10.1007/978-1-4842-6936-7_1

Collaboration in the Workplace

Collaboration has changed over the years from a rigid structure to a more flexible model that embraces technology and allows information workers to have more freedom and control over getting their work completed. Microsoft classifies information workers as employees who consume and create content. This includes nearly every department of an organization; some examples of content are budgets, employee records, project documents, technical guides, and forms. With that, not all companies embrace the model, and they prefer (sometimes strongly) that employees report to a company office location to perform their duties.

As we all are aware, the global pandemic of 2020 has brought on a new way of working. The Covid-19 pandemic quickly changed the way corporate leaders thought of remote work, the safety and well-being of their employees, and the acceptance of technology, which has fundamentally shifted the way we work today.

Overnight, information workers found themselves in a new way of working, and IT departments scrambled to find ways to connect people back to work. For many companies, Microsoft 365 was the chosen platform to enable information workers to be productive and have access to the information they needed.

As technology has evolved outside the workplace and made our lives arguably easier, technology has also evolved inside the workplace as we are aware of it. In today's workplace, you can have a video conference with someone halfway around the world and see and hear them in high definition. You can also search and retrieve email messages from years ago or get your mail on your mobile device with all the bells and whistles you expect.

Part of the allure of Microsoft 365 is that the content you are interested in is searchable and relevant. Think back 20 years ago and how you found information before the introduction of search engines, notably Google. To think I once used Microsoft Encarta or asked for a ride to the library to access their collection of *Encyclopedia Britannica* volumes, it boggles my mind to this day. Now Microsoft 365 is capable of searching across email, SharePoint, OneDrive, and the other applications to ensure you find the relevant item; it is even capable of searching within the document to improve its relevancy.

In some cases, a VPN connection is still required to access large systems such as an ERP system, a billing system, and custom-built applications that aren't available outside of the company through a proxy or some other means. I won't touch base on Azure, which is another Microsoft offering for companies looking to use IaaS (Infrastructure as a Service).

Today's collaboration tools allow for the sharing of information, which ultimately improves processes, boosts the bottom line, and delivers well-executed projects. Individuals working in a silo can't bounce ideas off each other or seek out other experienced individuals and so must bear the cost of a poorly executed project.

An excellent example of how collaboration works is to think of a group of university professors aligning their resources and experiences to deliver a well-received article or a world-changing vaccine. If they worked in their isolated environments, their outcomes and innovations might be much less impactful.

In the business world, teams collaborate around the launch of a new product, which involves teams from marketing, technology, sales, and leadership. This type of activity may include geographically dispersed teams or team members in other offices around the world. Technology must bring them all together so the objectives can be met and the product gets to market.

Part of the design and success of Microsoft 365 is that it allows companies to have a digital workplace. It allows companies and employees to have the tools to not only collaborate but get work done on their time on a cloud-based platform supported by Microsoft. It provides applications around the way people need to work, whether that is document-based, email, chat, or video collaboration; Microsoft 365 moves the common applications we use daily to the cloud and allows us to use the tools and applications we need to get our job done.

Let's dig into Microsoft 365 and discuss its elements and why it makes business sense to move to it.

What Is Microsoft 365?

Microsoft 365 is Microsoft's SaaS offering for email, collaboration applications, and Office ProPlus. SaaS stands for Software as a Service. The easiest way to understand the concept is that you simply sign into a website and access the software instead of installing it locally on your PC or Apple device. Popular examples of SaaS are not only Microsoft 365 but QuickBooks and Salesforce.

With SaaS, there generally is no software to install; the vendor maintains and supplies the software, updates, and hardware needed to run the software. In turn, you simply pay a monthly fee, and you have access to the software or platform.

Microsoft 365 is Microsoft's biggest software endeavor yet and has been years in the making. For over 25 years, Microsoft has been developing software to be installed on a company's servers within a company's data center. This includes not only Microsoft Exchange (email) but also products like Microsoft SharePoint, which was first released in the early 2000s. This approach required companies to buy and maintain expensive server equipment and needed the appropriate technical staff to support the systems.

Microsoft 365 changes the game by removing the need to buy expensive servers or ensure that the IT staff are trained to administer and support the software. By transitioning to Microsoft 365, IT departments and personnel can now focus on providing solutions that can help a business grow instead of managing software and infrastructure.

How Does It Work?

Microsoft maintains data centers around the world in many different regions to be able to offer this service. Each data center contains thousands of servers in perfectly stacked arrays with multiple electrical connections, cooling equipment, on-site support, and all in a highly secure facility with various levels of protection. Because Microsoft provides all the hardware, it also maintains an extensive disaster recovery plan. If one of the data centers were to experience an outage or catastrophic event, Microsoft 365 and its users would see minimum disruption and minimal downtime, if any. This model is also supported by a financially backed service-level agreement (SLA), ensuring that if Microsoft doesn't maintain its agreed SLA, there is a financial penalty for the company.

But all of this doesn't matter because of the beauty of all it is that you simply go to Office.com from any major supported web browser and log in with your credentials. Once authenticated, you will be presented with a variety of applications to choose from. From an end user perspective, that is 100% correct, but let's take a brief look at what must happen first to make it a seamless experience for the end user.

In most cases, your company's IT department has already done the heavy lifting. This includes signing up for Microsoft 365, configuring the service, and licensing the end users so they can access the appropriate applications. I do want to touch upon a few key points that can affect the Microsoft 365 experience:

- Microsoft 365 comes in a variety of license levels, each with a different per-user cost. This book will focus on Microsoft 365 for Business and Microsoft 365 for Enterprise; some applications will not be available for education, government, and nonprofit license levels. This is relevant because if an application we are discussing is not available to you, it could be because of the plan your company has subscribed to or a licensing issue.

- Some applications or features discussed in this book may not be visible to you because you may not have an appropriate license assigned to you to use them. If an application is not visible, your IT department may need to assign a license to you to use it.

- Companies have the option to determine when updates and new functionality get released to their respective tenants. This is known as the release preferences. By default, Microsoft sets all tenants to "standard release." This means that updates and applications are deployed when they are publicly available and not in beta. Companies have the option to set the Microsoft 365 tenant to "targeted release for everyone" and "targeted release for selected users." "Targeted release for everyone" means that everyone who is using Microsoft 365 in your organization will get Microsoft 365 updates during the first phase of deployment. This will introduce functionality and features before the majority of Microsoft 365 tenants get the updates. "Targeted release for selected users" allows updates and features to be deployed to a specific set of selected users. This is useful to test and review updates before they are deployed to everyone. Keep in mind that some updates only get deployed to the entire organization. The interesting part of this feature is that it allows Microsoft to be agile by monitoring support tickets and fixing issues before the update is deployed to everyone using Microsoft 365.

- If you do not have access to Microsoft 365 or if your company will not license the appropriate applications to you, Microsoft will allow a 30-day trial to be created, and you will have access to the applications discussed in this book. After 30 days, your account will be deactivated by Microsoft. You also will be able to purchase a single license monthly if you want to experiment for a longer period.

Why Should You Choose Microsoft 365?

Microsoft 365 combines the best of the Microsoft products with an amazing, proven infrastructure platform all for a price that makes it attractive to businesses. And because it is SaaS, the service is continually updated and made better each day. These new additions can be taken advantage of on day one without the typical installation and planning that traditional software requires.

Note   If you already have access to Microsoft 365 and the related applications, feel free to skip to the next section. This next section is intended for users who do not have access to a Microsoft 365 tenant or wish to create one simply as an exercise in conjunction with this book.

Creating the Microsoft 365 Trial Tenant

Open your favorite web browser and navigate to www.office.com. For this book, you will create a trial Microsoft 365 Business Standard account. On the Office.com website, select Products ➤ For business ➤ Plans & pricing. See Figure 1-1.

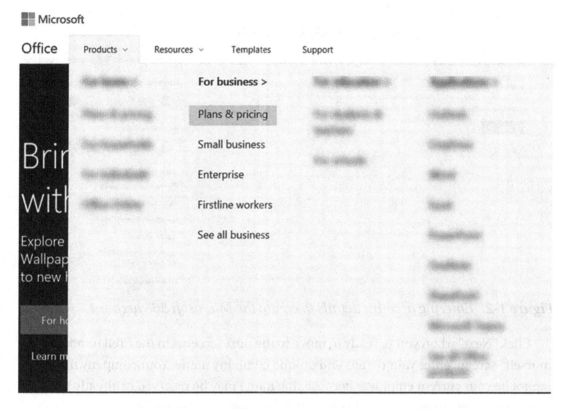

Figure 1-1. *Creating the trial account for Microsoft 365*

You will be presented with various business plans. Scroll to the bottom of the page and select "Try free for 1 month" within the Microsoft 365 Business Standard box. At the bottom of the column, click the "Try for free" button. Fill out the form, substituting your information instead of my information. For the purposes of this book, I used an Outlook.com email address for the trial but will revert to using my corporate tenant for the remainder of the chapters. Enter an email address you will like to use for the creation of the tenant. Do not use your corporate email address. See Figure 1-2.

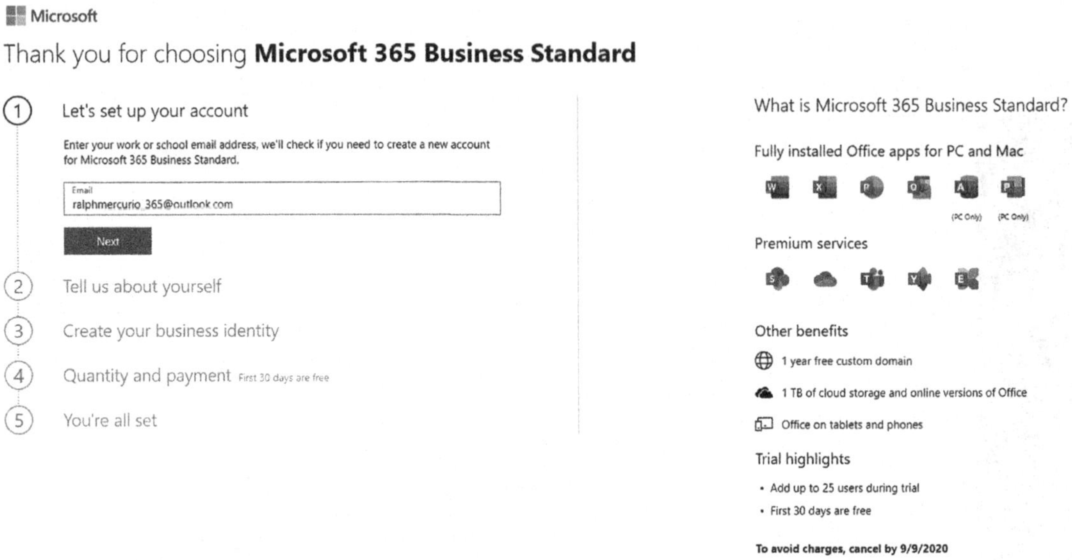

■■ Microsoft

Thank you for choosing **Microsoft 365 Business Standard**

(1)   Let's set up your account

Enter your work or school email address, we'll check if you need to create a new account
for Microsoft 365 Business Standard.

Email
ralphmercurio_365@outlook.com

Next

(2)   Tell us about yourself

(3)   Create your business identity

(4)   Quantity and payment   First 30 days are free

(5)   You're all set

What is Microsoft 365 Business Standard?

Fully installed Office apps for PC and Mac

W   X   P   O   A   P

(PC Only)   (PC Only)

Premium services

Other benefits

🌐 1 year free custom domain

☁ 1 TB of cloud storage and online versions of Office

📱 Office on tablets and phones

Trial highlights

• Add up to 25 users during trial
• First 30 days are free

To avoid charges, cancel by 9/9/2020

Figure 1-2. *Entering account details to create the Microsoft 365 account*

Click "Next" when you're ready to move to the next screen. On the "Tell us about
yourself" screen, enter your details and unique company name. Your company name
cannot be your current employer because that name may be reserved or already used.
Make up your company name. Click the "Next" button. See Figure 1-3.

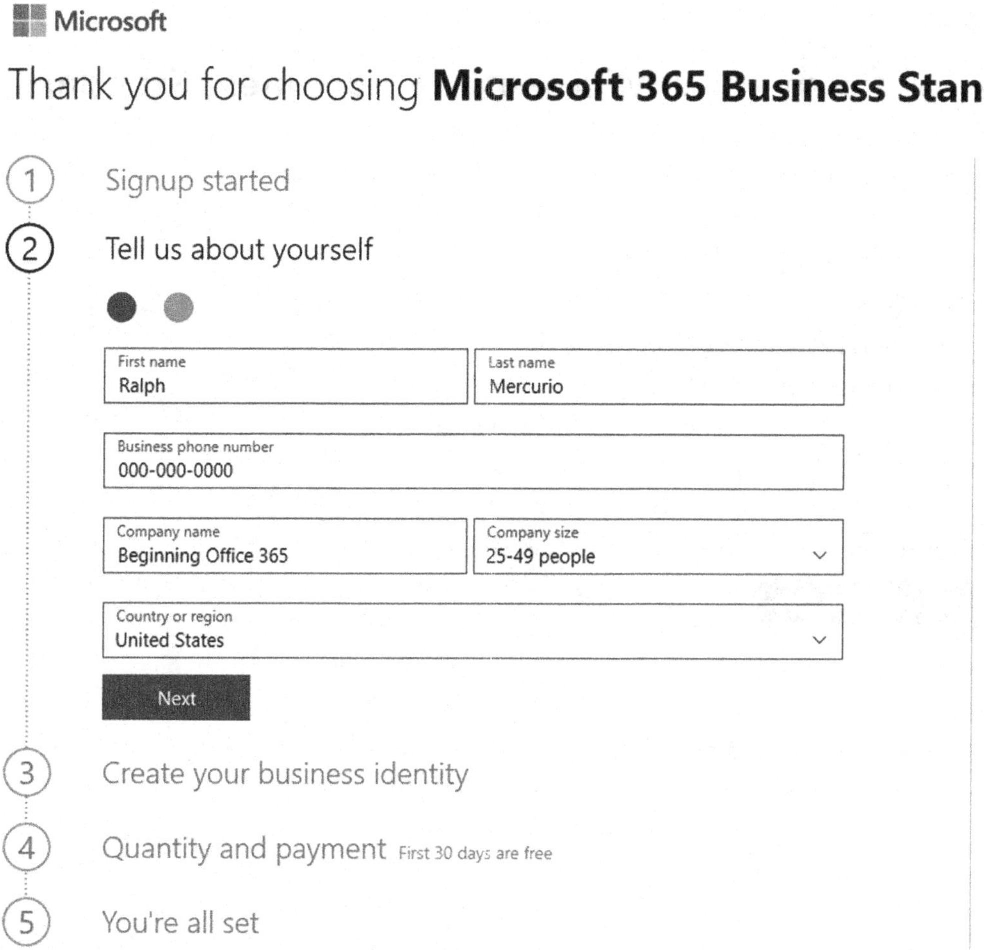

:: Microsoft

Thank you for choosing **Microsoft 365 Business Standard**

(1) Signup started

(2) Tell us about yourself

● ●

First name
Ralph

Last name
Mercurio

Business phone number
000-000-0000

Company name
Beginning Office 365

Company size
25-49 people ⌄

Country or region
United States ⌄

Next

(3) Create your business identity

(4) Quantity and payment First 30 days are free

(5) You're all set

Figure 1-3. *Create your Microsoft 365 account*

Enter your valid mobile number. The Microsoft service will call or text to verify the tenant requested is being created by a person and not a robot. See Figure 1-4.

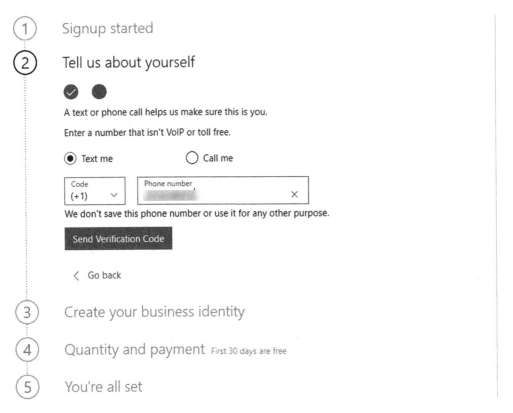

Figure 1-4. *Proving you are a real person*

It could take a few seconds for Microsoft to send the validation code. Just be sure you entered the correct phone number to authenticate. Once you receive your code, enter it on the following screen. See Figure 1-5.

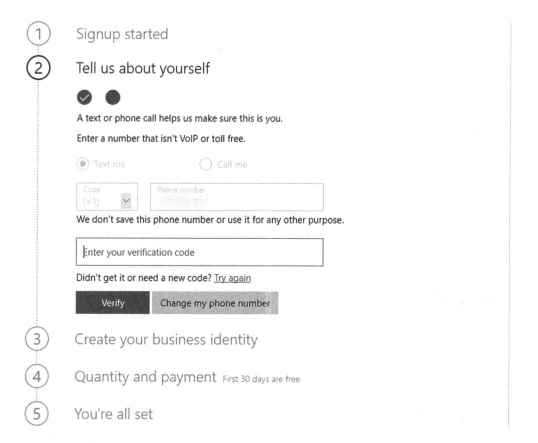

Figure 1-5. *Providing the Microsoft verification number*

Click "Verify." On the "Create your business identity" screen, enter a domain name. For this example, I didn't use my actual company domain name but created one for the trial only. Enter a domain name and then click "Check availability." If the name is available, you can then proceed to "Quantity and payment"; if not, enter a new name. See Figure 1-6.

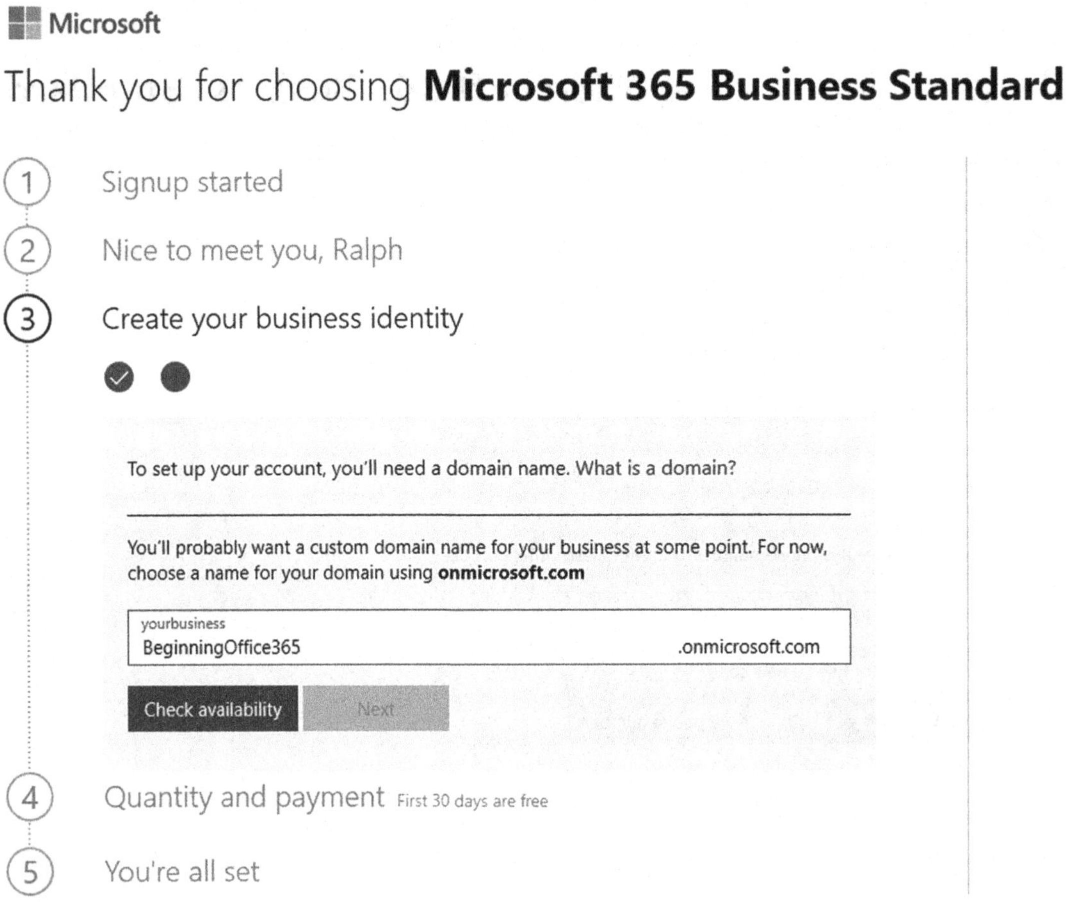

:: Microsoft

Thank you for choosing **Microsoft 365 Business Standard**

(1)   Signup started

(2)   Nice to meet you, Ralph

(3)   Create your business identity

    ✓ ●

To set up your account, you'll need a domain name. What is a domain?

You'll probably want a custom domain name for your business at some point. For now, choose a name for your domain using **onmicrosoft.com**

yourbusiness
BeginningOffice365   .onmicrosoft.com

[Check availability] [Next]

(4)   Quantity and payment   First 30 days are free

(5)   You're all set

Figure 1-6. *Create your business identity*

Enter your user ID and password, as seen in Figure 1-7. Be sure to store the credentials to the account. Once they are entered, click "Sign up."

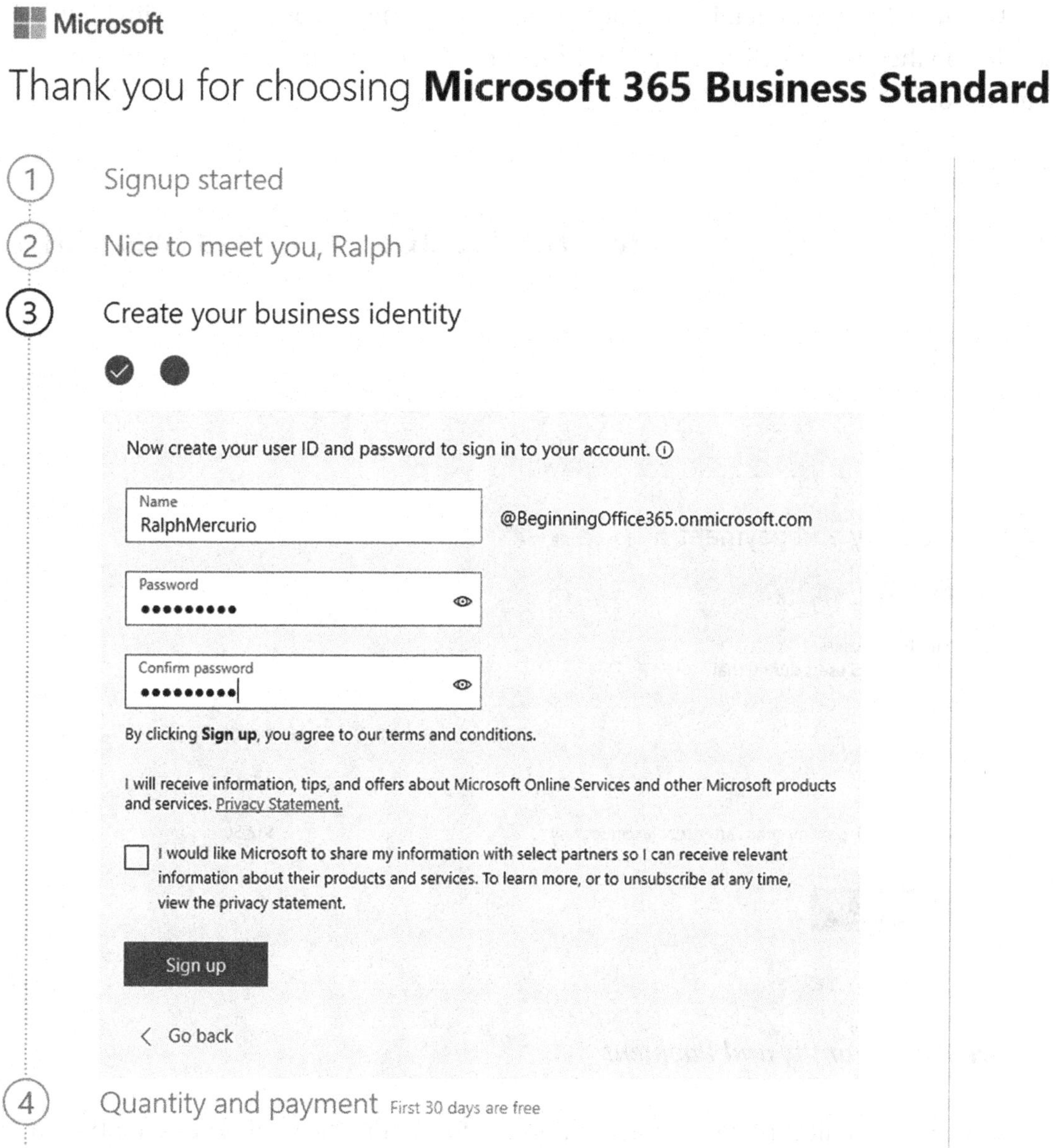

■■ Microsoft

Thank you for choosing **Microsoft 365 Business Standard**

(1)   Signup started

(2)   Nice to meet you, Ralph

(3)   Create your business identity

✓ ●

Now create your user ID and password to sign in to your account. ⓘ

Name
RalphMercurio

@BeginningOffice365.onmicrosoft.com

Password
●●●●●●●●●   👁

Confirm password
●●●●●●●●●| 👁

By clicking **Sign up**, you agree to our terms and conditions.

I will receive information, tips, and offers about Microsoft Online Services and other Microsoft products and services. Privacy Statement.

☐ I would like Microsoft to share my information with select partners so I can receive relevant information about their products and services. To learn more, or to unsubscribe at any time, view the privacy statement.

Sign up

‹ Go back

(4)   Quantity and payment First 30 days are free

Figure 1-7. *Create the first user*

Microsoft no longer offers a free trial without submission of a credit card for future charges. One option is to go ahead and provide payment details and then cancel the trial before billing begins in 30 days. This will give you access to a Microsoft 365 environment for the purposes of this book. If your company already uses Microsoft 365, you can also use that 365 tenant to familiarize yourself with the topics in this book.

To provide payment details and move forward with the 30-day free trial with billing starting on the 31st day, click "Next" on the Quantity and payment screen, as seen in Figure 1-8.

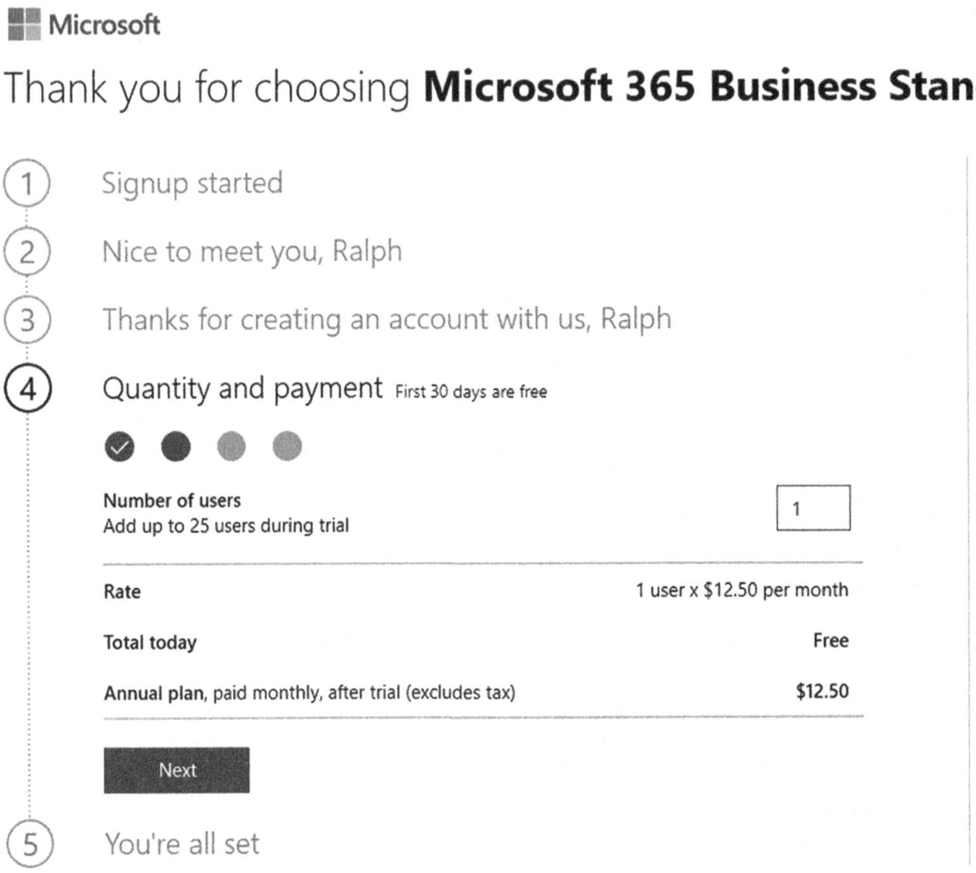

▊▊ Microsoft

Thank you for choosing **Microsoft 365 Business Standard**

(1)   Signup started

(2)   Nice to meet you, Ralph

(3)   Thanks for creating an account with us, Ralph

(4)   Quantity and payment First 30 days are free

   ✓ ● ● ●

   Number of users
   Add up to 25 users during trial   `1`

   Rate   1 user x $12.50 per month

   Total today   Free

   Annual plan, paid monthly, after trial (excludes tax) $12.50

   [Next]

(5)   You're all set

Figure 1-8. *Quantity and Payment*

Enter your credit card details and pertinent information. Be sure to pay attention to the three links above the Start Trial button. It not only informs you on the trial end date but also the cost if you fail to cancel on time. Microsoft also provides instructions on how to cancel the trial within the Microsoft 365 admin center. When ready, click "Start Trial" as seen in Figure 1-9.

Figure 1-9. *Provide payment details and start the trial*

Once the payment details are submitted and accepted, you will receive your fully qualified user ID and links to "Go to Setup" and "Manage your subscription" as seen in Figure 1-10.

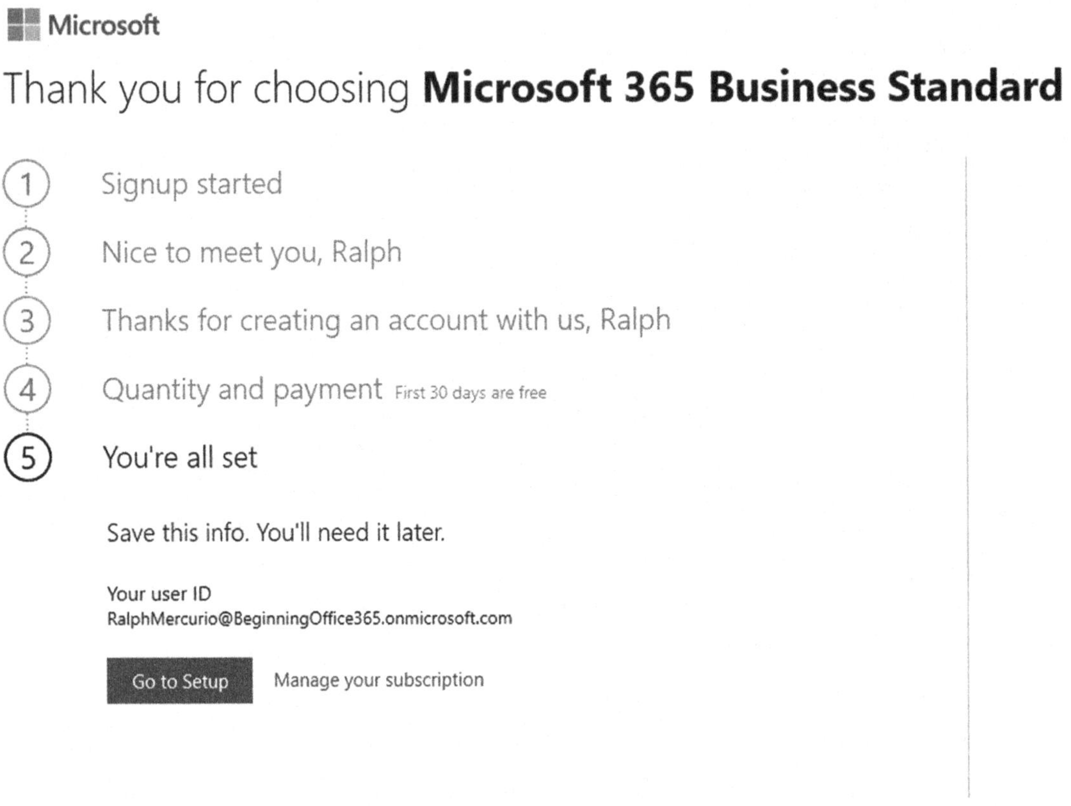

:: Microsoft

Thank you for choosing **Microsoft 365 Business Standard**

(1)   Signup started

(2)   Nice to meet you, Ralph

(3)   Thanks for creating an account with us, Ralph

(4)   Quantity and payment   First 30 days are free

(5)   You're all set

Save this info. You'll need it later.

Your user ID
RalphMercurio@BeginningOffice365.onmicrosoft.com

[Go to Setup]   Manage your subscription

Figure 1-10. *Confirmation screen*

Click "Go to Setup" to proceed and view your trial Microsoft 365 tenant. After a few moments, Microsoft will create the tenant and enter a setup screen. For the purposes of this book, do not set up a tenant as you will need a valid domain name, configure DNS and MX routing records, and various other IT administrative tasks. On the "Install Office" screen, click "Exit setup" in the lower right-hand corner, as seen in Figure 1-11.

Figure 1-11. *Exiting the Microsoft 365 setup*

You'll be redirected to the Microsoft 365 admin center, which is the heart of Microsoft 365. Within the admin center, you will have control over settings and users, as well as the administrative oversight of all Microsoft 365 applications. Please be sure you are comfortable with how to cancel your subscription to avoid being charged. To cancel your subscription, click "Billing" ➤ "Your products." You will see the option to cancel the trial under "More actions" under Buy now.

Logging into Microsoft 365 for the First Time!

Ready, set, go! Navigate to your favorite supported web browser to www.office.com and select the "Sign in" link located in the center of the page. If you already have access to a tenant and feel comfortable using it, enter the appropriate credentials. If you created a trial tenant as described, enter the email and password that were used during the creation of the subscription.

Once you authenticate, you will be presented with the Microsoft 365 screen. This screen contains some of the applications (see Figure 1-12) you are licensed to use, a rollup (see Figure 1-13) of documents you recently accessed, and a list of SharePoint sites you recently accessed (see Figure 1-13).

Note   Great care has been taken to ensure that the images are correct. However, with any SaaS offering, the product can be changed by the vendor at any time. Even though the product may change, the information will still be relevant.

Figure 1-12. *Microsoft 365 home screen*

The Office documents panel keeps track of recent or shared documents so you can quickly see what you might have been working on, while the Frequent sites will show the SharePoint sites you visit the most. See Figure 1-13 for both.

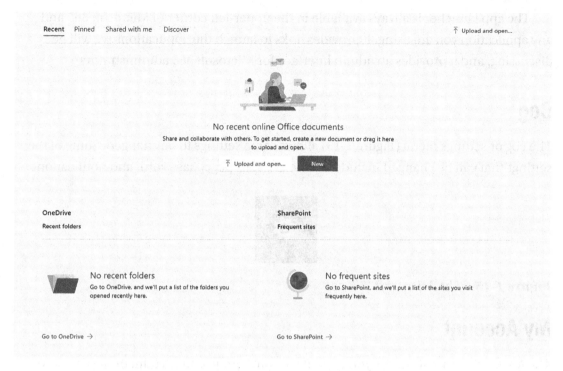

Figure 1-13. *Recently viewed documents and SharePoint sites*

The home screen also contains a few key areas that you can use to find applications and change your settings or Microsoft 365 experience.

App Launcher (the Waffle)

The app launcher (or waffle) holds all the applications you can access and will be on every Microsoft 365 screen regardless of which application you might be using. See Figure 1-14.

Figure 1-14. *The Microsoft 365 app launcher*

The app launcher is always available in the upper-left corner of Microsoft 365 and any application you are using. It provides links to launch the applications we will be discussing, and it provides an admin interface for Microsoft 365 administrators.

Cog

The cog or settings menu (Figure 1-15) allows some settings to be changed. Some of the settings that can be changed include the theme, start page, password, and notifications.

Figure 1-15. *The Microsoft 365 cog*

My Account

The My Account menu allows you to manage your profile and account or to sign out of Microsoft 365 completely. See Figure 1-16. When you click My Office Profile, it takes you to the Microsoft Delve page, which is a site where you can update your profile, including but not limited to birthday, contact numbers, About Me, projects, skills, expertise, schools, education, interests, and hobbies. The more you fill out, the better profile you create, and the easier it is for Delve to begin to catalog documents that you might want to see. A word to the wise: Only include personal information (birthday and others) if you feel comfortable sharing that information.

Figure 1-16. *My Account menu*

The My Account settings related to your account are Office ProPlus installs and which computer they have been installed on, personal info, and which licenses you are personally assigned.

The apps (Figure 1-17) collectively make up the collaboration applications of Microsoft 365. Yes, some are new, and some are powerful, but as we go through them, you will see that they need each other to either generate content or consume content. They can be accessed by clicking the app launcher shown in Figure 1-14.

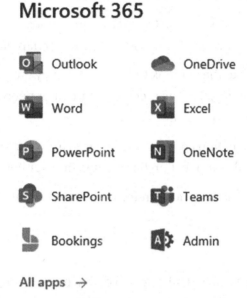

Figure 1-17. *The collaboration apps of Microsoft 365 via the app launcher*

Some of the applications aren't shown in the app launcher and are available by clicking the "All apps" link located below the Bookings application. Clicking this link shows every application, including some that are not discussed in this book.

Microsoft 365 Collaboration Applications

Now that I have discussed Microsoft 365 and you feel comfortable with what it is, how it works, and why you should use it, let me introduce each of the applications I will be discussing in the book.

Outlook

Outlook includes the following components:

- **Mail**: This application is your inbox for email communication. You can send/receive emails to/from anyone just as you do now.

- **People**: This is your standard Outlook address book but with some extended features, which I will discuss in a later chapter.

- **Calendar**: Just like the Outlook Calendar, you may have been using it for years. Use it to schedule meetings with other people, days you might not be in the office, and so on.

- **Tasks**: This application contains all the tasks from Outlook that you have created or the application has created on your behalf.

This version of Outlook is commonly referred to as web mail.

Office ProPlus

The newest version of the familiar Office tools you have been using has been upgraded to Office ProPlus, a continually updated version of Office. There are two flavors available to you as a subscriber to Microsoft 365. You can download and install the applications or use them through the web browser. In this book, I will refer to Office Online as the web version of Office, while client apps will be the version you download and use locally on your device:

- **Word**: Arguably the world's most widely used word processing program. Create documents, resumes, and other content using one of the world's most popular word processing programs.

- **Excel**: Create powerful spreadsheets, charts, and insights. A workhorse of the Office platform for years.

- **PowerPoint**: Create engaging presentations for meetings. Just don't make them too long.

- **OneNote**: Excellent application for taking notes, I use it almost every day, and it has replaced my little treasure trove of Post-It notes all over my desk.

- **Sway**: Create newsletters and other documents and share them easily.

- **Outlook**: Like Outlook in terms of functionality, but this version is installed on your device.

OneDrive

OneDrive allows you to store files in the cloud and access them from anywhere and on nearly every type of device. Items can be shared with users internally and externally; you can also view and edit documents in Office Online or the client apps of Office 2019.

SharePoint

One of the core pillars of collaboration in Microsoft 365, SharePoint offers document management, sites, and collaboration tools, and it integrates with Office 2019.

Microsoft 365 Teams

An explosive offering from Microsoft, Teams enables teams or smaller groups to work together in one application instead of working in different applications and then using a common application to collaborate. This differs from most applications because it is based on the concept of chat, not email.

Yammer

Similar to Teams, Yammer is designed to foster communication and disseminate information to the entire organization, ideally replacing email as the primary method. Employees can subscribe to groups and interact with other employees across the organization.

Power Automate

Power Automate allows users to create no-code workflows that can be used with the Microsoft 365 platform or as a connector to other external systems. This new application blurs the line and works across many applications.

Planner

Planner offers "light" project management via the ability to keep track of tasks and resources for small projects that don't require a project manager to manage the project.

Forms

Microsoft's form offering to tackle the issue of collecting information from end users, Forms gives you the ability to create forms and surveys and then view the results within an easy-to-use dashboard.

Power Apps

Power Apps allows for application development that works across multiple device platforms and easily connects to your data sources. Examples include an organization browser or address book or capturing meeting minutes. Power Apps includes templates and connectors to streamline the development of these applications. It's a groundbreaking application from Microsoft and can be used to easily deploy an application to solve a business issue.

Stream

Microsoft Stream provides a rich collaborative platform for video sharing in a secure manner. This platform allows video content to be published and searchable; it gives everyone in the organization the ability to create video content.

Power BI

This app strives to offer data analytics and dashboards to present data to make informed decisions, analyze trends, and become the reporting standard in Microsoft 365.

Summary

Microsoft has gone to great lengths in investing in and creating Microsoft 365. From the stability of the infrastructure, the disaster recovery planning perspective, and the affordable pricing structure, Microsoft 365 is a great tool to increase productivity, reduce administrative overhead, and empower users with the tools necessary to make their work successful.

If you are already using Microsoft 365 in your organization, then you are well on your way to understanding the collaboration apps mentioned earlier in this chapter. If not, I hope the walk-through of setting up a trial account was successful and now you are ready to explore the basics of the Microsoft 365 collaboration apps.

In the next chapter, you will explore SharePoint Online, a document-centric application that allows users to create and view SharePoint Online sites, manage documents, and create a collaborative document environment.

PART II

The Applications

CHAPTER 2

SharePoint Online

In the last chapter, you created the Microsoft 365 environment to begin your journey through the collaboration apps. The first app I will discuss is SharePoint, which has gone through a few iterations and with each release gets better and better. SharePoint is Microsoft's answer to document management, sites, and collaboration; it serves as an integration backbone for many of Microsoft's other products, such as OneDrive, Teams, and Power Automate.

Microsoft offers two flavors of SharePoint: SharePoint Online and SharePoint on-premises. In this book, we will focus on SharePoint Online, which is included with a Microsoft 365 subscription. SharePoint Online differs from SharePoint on-premises with regard to capabilities, but the foundation of both products is nearly identical from an end user perspective.

The Starting Line

SharePoint Online is accessible via the app launcher located in the upper left of the Microsoft 365 site, as shown in Figure 2-1.

© Ralph Mercurio and Brian Merrill 2021
R. Mercurio and B. Merrill, *Beginning Microsoft 365 Collaboration Apps*,
https://doi.org/10.1007/978-1-4842-6936-7_2

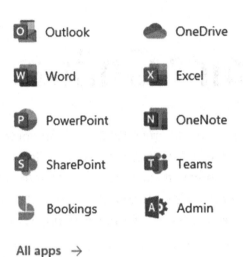

Figure 2-1. Accessing the SharePoint Online icon from the Microsoft 365 app launcher

Clicking the SharePoint icon opens a SharePoint site, which presents a single view of your particular SharePoint activity (Figure 2-2).

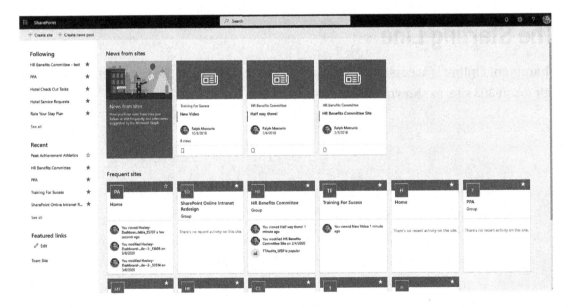

Figure 2-2. SharePoint portal site

This web page contains sites that you are following, recently visited sites, and a rollup of news articles from all the sites you access. All of this requires very little intervention on your part because the Microsoft 365 service aggregates and catalogs the activity for you seamlessly.

This view also contains Microsoft 365 Groups, which is discussed in Chapter 4. SharePoint sites and Microsoft 365 groups are closely related and share many of the same features and functionality.

Sites

The building blocks of SharePoint Online are sites. Sites allow users to create workspaces, which are used to organize content, disseminate information, or track projects. Sites can be created from various templates, each with a slightly different purpose or a way to convey information.

Team Site

The most widely used template available is a team site, which contains default document libraries, default lists, and default page templates for users to use to collaborate and share information. Later in the chapter, I will discuss each of the site components more in-depth.

Team sites come in two flavors: classic and modern. A classic team site (Figure 2-3) looks like a SharePoint 2013, 2016, or 2019 team site.

Figure 2-3. *SharePoint classic team site*

A modern team site contains many of the same components as a classic team site, but the look is different, as you can see in Figure 2-4.

Figure 2-4. *SharePoint modern team site*

While the look is different, it shares the same set of lists and libraries but with a few added features. The first change from all previous versions of SharePoint is that a modern team site also will have a corresponding Microsoft 365 group (Chapter 4) created as well. With the addition of the Microsoft 365 group, modern team sites also gain the conversation stream as well as an updated calendar feature. The second change is that Microsoft 365 groups are accessible in two ways: either via Outlook 2019 or Microsoft 365 Outlook or the SharePoint portal site.

Now that I have addressed the two available team site templates (classic and modern), let's discuss the rest of the available site templates before you create your first site. SharePoint Online includes the templates covered in the following sections.

Communication Site

A communication site (Figure 2-5) is a site template available in SharePoint Online and cannot be created as a subsite like the rest of the available templates.

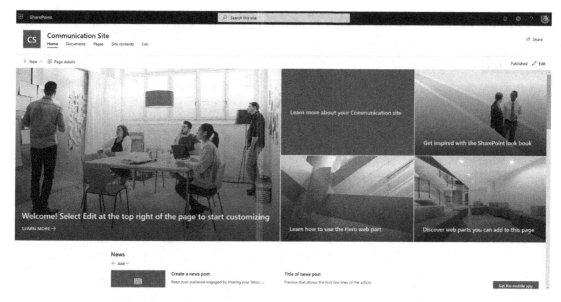

Figure 2-5. *Communication site*

This site template aims to foster communication by providing three different designs, which are also designed for the mobile experience. The three designs are

- **Topic:** Used primarily to share information

- **Showcase**: Used to share information and highlight a product or company event

- **Blank**: A blank site that can then be customized

Blog

A blog site (Figure 2-6) is used to convey ideas, conversations, and posts about a particular subject. Visitors can also post comments on any of the blog posts.

Figure 2-6. *A blog site*

The blog site can be selected under the Collaboration tab of the Template section when creating a new site.

Project Site

A project site (Figure 2-7) contains components that help manage a project in a concise site. The project site template can be selected from the Collaboration tab of the Template section when creating a new site.

Figure 2-7. *A project site*

Community Site

A community site (Figure 2-8) allows members of the site to discuss and comment on interests. It primarily works around the ideas of discussions and liking or rating discussion posts. This site template is accessible under the Collaboration tab of the Template section when creating a new site.

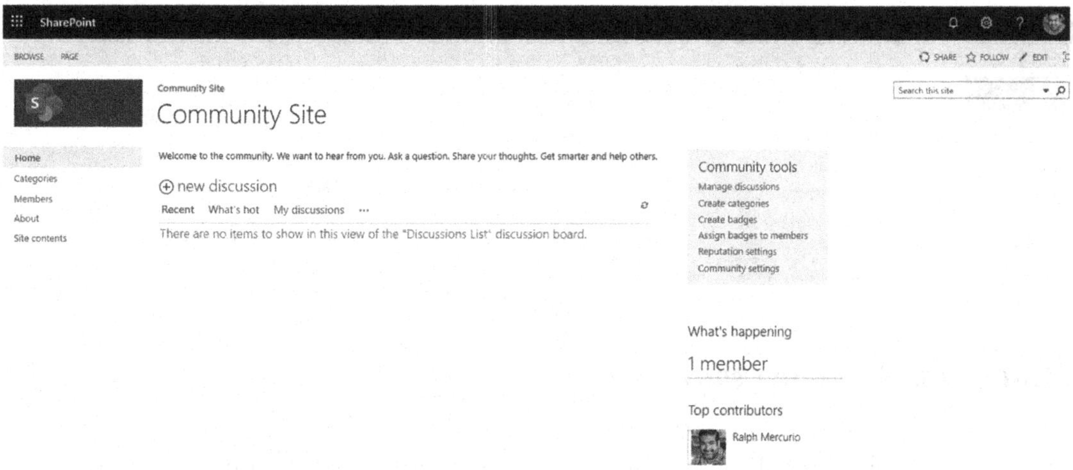

Figure 2-8. *A community site*

This site can only be created when the parent site is a classic team site. This template is not available for modern team sites.

Document Center

A document center site (Figure 2-9) allows for a location to centrally manage documents. The document center site is available under the Enterprise tab within the Template section when creating a new site.

Figure 2-9. *Document center site*

Records Center

A Records Center site (Figure 2-10) is used to manage records, which are permanent artifacts and have a retention period. Once a document becomes a record, it cannot be modified.

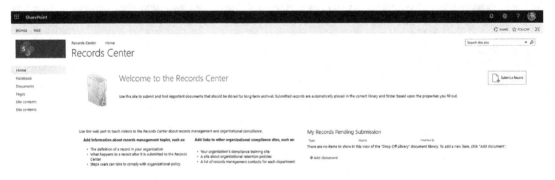

Figure 2-10. *A Records Center site*

Records Center sites also have specific rules that must be configured to ensure adherence to a specific record policy.

Business Intelligence Center

The Business Intelligence Center site (Figure 2-11) allows for the display of business intelligence (BI) content within SharePoint. The site template can be selected from the Enterprise tab within the Template section when creating a new site.

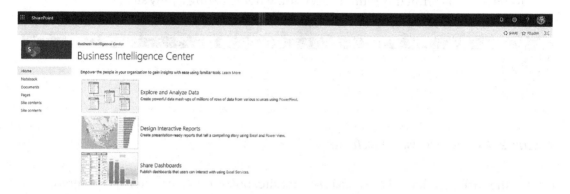

Figure 2-11. *Business Intelligence Center site*

This includes the ability to upload reports and leverage Excel services. This template does not provide BI dashboard capabilities.

Basic Search

A basic search site (Figure 2-12) provides a central site to execute searches from. It includes an advanced search page in addition to the basic search page. The site template can be selected from the Enterprise tab within the Template section when creating a new site.

Figure 2-12. *Basic search site*

This site does not have any associated lists and libraries with it because it is not meant for collaboration but rather to provide a basic search experience regardless of what SharePoint site the user is currently on.

Enterprise Search Center

The Enterprise Search site (Figure 2-13) provides an intranet approach to searching. Not only can it search for the same content as the basic search but it also provides specific searching for people, conversations, and videos. The site template can be selected from the Enterprise tab within the Template section when creating a new site.

Figure 2-13. *Enterprise Search site*

On the surface, it looks like a basic search site, but after a search term is entered, the Enterprise Search site will allow the search term to be refined through people, conversations, or videos, as shown in Figure 2-14.

Figure 2-14. *Enterprise search term refiners*

This site does not have any associated lists and libraries with it because it is not meant for collaboration but rather to provide an enterprise search experience regardless of what SharePoint site the user is currently on. This site can only be created when the parent site is a classic team site. This template is not available for modern team sites.

Visio Process Repository

A Visio Process Repository (Figure 2-15) is a site where Visio documents are stored. This site template can be created by selecting the "Visio Process Repository" template from the Enterprise tab when creating a new site.

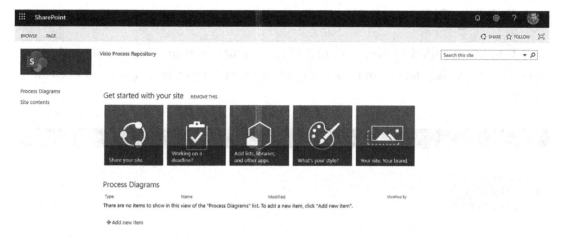

Figure 2-15. *Visio Process Repository site*

Publishing Site

The publishing site template (Figure 2-16) allows for content creators to create and edit pages in draft mode and publish them when ready for general consumption. The site template can be selected from the Publishing tab within the Template section when creating a new site.

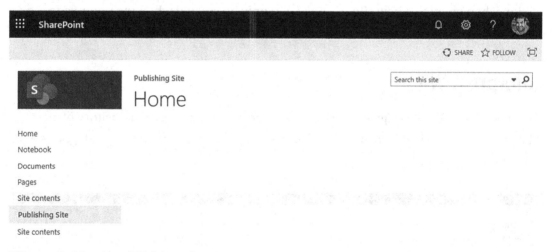

Figure 2-16. *A publishing site*

This site can only be created when the parent site is a classic team site. This template is not available for modern team sites.

Publishing Site with Workflow

A publishing site with workflow (Figure 2-17) is similar to a publishing site; the only real difference is that pages can be scheduled for publishing by leveraging an approval workflow.

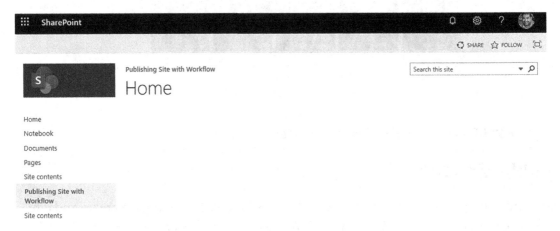

Figure 2-17. *Publishing site with workflow*

The site template can be selected from the Publishing tab within the Template section when creating a new site. This site can only be created when the parent site is a classic team site. This template is not available for modern team sites.

Enterprise Wiki

The enterprise wiki site (Figure 2-18) is used to create an enterprise repository of information in a wiki-style format. It allows content to be put into defined categories and page content to be rated.

Figure 2-18. *Enterprise wiki site*

The site has limited lists and libraries because most of the content are pages. This site can only be created when the parent site is a classic team site. This template is not available for modern team sites.

SAP Workflow Site

The SAP workflow site template (Figure 2-19) is, in my opinion, the least used site template out of all of them. It does require a SAP Duet subscription and allows SAP workflow steps to be disseminated from SharePoint.

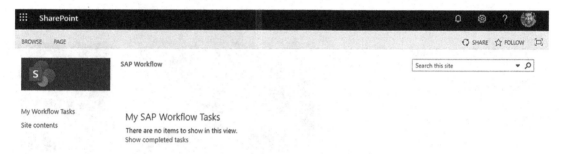

Figure 2-19. *A SAP workflow site*

The site template provides an interface for tasks through SharePoint, and the user works on the SharePoint site. This integration is useful if Duet and the associated business logic of documents that go along with the workflow tasks exist.

Creating a Site

Before creating any sites, try to envision what your site hierarchy will look like and how you want the site to function. A bit of planning around site structure will alleviate site sprawl, create a logical hierarchy, and allow for specific sites to be in particular site collections.

Creating sites is a simple process in SharePoint Online as long as the user has the correct rights assigned to create sites. As you progress through this book, you'll create a modern team site, and a Microsoft 365 group (Chapter 4) will also be created. This means that, since Microsoft 365 groups are created within Outlook, they will also create a corresponding SharePoint site. I know it's a little confusing, but remember that planning is the key to ensuring that sites are not duplicated.

Communication Site

To create a communication site, select "+ Create site," near the top of the SharePoint portal site, as depicted in Figure 2-20. You can access this site by clicking SharePoint in the app launcher.

Figure 2-20. *SharePoint creation interface from the SharePoint portal site*

Clicking the link opens the creation interface and presents you with two options: Team site and Communication site. Select Communication site by clicking the image.

1. Choose a design based on your specific requirements. You can choose from the following layouts: Topic, Showcase, and Blank.

   Enter a site name within the Site Name text box. As you type the site name, SharePoint will fill out the Site Address field, removing spaces or special characters. If you do not want the generated site address, click the pencil and edit accordingly.

2. Enter a site description if desired; it is not a required field.

3. Click the Finish button, and the site will be created in the background.

4. Once the site is created, you will be automatically navigated to the site.

Modern Team Site

Creating a modern team site is a nearly identical process to creating a communication site. To create a modern team site, select "+ Create site" near the top of the SharePoint site, as shown in Figure 2-20, and select Team site by clicking the corresponding image.

1. Enter a site name within the Site Name text box.

2. As you type the site name, SharePoint will fill out the Group email address field, removing spaces or special characters. If you do not want the generated group email address, click the pencil and edit accordingly.

3. Enter a site description if desired; it is not a required field.

4. Choose a privacy setting, either public or private:

   • **Public**: Anyone in the organization can view the site.

   • **Private**: Only a select group of specified individuals can view the site.

5. Click the Finish button, and the site will be created in the background.

During the creation process, you also can add additional owners and additional members. I will discuss basic permissions later in this chapter. Once the site is created, you will be automatically navigated to the site.

Classic Experience Team Site

Classic experience team sites are slowly being phased out of SharePoint Online. Classic experience team sites will slowly be transitioned to modern team sites, and eventually, only modern team sites will be able to be created. Classic experience team sites have been around for quite a while and hence have quite the following from the community and SharePoint users.

Classic experience team sites can be created either as a subsite of a modern team site or as a subsite of the SharePoint aggregate site, as depicted in Figure 2-20. The process is the same for creating classic team sites and begins by selecting the cog (gear) in the upper-right corner.

1. Choose Site Contents from the cog menu.

2. Select the "+ New" drop-down menu below the title of the site, as seen in Figure 2-21.

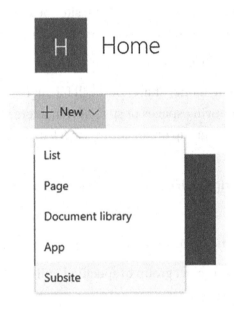

Figure 2-21. *Creating a new subsite*

3. The New SharePoint Site form will open. Fill out the details as needed:

   a. **Title and Description**: Give your site a title and description.

   b. **Web Site Address**: Unlike when creating modern or communication sites, you must specify the address here. You can't change the beginning of the URL. Avoid spaces or special characters here.

   c. **Template Selection**: Choose Team Site (Classic Experience).

    d. **Permissions**: You can inherit permissions or create new permission groups for your users. I will discuss permissions later in this chapter.

    e. **Navigation Inheritance**: You can choose to use the same global navigation as the parent site or not.

4. Once you have filled out the form, click the Create button.

Creating Non-team Sites

As you can see, creating sites is a pretty straightforward and simple process. The only gotcha is that specific site templates can only be used when the parent site is a classic team site. To make a non-team site, follow these instructions:

1. Choose Site Contents from the cog (gear) menu in the upper-right corner.

2. Select the "+ New" drop-down menu below the title of the site, as shown in Figure 2-21.

3. The New SharePoint Site form will open, and you can proceed to fill out the details as needed:

    a. **Title and Description**: Give your site a title and description.

    b. **Web Site Address**: Unlike when creating modern or communication sites, you must specify the address here. You cannot change the beginning of the URL. Avoid spaces or special characters here.

    c. **Template Selection**: Choose the site template you want to use. An explanation of each of the templates is included earlier in this chapter.

    d. **Permissions**: You have the ability to inherit permissions or create new permission groups for your users. I will discuss permissions later in this chapter.

    e. **Navigation Inheritance**: You can choose to use the same global navigation as the parent site or not.

4. Once you have filled out the form, click the Create button.

Lists and Libraries

Now that I have covered the different kinds of sites, let's discuss lists and libraries, which are the foundational building blocks of sites. Think of lists and libraries as the walls of a building and sites as the foundation upon which everything is built.

Note   The following are only available by selecting "App" from the + New menu on a site.

Lists

SharePoint Online offers preconfigured lists or libraries. The following sections cover each of the available templates and a brief explanation of each list and library template.

Announcements

An announcement list is a predefined list that allows you to create an item and other types of news-related items. The announcement list is generally used to show announcements, which can be set to expire on a preselected date.

Calendar

The calendar list is a SharePoint calendar that can be used by the team to add events and schedule meetings within a SharePoint site. The calendar can also be connected to Outlook to enable seamless editing through Outlook.

Contacts

The contacts list is similar to an address book, and contacts can be added through Outlook. The contacts list can hold employees, vendors, or partners and keep their information centralized.

Custom List

A custom list is merely a list with minimal preconfigured columns. This is a blank list that can be configured in any way you see fit to support the business requirement.

List in Datasheet View

A custom list in a datasheet is the same as a custom list except you can edit the list in an Excel-like format, making data entry a lot easier.

Discussion Board

A discussion board is a preconfigured list template that supports discussions and conversations. The list can also be configured to require approval before any post becomes viewable by all.

External List

External lists are out of scope for this book but connect to external content types, which in turn connect to a SQL database, for example. They can present a SQL database view as a SharePoint list and allow data to be added, deleted, or modified in a SQL database.

Import Spreadsheet

The import spreadsheet list template allows you to upload an Excel spreadsheet and use the headers of the sheet as column types. It imports the data from Excel and creates nearly identical columns.

Issue Tracking

An issue tracking list allows you to track issues that can be assigned to be prioritized and completed; you can also assign statuses.

Links

The links list template allows a list of links to be created. The links list contains a URL column where the website address is stored.

Promoted Links

Similar to the preceding links list, the promoted links list will display the links in a graphical tile-based format.

Survey

You can create a list of questions in a survey format. I discuss Microsoft Forms in Chapter 10, which provides a much better interface to create surveys and view responses.

Tasks

A tasks list allows tasks to be created plus details like whom the task is assigned to, a due date, progress, and a few other fields.

Libraries

Libraries act and share a lot of the same features as lists such as columns, views, and the ability to organize the data. The significant difference between lists and libraries is that libraries are geared toward containing some sort of content such as documents, reports, or images. In the next few pages, I will list the available out-of-the-box library templates and provide a brief description of their purposes.

Asset Library

An asset library is similar to a picture library but is geared to manage assets such as images and audio or video files.

Document Library

A document library is a library with minimal preconfigured columns. This is a blank library that can be configured in any way you see fit to support the business requirement.

Form Library

A form library template is a library that is used to store InfoPath forms, which could be employee forms, status reports, or business forms. With InfoPath being deprecated and the industry moving to Microsoft Power Apps to create forms, this library is slowly being phased out.

Picture Library

The picture library template contains columns that correspond to images and provide different views into the library. I will discuss views later in this chapter.

Site Mailbox

The site mailbox is a deprecated library template; it was used to connect an Exchange mailbox to SharePoint. The recommendation is to use Microsoft 365 Groups going forward.

Wiki Page Library

This library supports wiki pages and the ability to create a wiki using text and images.

List and Library Columns

Every list or library contains columns. These columns can be a variety of types and are used to store information about the item or content. For example, many lists and libraries contain Modified, Modified By, Created, and Created By columns, which are used to store details about the user and date of modification. In fact, these types of columns have been around for years because Windows uses them to store information. The only real difference is now they are more visible and are used more frequently in SharePoint and in every other Microsoft 365 application such as OneDrive for Business.

Every list or library contains columns, which can be created from a wide variety of types. Different types of columns can be added to a list or library, and the column dictates what information it accepts. Table 2-1 contains a list of the available columns and their associated type.

Table 2-1. *SharePoint Columns by Type and Associated Data Type*

Type	Data Type	Notes
Single line of text	Text	Only accepts plain text
Multiple lines of text	Text	Accepts either plain or enhanced rich text
Choice (menu to choose from)	Text	Choose from drop-down, radio buttons, or checkboxes
Number (1, 1.0, 100)	Numeric	
Currency ($, ¥, €)	Currency	
Date and time	Date and time	
Lookup (information already on this site)	Text or numeric	Only available on the current site, cannot look up information on other sites
Yes/no (checkbox)	Text	Can only be yes/no; no other entries are allowed
Person or group	Person	Finds a person in Active Directory or a SharePoint group
Hyperlink or picture	URL	
Calculated (calculation based on other columns)	Formula based	
Task outcome	Text	Can be a choice field or calculated value
External data	External content types	
Managed metadata	Term set	

Most of the columns also can be set to Required or enforce unique values. To set one of these settings within the column, make sure to mark the appropriate radio button when creating the column.

Creating Columns

To create a column in a list or library, open the list or library first. In this example, you are going to create a column in the document library of a modern team site. If you didn't create a modern team site earlier in this chapter, please go ahead and do so now.

On the modern team site, click Documents in the left-hand navigation control (otherwise known as the quick launch). The window will refresh, and you will be presented with a view of the document library. In the main area, to the right of Modified By, click the + sign. You'll be presented with 11 frequently used field types ranging from a single line of text to currency. If the field type you are interested in is not listed, click the More option.

Let's create a choice field (you can select any column type) and create your first library column. Clicking "Choice" opens the "Create a column" form (Figure 2-22). Fill in the fields.

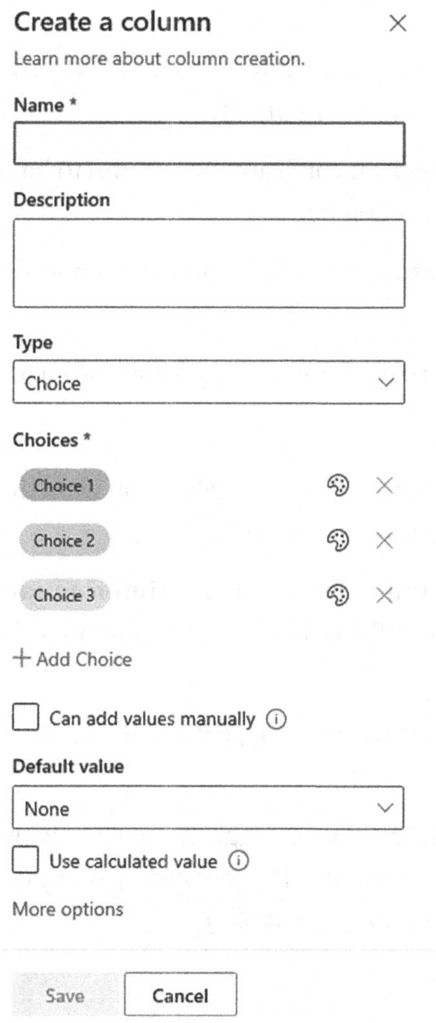

Create a column   ×

Learn more about column creation.

Name *

Description

Type

Choice   ∨

Choices *

Choice 1

Choice 2

Choice 3

+ Add Choice

☐ Can add values manually ⓘ

Default value

None   ∨

☐ Use calculated value ⓘ

More options

Save   Cancel

Figure 2-22. *The "Create a column" form for a choice column*

On the "Create a column" form, the Name and Choices fields are required, as denoted by the asterisk. The fields and their description are listed in the following:

- **Name**: Name of the column.

- **Description**: Enter a description of the purpose of the column.

- **Type**: Choice type selected; remaining fields are based on the Type field.

- **Choices**: Enter the choices for the column. You can select the backfill color as well. The backfill color is used within the list as a visual indicator.

- **Can add values manually**: Allows a user to add a choice to the choices drop-down menu manually.

- **Default value**: Specify if you want the column to have a default value when a document is uploaded or created.

- **Use calculated value**: Allows a formula to compute the value for the column.

- **Display choices using**: Choose Drop-Down Menu or Radio Buttons.

- **More options**

  - **Allow multiple selections**: Toggle if you want the user to be able to select more than one choice.

  - **Require that this column contains information**: Toggle if the field must be filled out for the document to be created or uploaded.

  - **Enforce unique values**: Toggle if you do not want multiple items to have the same value.

  - **Add to all content types**: Toggle if you want to add the column to all content types. (It will be a column in any content type associated with the current list.)

- **Column Validation**

  - **Formula**: Validate the choice selected by using a formula.

  - **User message**: Based on the formula, show a message.

I populated the form with the values shown in Figure 2-23.

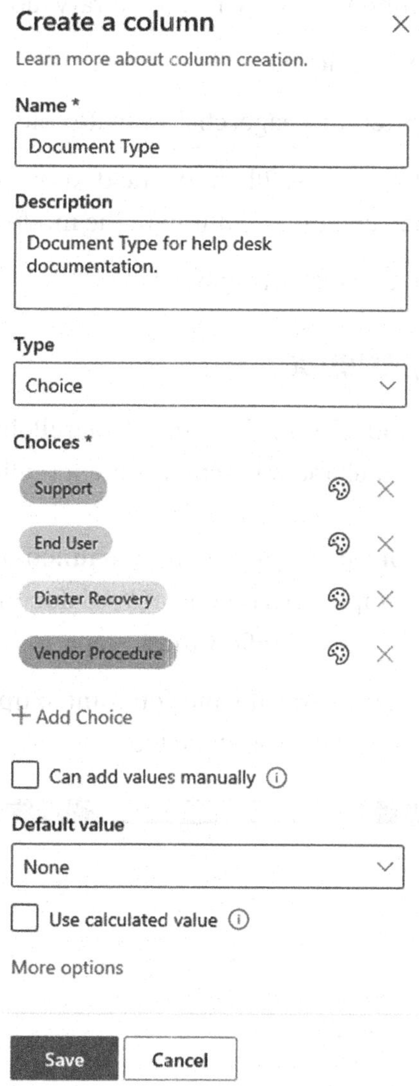

Create a column   ✕

Learn more about column creation.

Name *

Document Type

Description

Document Type for help desk
documentation.

Type

Choice   ⌄

Choices *

Support   🎨 ✕

End User   🎨 ✕

Diaster Recovery   🎨 ✕

Vendor Procedure   🎨 ✕

╋ Add Choice

☐ Can add values manually ⓘ

Default value

None   ⌄

☐ Use calculated value ⓘ

More options

Save   Cancel

Figure 2-23. *Choice column form populated with values*

Click the Save button, and the column will be created and be added not only to the
library but to the view as well. This process is the same for all column types regardless of
if they are lists or libraries. The procedure is slightly different for classic experience team
sites and is covered next.

To create a column in the classic experience, follow these steps:

1. In the SharePoint ribbon, click the List or Library tab.

2. Click the Library Settings icon.

3. In the middle of the Settings page, click "Create column."

4. On the Create a column page, fill out the fields as needed. They are the same as when creating a column in the modern interface.

5. Click the OK button to create the column.

Document Library Experience

As of now, I have covered the foundation elements of SharePoint Online: sites, lists, libraries, and columns. The next element is actual content (Office documents, images, and other files) and list items.

Uploading a document is one of the most common functions that we all do in SharePoint Online. For this example, let's upload a Word document to a document library on a modern team site. To do so, follow these steps:

1. On the modern team site, drag the file you want to upload directly onto the Documents web part, as depicted in Figure 2-24.

Figure 2-24. *The drag file interface on a document library*

2. The file will upload directly to the library.

Now that a document has been uploaded to a document library, let's explore the available options not only at the library level but also at the document item level. A document library contains a few key areas, as shown in Figure 2-25.

Figure 2-25. *A document library*

A document library contains a menu bar consisting of New, Upload, Quick edit, Sync, Export to Excel, Power Apps, Automate (formerly Flow), and the ability to switch views and filter. The central area where documents are stored contains columns that describe the attributes of the file (metadata). Another area offers item functions, which are accessible from the three dots next to the file. Let's explore each of these areas a little more in-depth because they form a foundation for a lot of other Microsoft 365 applications.

The first area to explore is the menu bar. This menu bar contains actions that allow you to do a variety of things, and some actions can be performed on more than one file at a time. The following list offers a description of the available actions:

- **+ New**: Creates a new document. It integrates with Office Online to create documents inside the browser. I discuss Office Online in further detail in Chapter 7.

- **Upload**: Uploads an existing file, folder, or template to the document library from your device.

- **Quick edit**: Allows you to edit the column values of documents to quickly change their metadata in bulk without having to edit each item individually.

- **Sync**: Allows OneDrive for Business (Chapter 3) to sync the contents of the library with your device.

- **Export to Excel**: Exports the library to Excel. This export does require Excel to be installed, and you can't import it back. It also will not download the documents; it just links back to the document library via a URL.

- **Power Apps**: Allows you to customize the form to align it with a business process. We will discuss Power Apps in a later chapter.

- **Automate**: Power Automate allows workflows to be created and executed against content. I introduce Power Automate and the basic concepts in Chapter 11.

- **…**: Refer to the three dots as an ellipsis.

- **Alert me**: Sets up alerts on changes in the library. An email will be sent with the subscribed changes.

- **Manage my alerts**: Allows you to add/edit/remove alerts that have been created by you.

- **All Documents**: The standard and default view on all document libraries. This view shows all documents and created columns. In the next section, I will discuss creating and using your own specified views.

- **Filters**: If filters are available on a view, you can filter the documents based on the parameters specified. The filters are denoted by the funnel icon.

- **Details**: Clicking the icon (question mark) shows a stream of recent activity. If a document is selected and the icon is clicked, it shows details surrounding a file such as permissions and metadata.

The second area is where documents are stored. This area is where you create new columns, as described earlier in this chapter, and edit the associated metadata of documents by either selecting the item and editing the properties or using the Quick edit action in the document library menu bar.

The third area is where the core SharePoint actions are located and are used to manipulate the documents. Clicking the three dots next to a file (ellipsis) opens a new menu with a variety of options. Each one of these options has a unique purpose, and the easiest way to familiarize yourself with the options is to review the following list:

- **Open**: Opens the document. If it is a recognized file type, you will get the option to open in Office Online or locally installed Office.

- **Preview**: Previews the document in Office Online.

- **Share**: Allows sharing the document with users inside the organization, users with existing access, and specific people. You can also share the document with anonymous users if it has been configured by the SharePoint administrator to do so.

- **Copy link**: You can copy the link, and then the link can be sent to a user via email or MS Teams.

- **Manage Access**: Allows one to share the file or restrict access.

- **Download**: Allows you to download the file to your local device. Once it is downloaded and you make changes to the item, it will not sync or be saved back.

- **Delete**: The document will be deleted and sent to the recycle bin.

- **Power Automate**: Allows you to start a Power Automate that has been already created. Power Automate can also integrate with other Microsoft 365 applications.

- **Pin to top**: Pins the document to the top of the library, so it is always in the first position.

- **Move to**: Moves the document to another library on the site.

- **Copy to**: Makes a copy of the document and stores it in a different library on the site.

- **Version history**: Shows a stream of changes in the document and can restore a previous version.

- **Alert me**: Sends an alert when there is a change, someone else changes a document, someone else changes a document created by you, and someone else changes a document last modified by you. The alert can be sent immediately, daily, or weekly. These alerts will also apply to the entire library.

- **More >**

- **Properties**: Shows the properties of the file, including the default columns and columns created to support different metadata.

- **Workflow**: Power Automate a legacy workflow on the document. These workflows are slowly being replaced by Flow, but you can create workflows in SharePoint Designer 2013 until further notice. This is still available because Flow has not reached the same maturity as Workflow, which has been in existence for over 10 years.

- **Compliance details**: Displays any compliance parameters around the document including if it is on legal hold or if it is in a different retention stage.

- **Check out**: Sets the document to a status of checked out. While the document is in a checked-out status, no other user can edit the file until it is checked back in. You must check in the document once you are done with your changes.

- **Details:** Shows a stream of recent activity and details surrounding a file such as permissions and metadata.

List Experience

Lists and libraries are very similar; the only measurable difference, beyond some minor differences in actions, is that lists are used to store items and not content (files). Looking at a list in Figure 2-26, you can see that it looks very similar to what I just discussed.

Figure 2-26. *A SharePoint Online list*

A list shares the same structure as a library. Power Apps allows you to customize the Add item and Edit item forms to provide a more robust business form than the standard SharePoint forms. Another change is in the available actions when selecting the ellipsis next to a list item. The following list details the available actions and their intended purpose:

- **Open**: Opens the item in view mode. You are then able to edit the values of the columns by clicking the corresponding text box.

- **Edit**: Opens the item in edit mode.

- **Share**: Allows the sharing of the item with users inside the organization, users with existing access, and specific people. You can also share the item with anonymous users if it has been configured by the SharePoint administrator to do so.

- **Copy link**: You can copy the link, and then the link can be sent to a user via email or MS Teams.

- **Copy field to clipboard**: Copies the fields of the item to the clipboard so that you can paste them into another document or application.

- **Manage Access**: Allows one to share the file or restrict access.

- **Delete**: The item will be deleted and sent to the recycle bin.

- **Power Automate**: Allows you to start a Power Automate that has been already created. Power Automate can also integrate with other Microsoft 365 applications.

- **Alert me**: Sends an alert when there is a change, someone else changes an item, someone else changes an item created by you, and someone else changes an item last modified by you. The alert can be sent immediately, daily, or weekly. These alerts apply to the entire list.

- **More >**

  - **Workflow**: Allows you to start a legacy workflow on the item. These workflows are slowly being replaced by Flow, but you can create workflows in SharePoint Designer 2013 until further notice. This is still available because Flow has not reached the same maturity as Workflow, which has been in existence for over 10 years.

61

- **Compliance Details**: Displays any compliance parameters around the item, including if it is on legal hold or if it is in a different retention stage.

- **Details:** Shows a stream of recent activity and details surrounding a file such as permissions and metadata.

In summary, lists and libraries are very similar. The best way to gain an understanding of all the features, which are too many to cover in this introductory book, is to create them and explore them. If you have any questions, please feel free to email me. I can't promise an immediate response, but I will try to respond in a timely manner.

Views

Views allow us to manipulate data, whether in lists or libraries, to show or hide data that does not fit the story we are trying to tell. If you look at any data, the data is rarely ever presented in a flat file. Usually, there is some grouping or filtering to show the data that we want to present. For example, if you have a list of orders for a product company, it might be best to show that data grouped by location and filtered above a certain order cost. In this next section, you will explore the standard views of SharePoint and learn how to customize a view in a way to suit your needs.

The standard view that comes with a list or library is titled "All Items or All Documents." This view will render all items or documents in a single view with no data logic applied. These views are great for when there is a limited number of items or documents, but once the content grows, these views become very useless unless you filter.

Note   You can always sort the column values and filter when applicable to show different data in the standard view. However, a better practice is to create a set of views that support the business need of the list, so they are always available and users do not need to spend time filtering a list manually.

Filtering on demand works well to quickly create a view of the data that you are interested in. Another approach is to create views that everyone is interested in. For example, for a help desk ticket list, the view could be open tickets, closed tickets, high-priority tickets, and tickets not started. This allows anyone using the application to quickly switch between different views to find the data they need.

In this example, let's create a new list called "Project Contacts." You will need to create the columns such as "Project Name" (rename title column), "Project Contact" (single line of text), and "Role" (choice).

Once the columns are created, populate the list with a few projects and create a view to show all projects grouped by Role.

To create the view, follow these steps:

1. In the list, click the down arrow next to "All Items."

2. Click "Save view as."

3. Save it as "Grouped by Role" and click the Save button.

4. Select the down arrow again, and the Grouped by Role view should have a checkmark next to it. If it doesn't, select the view you created in Step 3.

5. In the same drop-down menu, select "Edit current view."

6. The Edit view page allows you to configure the view on a variety of factors. In this example, scroll down to Group By and set First group by the column to Role.

7. Scroll to the bottom of the Edit view page, and click the OK button.

When you look at the list again, you will notice that the items are grouped by Role, and you can easily see how many projects are assigned to each Role. When creating the view, you may have noticed that there are many other options that can be used to configure a view. The available options are as follows:

- **View Name**: Specify the name of the view.

- **Web address of this view**: Specify the URL. If needed, SharePoint will create a default value.

- **Make this the default view**: Check the checkbox if you want this to be the default view that every user will see when they access the list. If not checked, the view will be available for a user to select.

- **Columns**: Select or deselect any columns you do not want to show in the view. At a minimum, one column must be checked.

- **Sort**: You can sort the list by two columns in either ascending or descending order. You cannot sort by more than two fields.

- **Filter**: Set a filter or multiple filters and use and/or logic to create a sophisticated filter. You can also use different mathematical equations such as "is equal to" or "less than or equal to."

- **Tabular View**: By default, this checkbox is checked and allows an item to be checked so that multiple items can be selected for bulk actions.

- **Group By**: Select at most two columns and group items by a column value. Each Group By field can also be sorted in either ascending or descending order. You can also set the groups to be collapsed or expanded when a user accesses the list and the associated view.

- **Totals**: In views, you can sum all the values of a column and have it displayed in the view. You can choose from Count, Sum, Average, Maximum, Minimum, Std Deviation, and Variance. The available options are based on column type and only not the default columns such as Created or Modified By.

- **Style**: With a view, you can apply a style to change the way the list or library looks. If there are a lot of columns in your view, the Shaded Style will make it easier to read.

- **Folders**: You can specify whether to show folders or not to show folders at all. This pertains more to libraries than lists. Also, if you use folders within a library, it limits the ability to use grouping and filtering.

- **Item Limit**: Specifies the number of items to show in the view and displays either in batches or within limit overall.

- **Mobile**: Every list or library has mobile settings. The first setting allows you to limit the number of items returned and set a field that will allow you to edit the item.

With these settings, you can create straightforward views or complex views. A word of caution: Be careful with the filter rules because a wrong filter condition can render zero items returned and becomes quite frustrating to find and resolve.

Permissions

The SharePoint permissions model has always been a bit cumbersome because of the many places where permissions can be changed from sites, libraries, and items. With modern team sites, permissions management has been streamlined so adding users, whether they are a user of the organization or a guest, is now a lot easier.

On a modern team site, the permissions are accessible via the Share link in the right corner, as shown in Figure 2-27.

Figure 2-27. *Viewing members of a site*

Add organizational users (coworkers) by clicking "Share" as described in the preceding. In the dialog, click "Share" and begin typing their name or email address. As you type the name or email address, the matches will begin to populate, and you can select the user from the list of suggestions. Click the Save button, and the user will be saved and given the permission level in the drop-down box (Read, Contribute, Edit, Full Control). The Read permission level allows the user to read only; they cannot add content or make any changes to the site. The Contribute permission allows a user to add/delete content to/from the site. The Edit permission allows not only all the permissions associated with Contribute but also the ability to add/delete lists and libraries. The final permission level of Full Control allows a user to make any changes on the entire site including permissions.

Note   External users such as guests are governed by the external sharing policy of the tenant. The policy would need to be altered for the entire tenant to allow external users access when assigned.

In most cases, I would say to leave the permissions as is and not modify them because modifying them can indirectly cause users to lose access to the site or grant users too much permission. There are business cases where modifying the permissions is necessary, as in the case of employee reviews or a confidential site where permissions need to ensure that employees have the right level of access.

To modify the permissions in an advanced scenario, click "Site permissions" located in the Microsoft 365 settings menu (cog or gear icon in the upper-right corner). Clicking "Site permissions" will open the Site permissions dialog. In this dialog, you can modify permissions of the SharePoint group such as to be Read or Full Control. This is accomplished by selecting the down arrow of the group and choosing the appropriate permission, as shown in Figure 2-28.

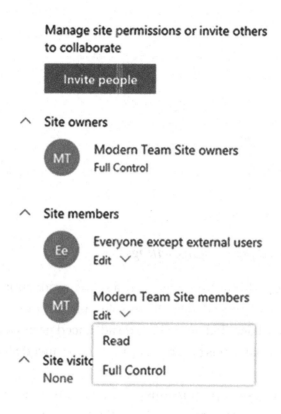

Figure 2-28. *Site permissions dialog*

This where most permission changes are done if needed. If the business requirements require that a different permissions scheme be created, that can be done by clicking the "Advanced permissions settings" link shown in Figure 2-28.

For those users who are familiar with SharePoint 2013, 2016, or 2019 permissions management, the advanced permissions settings look identical to Figure 2-29.

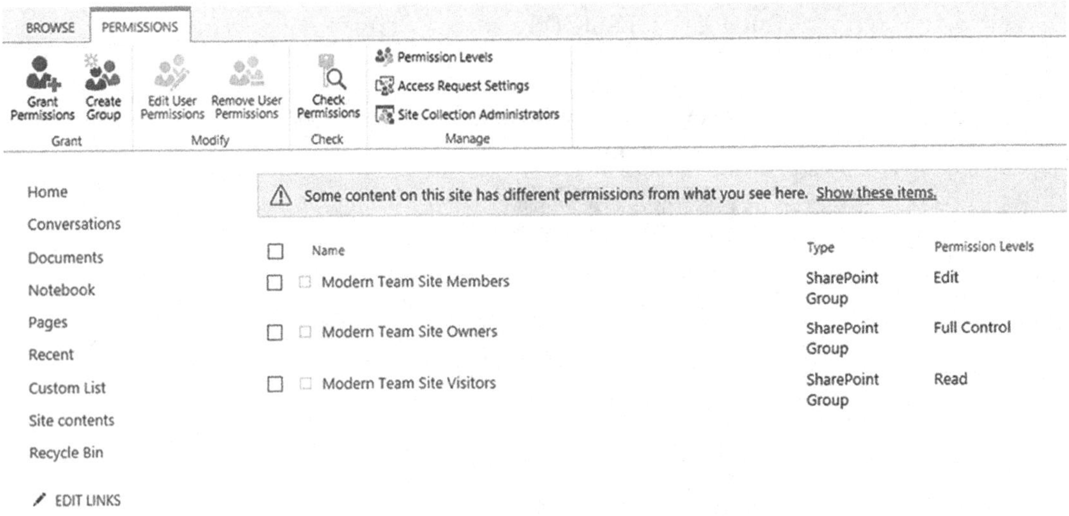

BROWSE	**PERMISSIONS**				

Grant Permissions | Create Group | Edit User Permissions | Remove User Permissions | Check Permissions | Permission Levels / Access Request Settings / Site Collection Administrators

Grant | Modify | Check | Manage

Home

Conversations

Documents

Notebook

Pages

Recent

Custom List

Site contents

Recycle Bin

⚠ Some content on this site has different permissions from what you see here. Show these items.

	Name	Type	Permission Levels
☐	☐ Modern Team Site Members	SharePoint Group	Edit
☐	☐ Modern Team Site Owners	SharePoint Group	Full Control
☐	☐ Modern Team Site Visitors	SharePoint Group	Read

✏ EDIT LINKS

Figure 2-29. Advanced permissions settings

Part of the purpose of this book is to provide a solid introduction to all the Microsoft 365 collaboration applications and not to focus solely on one application more than another. Because of this, I decided not to include advanced permissions in this book because that is a topic that is best reserved for an advanced SharePoint Online publication.

For classic experience sites, permissions are modified through a slightly different procedure. This procedure is the same as it is in Microsoft's SharePoint 2013, 2016, and 2019 on-premises products. Again, advanced permissions are best reserved for a non-introductory book.

As a best practice, in most scenarios, you manage the permissions through the Group membership dialog described at the beginning of this section. If advanced permission changes are needed, please consult with your Microsoft 365 administrator prior to doing so.

Pages and Web Parts

Now let's explore pages. Pages hold all the sites together and give the user an interface to connect to. SharePoint pages can be customized to include specific web parts, which can be used to show a user a different presentation of data or specific lists or libraries.

I will focus on editing a modern team site instead of a classic experience site. This is partly because modern team sites will always have a different set of web parts and are becoming the standard site template for Microsoft 365.

Before you dive into editing a site, I want to briefly touch upon the available web parts and their uses because they have significantly matured throughout the years:

- **Text**: Adds text to the page. Allows for typical text formatting options.

- **Image**: Adds an image to the page.

- **File viewer**: Embeds a file onto the page. It can be a .pdf, .docx, .xlsx, or another supported file type.

- **Link**: Adds a link to the page. Will show a preview of the website that the URL points to.

- **Embed**: Allows for embedded code to be added to the page. For example, you can embed a YouTube video. YouTube will generate the embedded code automatically on the website.

- **Highlighted content**: Shows content based on a variety of metadata.

- **Bing maps**: Adds a Bing map to the page and shows a location.

- **Button**: Graphical way to add a button for a user to click to navigate to other content.

- **Call to Action**: Allows to quickly grab the attention of the user to perform some action or notify them of something important.

- **Code Snippet**: Used to display programming code as text so it can be viewed in a noninteractive format.

- **Conversations**: Able to display Yammer content.

- **Countdown Timer**: Will display a countdown timer configured by the user.

- **Divider**: Inserts a line (divider) between web parts.

- **Document Library**: Displays the items of a selected document library.

- **Events**: Displays upcoming events or calendar entries.

- **Group Calendar**: Creates a calendar that all team members can add events to.

- **Hero**: Adds the Hero web part to the page. The Hero web part allows content to be visually displayed and highlighted. This web part was introduced in the communication site.

- **Highlights**: Displays dynamic content based on filters and/or content types.

- **Image Gallery**: Shows a gallery of images.

- **Kindle Instant Preview**: Allows the insertion of a Kindle book (preview only).

- **List**: Displays the items of a selected document list.

- **List Properties**: Connects to an existing list web part on the same page and displays the items of that list.

- **Markdown**: Allows you to add text and format it using Markdown language. This language is used to create simple-to-read text files.

- **Microsoft Forms**: Adds a survey to the site. Surveys are used to gather responses to a questionnaire. Microsoft Forms and surveys are discussed in Chapter 10.

- **Microsoft Power Apps**: Allows you to embed a PowerApp into a page for consumption.

- **News**: Allows one to post and configure a news center where news articles can be posted and consumed.

- **Microsoft (Office) 365 Video**: This is being removed and replaced with the Microsoft Stream web part.

- **Page**: Provides details about the page.

- **People**: Allows one to display selected users and their basic information.

- **Power BI**: Allows one to embed a Power BI report on the page.

- **Quick chart**: Allows one to add simple charts (column or pie) to a page.

- **Quick links**: List of links.

- **Recent Documents**: Displays recently added/modified documents.

- **Saved for later**: Is a new webpart which allows users to "pin" pages and documents for users to see.

- **Stream**: Embeds a video from a Microsoft Stream channel. Microsoft Stream is a video sharing platform that is integrated into the Microsoft 365 suite.

- **Twitter**: Allows one to embed a Twitter feed.

- **Weather**: Allows one to embed the weather for a location.

- **World clock**: Displays time zones.

- **YouTube**: Allows the embedding of a YouTube video.

Editing Pages

Editing pages in SharePoint Online is a simple task. The only trouble you will run into is figuring out which web parts to use or what page layout to use. To put the page into edit mode, select the Edit button in the upper-right corner, as shown in Figure 2-30.

Figure 2-30. *Putting the page into edit mode*

Clicking the Edit button puts the page into edit mode. The interface will look like Figure 2-31. The layout contains some key components that I will highlight.

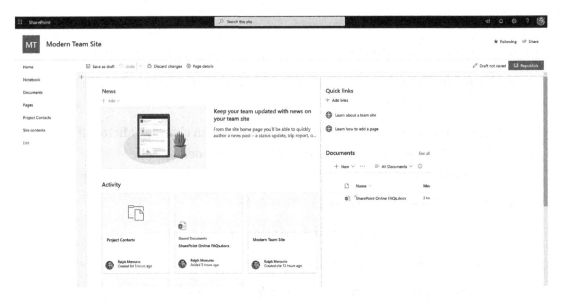

Figure 2-31. *The edit interface*

At the top of the page layout beneath the Modern Team Site title, you will notice three buttons: "Save as draft," "Discard changes," and "Page details." "Save as draft" saves all the changes you made but does not publish the page to be visible and allows you to work on the page over the course of time without having to make all the changes at once. If you made a mistake and just want to start fresh, clicking "Discard changes" closes the page and allows you to reopen the page and start anew. It doesn't save any of your changes – even before you made a mistake in editing the page. The final button, "Publish/Republished," located on the rightmost side publishes the page and makes it visible to all users.

In this edit mode, you can edit either sections or web parts. In Figure 2-31, News and Activity are web parts, while the section is the zone that contains both of the web parts. If you ever edited pages in other versions of SharePoint, the section is similar to the web part zone or the wiki zone on SharePoint pages.

In the edit view, you can change the layout of a section, move the section, or delete the section completely from the page. The edit section icons are to the left of the section and are listed in a vertical format, as shown in Figure 2-32.

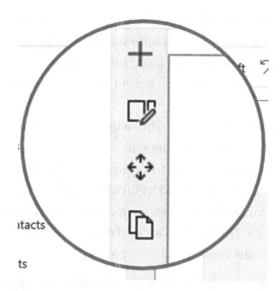

Figure 2-32. *Editing a section of a page*

The first icon allows you to add a section. Each page can have different sections as listed in the next paragraph.

The second icon allows you to change the layout of the section to one of five section layout choices. After you make your selection from the following available choices, click Save, and the section will switch to the selected layout:

- **One column**: One single column. Web parts will stack vertically on each other.

- **Two columns**: Two equal columns. Web parts will stack vertically on each other.

- **Three columns**: Three equal columns. Web parts will stack vertically on each other.

- **Vertical Section**: This option will add a vertical column on the right side running the length of the page.

- **One-third left column**: The section will be divided into two columns with the left column taking up one-third of the section.

- **One-third right column**: The section will be divided into two columns with the right column taking up one-third of the section.

The third icon is the Move Section icon. This icon allows the section to be reordered on the page. When moving a section, the entire section moves, including the web parts within the section. To move a section, click and hold the Move Section icon with your right mouse button. While the right mouse button is held, move the section anywhere on the page.

The fourth icon is the Duplicate icon. This action allows you to duplicate the currently edited section where the icons appear.

The fifth and final icon available when working with sections is the trash can icon. Clicking this icon removes the section and its included web parts from the page and deletes it all. You will no longer be asked for a confirmation during delete. If you deleted the section in error, click the Undo action located near the topmost section. If you need to restore a page to a previous version, follow these steps:

1. Click Page details in the edit bar below the title of the site.

2. Select "Version history" from the menu.

3. Select the three vertical dots (ellipsis) next to the version you want to restore. You can Compare the selected version, Delete, or Restore.

Manipulating Web Parts

To add a web part to a section, make sure the page is in edit mode. If it is not, please follow the steps in the previous section to put the page into edit mode. Much like editing sections, adding web parts is a simple process. When hovering within a section, the "Add web part" dialog (as denoted by the red circle with a plus sign) will appear, allowing you to add any number of web parts; see Figure 2-33.

Figure 2-33. *The "Add web part" interface*

Clicking the "Add web part" will load the available web parts that can be added to a page. I listed out the web parts in a prior section, and the choices presented now are quite exhaustive.

Let's add the Text web part to the section from the "Add web part" dialog. Adding the Text web part to the section will not only add the web part but also put the web part in edit mode, as shown in Figure 2-34.

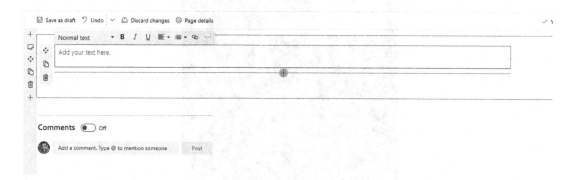

Figure 2-34. *Text web part in edit mode*

Because this is a Text web part, the familiar text styling tools appear. To add text, simply type your desired text and then style it with the available tools. Every web part also can be moved to another section or within the section by clicking the Move Section icon or can be deleted by clicking the trash can icon.

The other web parts all work in a similar manner: add them to a section, edit as needed, and save your changes. Go ahead and explore them all, see what works for your needs, and be sure to save your changes.

SharePoint Mobile App

Microsoft 365 is designed to work across a variety of browsers and devices. This includes mobile devices on the Android, Apple, and Microsoft platforms. Microsoft released a SharePoint mobile app that allows you to connect to SharePoint Online sites, document libraries, and resources all with your phone.

To install the SharePoint mobile app, access the respective app store for your device. The following instructions are from the iPhone perspective, but the instructions and experience are similar regardless of the mobile platform. Access your respective store and search for "Microsoft SharePoint." Figure 2-35 depicts the app available in the Apple Store.

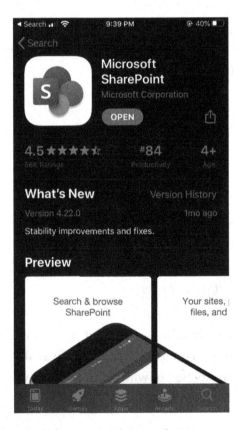

Figure 2-35. *SharePoint mobile app in the Apple Store*

Proceed to download and install the SharePoint mobile app. Once the app is installed, go ahead and open it. Upon opening the app, it will prompt you for your Microsoft 365 email address and password. By entering your credentials, it connects the mobile app to Microsoft 365 and will display the same information as the SharePoint portal site, which is accessible from the Microsoft 365 app launcher in the browser.

The SharePoint mobile app will display the Frequent sites, People, Recent files, and Featured links. You will also be able to use the News and Find icons and see content you have recently worked on. Figure 2-36 shows the main interface of the SharePoint mobile app.

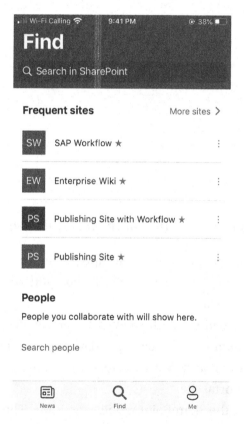

Figure 2-36. *SharePoint mobile app interface*

Clicking a frequent site or a site you are following opens the respective site in the mobile app. Figure 2-37 depicts a modern team site in the mobile view; even though it is not identical to viewing a modern team site in a browser, the functionality is roughly the same.

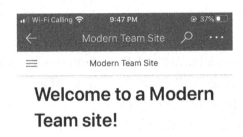

Figure 2-37. *Modern team site in the SharePoint mobile app*

The other aspects of the SharePoint mobile app pull information from Microsoft 365. For instance, clicking the Find icon in the app will allow you to search and find content and people within the organization.

Clicking the News icon gathers all the news articles that have been published within the modern team sites. I didn't cover creating and maintaining news articles in this book, but go ahead and give it a try. You can create news articles on modern team sites or within the SharePoint portal site.

The last component of the SharePoint mobile app is Me. The Me icon within the SharePoint mobile app allows you to modify your Microsoft 365 profile as well as see an activity stream of your actions, files, and created content in Microsoft 365.

Summary

SharePoint Online is a workhorse application. It can help with document management and be the company's intranet, a place to search and find content, or a project management site with user tasks and documentation. SharePoint can be really whatever you need it to be and does so with elegance and ease.

Using lists and libraries to organize content with appropriate columns and views allows for data to be stored in a single location and provides business views into the data; by specifying metadata, you make the search experience even better. The metadata of an item gives the SharePoint Online search engine the ability to categorize an item and create a robust index, which ultimately gives you the best search experience possible.

Modern team sites and communication sites are modern templates that have been redesigned completely and allow for a mobile experience as well as new integrations with other products to bring information into a single site. This robust integration is only going to get stronger in the future.

OneDrive for Business, which is discussed in the next chapter, is built on the backbone of SharePoint Online document libraries, and you will notice that OneDrive functions in a similar manner and is centered around the document experience.

CHAPTER 3

OneDrive

In the last chapter, I discussed SharePoint Online and how it can help organize content around document libraries and sites at the organization level. In this chapter, I will discuss OneDrive, which allows content to be stored in Microsoft 365 and always available. OneDrive will allow you to store up to 1 (one) terabyte (TB) of content, which is then accessible from any Internet-connected device. OneDrive is geared toward the individual user, and there are two flavors currently offered by Microsoft: OneDrive and OneDrive for Business. I will focus on OneDrive for Business because it is included in your Microsoft 365 subscription, whereas OneDrive is targeted at consumers purchasing home subscriptions of Microsoft 365. For our purposes and discussion, I will refer to OneDrive for Business as just OneDrive.

OneDrive is meant as a serious contender for file storage instead of using a local drive or a network location. As Internet-connected devices become more common and the Internet becomes available almost anywhere, it makes sense to store and access your files in the cloud. Microsoft also released a mobile version of OneDrive and introduced new features on the Windows 10 platform that significantly improve the storage, syncing, and accessing of your OneDrive files.

Where Is OneDrive Located?

Over time, OneDrive has been tightly integrated into Windows, Office, and mobile devices to allow ease of use and further adoption of the platform. The first and foremost way to access your OneDrive content is to use any modern web browser and access it directly from the app launcher (Figure 3-1) in Microsoft 365.

© Ralph Mercurio and Brian Merrill 2021
R. Mercurio and B. Merrill, *Beginning Microsoft 365 Collaboration Apps*,
https://doi.org/10.1007/978-1-4842-6936-7_3

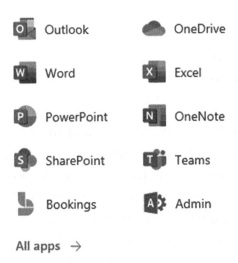

Figure 3-1. OneDrive located in Office 365 app launcher

Clicking the OneDrive icon opens OneDrive; I will discuss it further in the next section.

OneDrive also includes a sync client (Figure 3-2) that integrates into Windows Explorer and syncs content, additions, changes, or deletions with your OneDrive account.

Figure 3-2. OneDrive sync client (blue cloud) installed on Windows 10

OneDrive is also tightly integrated with the Microsoft Office suite and allows for opening and saving files directly from OneDrive. This integration is beneficial because you do not need to download files but can browse directly in OneDrive from the Office applications. Office Online, which offers the web versions of Word, Excel, PowerPoint, is also tightly integrated with OneDrive. I will discuss this further in Chapter 7.

Android and Apple mobile apps are available and allow you to browse and open files located in OneDrive. In conjunction with the mobile version of Office, you can also create and edit documents on your mobile devices, fortunately (or unfortunately), creating a modern workplace where you do not need to be in the office to work.

OneDrive via the Browser

As I demonstrated in the previous section, accessing OneDrive via the app launcher opens OneDrive. The OneDrive layout includes the content shown in Figure 3-3.

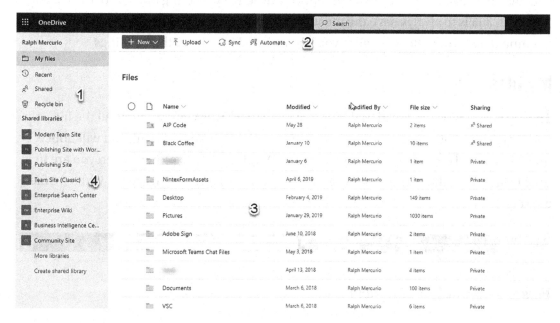

Figure 3-3. *OneDrive layout*

Each of the areas depicted by a number is explained in the following and elaborated on further in this chapter:

- Area 1 allows you to change the view to show My files, Recent, Shared, and the Recycle bin.

- Area 2 depicts the OneDrive menu, which shows/hides options based on your item selection.

- Area 3 is the main area of OneDrive where files and folders appear. It's like Windows Explorer.

- Area 4 shows the recent SharePoint sites or Microsoft 365 groups and allows you to quickly access the document portion of those sites or groups.

Views

Area 1, shown in Figure 3-3, allows you to show different views in OneDrive. This is useful because as your OneDrive grows and as you add more and more content, it can become cumbersome to view the content you're actively working on. Part of the goal of Microsoft 365 is to always have the most recent content available. The OneDrive views attempt to help you; select the view you want by clicking one of the headings.

My files

The My files view is the bread and butter of OneDrive. This view contains all the files and/or folders that you upload or create in OneDrive. Looking around, you will notice that it is a mix of SharePoint functionality and Windows File Explorer. When you are in the My files view, the context menu shows the options shown in Figure 3-4 when no files are selected.

Figure 3-4. *OneDrive My files view*

The New option allows you to create a Word or Excel document, PowerPoint presentation, or OneNote notebook using Office Web Apps (discussed in Chapter 7) and save the file directly in OneDrive. You can also create two other items: forms for Excel and a link. Forms for Excel allow you to develop web-accessible forms and collect the responses from all participants. A OneDrive link is a hyperlink to an existing item or web page. The link then is stored in your OneDrive with a .url file extension.

The Upload option allows you to upload either files or folders directly to OneDrive. The upload interface is like the SharePoint upload interface and allows the selection of multiple files or folders. You can also drag a folder or file from your local device and upload it into OneDrive. Simply right-click the item and drag it onto the browser window where OneDrive is open.

The next option, Sync, syncs the contents locally to your PC utilizing the OneDrive sync application. This application, which is discussed later in this chapter, allows for the contents of OneDrive (selected or all items) to be copied locally to your device. This device can be a laptop, desktop, tablet, or mobile device.

The next option, Automate, allows workflows to be created to perform a certain set of actions when an event (i.e., upload) occurs. I will discuss Automate in Chapter 11 because it is a newer product in Microsoft 365, and I first need to lay the foundation so you can understand the impact and its use within Microsoft 365.

The final set of icons is located to the right of the context menu: Sort, view options, and details. The Sort option allows you to sort the contents of OneDrive by the fields shown in Table 3-1.

***Table 3-1.** Sorting Attributes*

Sort Attribute	What It Does
Type	Sorts based on file extension (.docx, .pdf, etc.)
Name	Sorts alphabetically
Modified	Sorts by time stamp
Modified By	Sorts by user who last modified the document
File Size	Sorts by file size
Ascending	Sorts alphabetically or by increasing number
Descending	Sorts reverse alphabetically or by decreasing number

Note   One thing to be aware of is that for the most part, folders will always be first in any sort order, followed by files.

The Tiles preview (Figure 3-5) located within view options allows you to view the contents of OneDrive graphically vs. the standard details view that you see when OneDrive loads. This is useful if you are looking for an icon or from a readability standpoint.

Figure 3-5. *Tiles preview for OneDrive*

The last icon is the details icon, and it has two unique views. If no item is selected, clicking the details icon displays the stream of recent changes that took place in your OneDrive. This recent stream is a history of what happened. However, you cannot revert any recent change from this window. If you select an item and then click the details icon, it will show a preview of the contents of the file but not for every file type. For instance, .mp4 or .wav files will not render a preview, but Office and PDF files will.

As part of the details, you can see who has access, and you can grant or revoke access. Below the access details are the recent changes, including the history of changes to the item. The last section is the information details, such as the type, modified date/time, path (location), and size.

Recent

The Recent view displays a sorted list of files or folders starting with the most recently accessed item (Figure 3-6). It sorts in a descending order (most recently accessed first) on the Last accessed column.

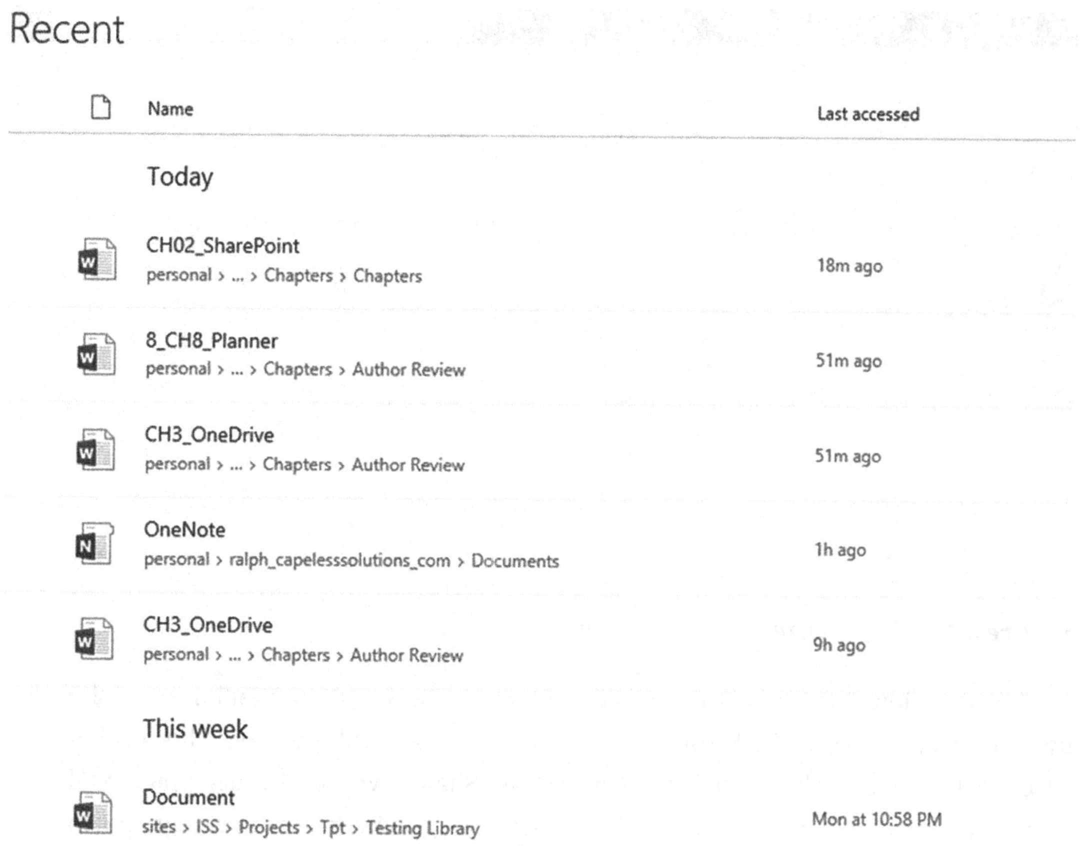

Recent

	Name	Last accessed

Today

CH02_SharePoint
personal > ... > Chapters > Chapters   18m ago

8_CH8_Planner
personal > ... > Chapters > Author Review   51m ago

CH3_OneDrive
personal > ... > Chapters > Author Review   51m ago

OneNote
personal > ralph_capelesssolutions_com > Documents   1h ago

CH3_OneDrive
personal > ... > Chapters > Author Review   9h ago

This week

Document
sites > ISS > Projects > Tpt > Testing Library   Mon at 10:58 PM

Figure 3-6. *OneDrive Recent view*

This view is beneficial because it allows you to quickly see the recent items first because those are the items that you are likely to share or continue to work on.

Shared

The Shared view of OneDrive includes two child views. The first view is "Shared with me," and the second view is "Shared by me" (Figure 3-7).

Figure 3-7. *The "Shared with me" view*

The first view, "Shared with me," allows you to see any content that has been shared by other people and to which you have been given some level of access. This level of access can be read-only or edit. When an item is "Shared with me," the recipient will receive a link to the item and will be able to perform certain actions as designated by the owner of the item. The magic here is the file will and does reside on the owner's OneDrive, reducing the number of copies or email attachments.

The second view, "Shared by me," shows all the items that have been shared by the OneDrive owner. The power of this view is that you can quickly see what content is being shared and if you need to stop the sharing of the content and remove access for a user. In theory, this is great; it aims to cut down on information leakage or unauthorized access, but if the recipient saved a copy, this wouldn't protect the content.

Note   Protecting content once it leaves your Microsoft 365 environment is the work of Azure Rights Management and is out of the scope of this book.

To view details about an item that is shared, the first step is to highlight the item by clicking the row. Once the row is highlighted, the context menu will change, as shown in Figure 3-8.

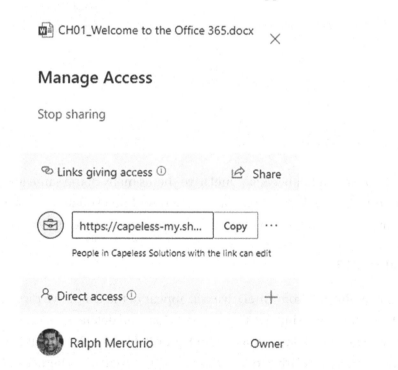

Figure 3-8. *Managing access to a file*

Clicking "Manage access" opens a details pane. This details pane, shown in Figure 3-9, gives basic information about the sharing access. Currently, `CH01 WelcometotheOffice365.docx` is only shared with my organization, and a single user has edit rights. You can quickly tell which user has edit rights by hovering over the user image; in a moment, the user's name and email address will appear.

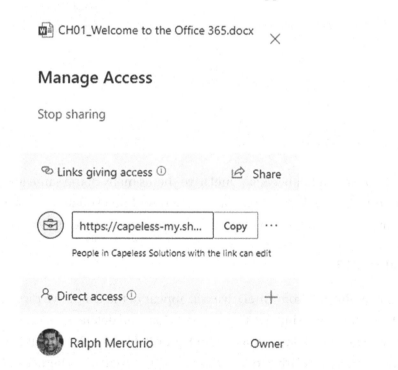

Figure 3-9. *The Manage access details pane*

By clicking "Stop sharing," you can immediately remove all permissions from the item, and only you (the OneDrive owner) will have rights to the file.

Clicking "Share" opens the Microsoft 365 sharing interface and allows you to send a link to an individual (Figure 3-10).

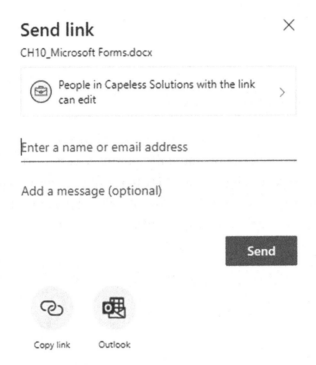

Figure 3-10. *Sharing an item*

This looks familiar because OneDrive shares many of the same features as well as frameworks. This reduces development costs for Microsoft and allows the company to tailor and create products to serve different segments of the enterprise.

Recycle bin

Any content deleted from OneDrive will appear in the OneDrive recycle bin. In OneDrive, the recycle bin has two stages. When you delete an item, it will appear in the recycle bin for 90 days, as shown in Figure 3-11. After 90 days, it will be moved automatically by OneDrive to the second-stage recycle bin where it will be available for another 90 days. After 180 days, it will be marked for permanent deletion.

Recycle bin

	Name ∨	Date deleted ↓ ∨	Deleted by ∨	Created by ∨	Original location
	Document1.docx	2/22/2018 12:13 PM	Ralph Mercurio	Ralph Mercurio	personal/ralph_capel
	Book2.xlsx	1/12/2018 11:38 AM	Ralph Mercurio	Ralph Mercurio	personal/ralph_capel
	OneDrive - Capeless Solutions - Shortc...	12/12/2017 8:08 PM	Ralph Mercurio	Ralph Mercurio	personal/ralph_capel

Can't find what you're looking for? Check the Second-stage recycle bin

Figure 3-11. *The recycle bin and accessing the second-stage recycle bin*

The second-stage recycle bin is available by scrolling to the bottom of the recycle bin and selecting the second-stage recycle bin.

Clicking the second-stage recycle bin changes the view, as shown in Figure 3-12, and displays the second-stage recycle bin.

Second stage recycle bin

	Name ∨	Date deleted ↓ ∨	Deleted by ∨	Created by ∨	Original location

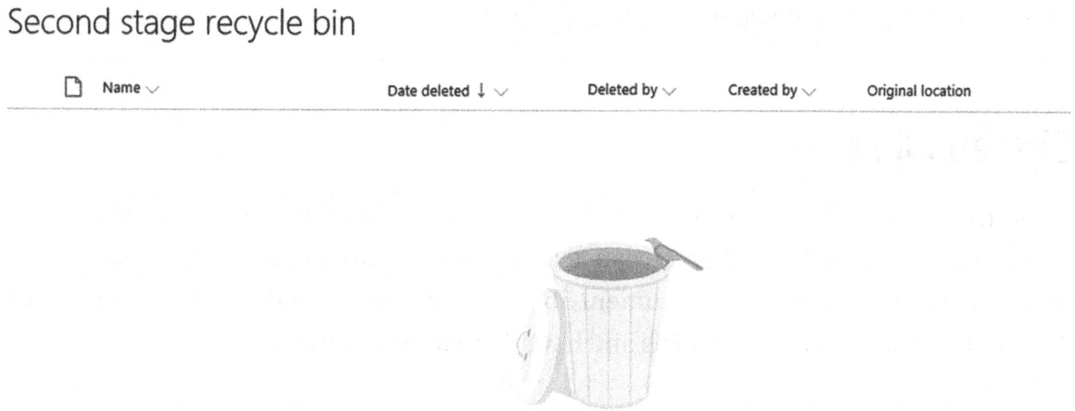

Figure 3-12. *Second-stage recycle bin*

Here, you will be able to restore files if any where there.

Restoring a file from either the first- or second-stage recycle bin is an easy process. To do so, simply click the item and choose "Restore" from the context menu, as shown in Figure 3-13.

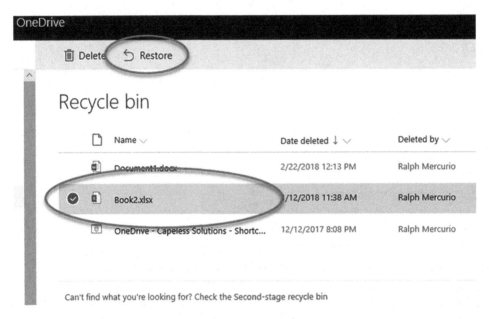

Figure 3-13. *Restoring an item from the recycle bin*

Note   If you manually delete a file from the recycle bin, you will not be able to restore or find it in the second-stage recycle bin.

Shared Libraries

Below the available OneDrive views, OneDrive catalogs and keeps track of the Microsoft 365 groups and SharePoint sites you can access. Clicking into a SharePoint site or Microsoft 365 group opens the document library on the corresponding site/group. Once the library opens, you can add items and have them available immediately.

Working with Items in OneDrive

OneDrive is very closely related to SharePoint Online document libraries and works similarly. OneDrive offers a myriad of actions depending on how and what you do within the OneDrive interface. By hovering over an item, two options appear: a Share link and an ellipsis (Figure 3-14).

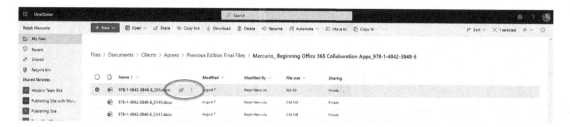

Figure 3-14. *Share and ellipsis icons of a OneDrive document*

Clicking the Share icon allows you to share the item through the Microsoft 365 sharing interface. This interface allows the item to be shared with the following:

- People within your organization

- People with existing access

- Specific people

You also have the ability to specify if the permission allows for editing or viewing only. You can also create a shareable link and send it directly to specific user(s).

Clicking the ellipsis (three vertical dots), as shown in Figure 3-14, renders a menu with a myriad of options. This context menu (Figure 3-15) shows the various options or actions per the selected item in your OneDrive, as shown in Table 3-2.

Figure 3-15. *OneDrive item context menu*

Table 3-2. *Context Menu Explanation*

Context Menu Option	Action
Open	Opens the item in the corresponding application, if available and known
Preview	Renders a preview within the web browser. If it is an Office document, OneDrive will attempt to use Office Online
Share	Allows the item to be shared with the following: People within your organization People with existing access Specific people
Copy link	Creates a direct link to the item to share or access it

(*continued*)

Table 3-2. (*continued*)

Context Menu Option	Action
Manage access	Can see who has access, has the ability to revoke access, or can share
Download	Downloads the item
Delete	Deletes the item, sending it to the first-stage recycle bin
Move to	Allows the file to be moved anywhere in the current OneDrive file/folder structure. The item will be moved, not copied, to the new location
Copy to	Allows the file to be copied anywhere in the current OneDrive file/folder structure. The item will be copied, not moved, to the new location.
Rename	Renames the item to a new file name
Automate	Starts an Automate to perform a set of actions. Automate is discussed in detail in Chapter 12
Version history	Shows previous versions and allows for a restore of a previous version if needed
Details	Shows the details of the item, including properties and shared information

Do not be overwhelmed by the available choices. In the previous chapter, I covered the context menu from the SharePoint perspective, and it is closely related to the available context menu in OneDrive.

OneDrive Sync Client

OneDrive also offers the ability to sync the contents of OneDrive with a OneDrive folder on your local device. A benefit of this architecture is that in the absence of an Internet connection, you will still be able to access and consume your files. Any changes you make will automatically sync once an Internet connection is reestablished.

The OneDrive sync client is available on Windows, Apple, tablets, and mobile devices through either the respective app store or a download from Microsoft. Now, I'll guide you through the process of an install and a basic configuration of the OneDrive client for reference. I suggest checking with your information technology department if there are any policies or special configuration needed within your enterprise.

Installing OneDrive on Windows 10

The OneDrive sync client works on Windows 7 and higher versions, but Microsoft released an important update with the Windows 10 Creators Update that allows for selective syncing of items to your local workstation. This is important because OneDrive offers 1 TB of online storage and you may not want to keep all of that content locally on your device. Also, if the hard drive isn't very big, you also run the risk of eventually running out of space and needing to upgrade to a larger hard drive.

The first step in the install process is to download the OneDrive sync client. The download link is available via a hyperlink in the lower-left corner of OneDrive titled "Get the OneDrive apps." Clicking the link opens a new web browser tab, and you can download the OneDrive sync client. Once you give permission to install OneDrive after downloading, it will automatically install, as shown in Figure 3-16.

Figure 3-16. *Installing the OneDrive sync client*

Once OneDrive finishes, a gray cloud will appear by the system time, and you will need to sign into Microsoft 365 to activate the OneDrive sync client. To sign in, left-click the gray cloud and sign in. Once you click "Sign in," OneDrive will begin the configuration process and ask you for your email account associated with Microsoft 365. Figure 3-17 shows the first step in configuring the OneDrive sync client.

Figure 3-17. *Signing into OneDrive via the OneDrive sync client*

Once you enter your email address, choose the appropriate platform to authenticate to OneDrive. In my case, it was Work. As discussed before, OneDrive comes in two flavors: personal or business. The OneDrive sync client works the same in either version, but OneDrive for personal storage is not integrated into Microsoft 365, and I have exclusively discussed OneDrive for Business in this chapter.

Once authenticated, the OneDrive client will create a default folder where it will sync the contents of your OneDrive account to your local device. Part of the simplicity of the OneDrive sync tool is that any content that you want to sync must be in the default OneDrive folder. You cannot sync folders or content that is stored outside of this folder.

Accepting the defaults, the OneDrive sync client will sync an exact copy of your OneDrive account to your device. In more advanced scenarios, you can selectively sync OneDrive folders instead of syncing your entire OneDrive account.

Now that OneDrive has been configured using the default configuration options, you will notice that the gray cloud has now turned blue and a OneDrive folder is now available within Windows File Explorer. You can save files directly into the OneDrive folder or drag files into it using Windows File Explorer.

Note   The following steps are specific to Windows 10 and having the Creators Update installed only.

Now that you have completed the basic steps, let's explore some of the features of the OneDrive sync client. The first feature I want to discuss is the ability to selectively sync content to the local device. By default, this feature is not enabled, and all content is synced between the two locations. To enable the selective sync, right-click the blue OneDrive cloud in the system tray (next to the system time) and select "Settings." Click the Settings tab, check the "Save space and download files as you use them" box shown in Figure 3-18, and click OK when complete.

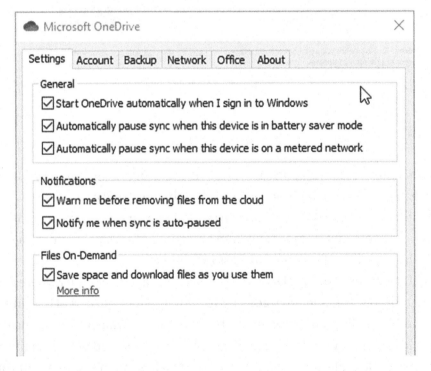

Figure 3-18. *Enabling Files On-Demand*

Now that the feature is enabled, you can selectively enable Files On-Demand for the items you want. To do so, open the OneDrive default folder as designated by the blue cloud in Windows File Explorer.

With Files On-Demand enabled, three options become available to sync files. The three options are "online only," "locally available," or "always available." These settings are controlled by selecting the file or folder in Windows File Explorer and choosing the corresponding option.

First, to mark a file as "online only," open Windows File Explorer and navigate to the OneDrive folder. Right-click the item and choose "Free up space." This will change the status of the item from a green icon to a blue-outlined cloud icon. See Figure 3-19.

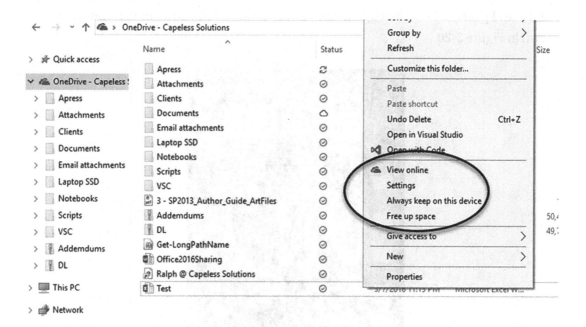

Figure 3-19. *Marking a file as "online only"*

The second option, "locally available," is when you open a file that was previously marked as "online only." This will cause OneDrive to download the file and change from a blue-outlined cloud icon to a green checkmark. Once you are done working on the file and want to set it back to "online only," follow the preceding steps.

The third option, "Always keep on this device," will ensure that the file is never marked as "online only" and that a copy is stored on your device. This is denoted by a solid green circle with a white checkmark.

Note   Deleting an "online only" file from your local machine will delete it from your OneDrive in Microsoft 365. The file will be available in the recycle bin if you need to restore it.

Experience Mobile OneDrive

Microsoft also released an app for both Android and iPhone platforms. The OneDrive client for these devices is available in the respective app stores. To access your OneDrive via your mobile device, open the downloaded app and sign in with your Microsoft 365 user ID and password. Upon logging into the app, you will notice a familiar interface, as shown in Figure 3-20.

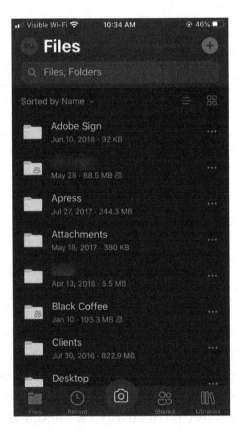

Figure 3-20. *OneDrive mobile interface*

The OneDrive for mobile interface contains multiple views such as Files, Recent, Shared, and Libraries. You can also select the appropriate options by clicking the ellipsis on the specific file. Not every option is available, such as starting an Automate, which currently can only be done from the browser.

Another setting that is similar to Files On-Demand is that by default all items are available online only in the mobile version. This is by design because it limits the initial download of content and you can then stream files as needed and sync the changes back to your OneDrive. If you want to download an item and have it available when an Internet connection may not be available, click the ellipsis and choose "Make Available Offline," as shown in Figure 3-21.

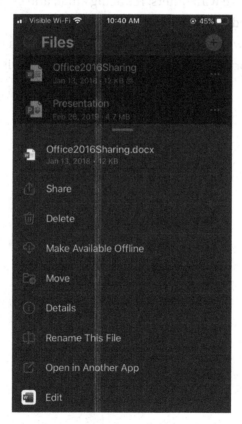

Figure 3-21. *Making a file available offline*

Summary

Microsoft OneDrive offers you 1 TB of storage that is secure and always available to you regardless of device or location as long as you have an Internet connection. By using OneDrive, you are almost guaranteed that you will not lose content via a hardware failure.

With OneDrive, not only is the content safe and secure but it becomes part of the Office 365 ecosystem and you can use the Office Online apps to view or edit your documents. This integration ensures that you have unfettered access to consume your content on your terms. Another important feature is the ability to selectively share content from your OneDrive with others, reducing email and ensuring that multiple versions do not get created.

In the next chapter, I will cover Microsoft 365 Groups, which is a new feature of Microsoft 365; it allows for a collaborative group experience built on Outlook and SharePoint.

CHAPTER 4

Microsoft 365 Groups

In the previous chapter, I discussed OneDrive, which allows content to be stored in Microsoft 365 and always available. In this chapter, I will discuss Microsoft 365 Groups, which brings email, calendars, SharePoint sites, Planner, OneNote, and the ability to integrate other third-party sources into a single, concise application. Microsoft 365 Groups is the ultimate tool for teams to collaborate and share information. This application mash-up aims to bring together people from inside or outside the organization and collaborate using the familiar tools of Microsoft 365.

Before I dive into Microsoft 365 Groups, let's discuss what Microsoft 365 Groups is not. These groups are not the same as SharePoint groups; as I mentioned earlier, SharePoint groups focus on permission-based access to your SharePoint sites.

Where Are They Located?

Microsoft 365 Groups is accessible via the Outlook icon (Figure 4-1) from the Microsoft 365 app launcher or within Outlook 2019 (Figure 4-2). You can access the Microsoft 365 app launcher by logging into Office.com from any supported web browser. Any group of which you are a member will show in the Outlook left navigation and be accessible. Below the Groups heading are three more options: New group, Discover groups, and Manage groups. These three options are used to find groups and to create your own groups for use.

© Ralph Mercurio and Brian Merrill 2021
R. Mercurio and B. Merrill, *Beginning Microsoft 365 Collaboration Apps*,
https://doi.org/10.1007/978-1-4842-6936-7_4

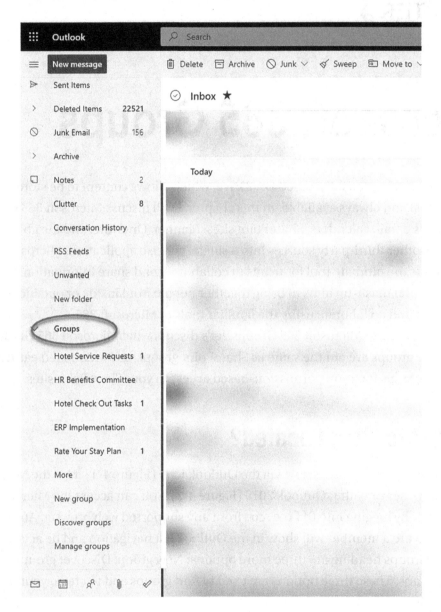

Figure 4-1. *Accessing Microsoft 365 Groups from the Outlook icon in the Microsoft 365 app launcher*

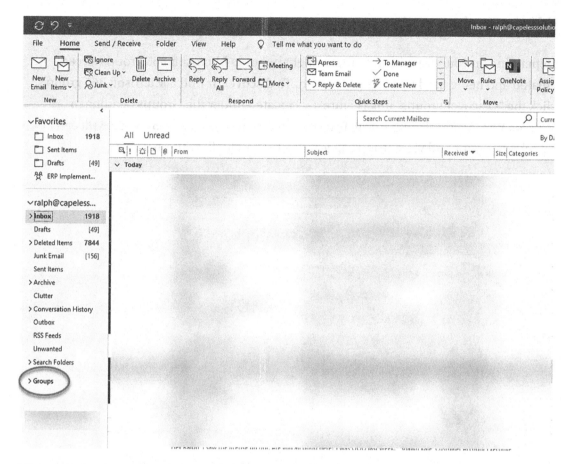

Figure 4-2. *Accessing Microsoft 365 Groups from Outlook 2019*

Note   The interesting notion about Microsoft 365 groups is that they do not rely on IT departments for creation. In Microsoft 365, you can create a group and use it as you see fit to solve your particular challenges. With that, you should follow any governance or guidelines that your IT department has published around the creation and usability of Microsoft 365 groups. There may be requirements or record retention laws around protecting and archiving any of the data in a group.

Discovering a Group

Depending on your organization, there might be some Microsoft 365 groups already created and being used by the organization. To discover or find a Microsoft 365 group, click the "Discover groups" link (Figure 4-1) located under the Groups heading in Outlook Web Access. Doing so will bring up an interface (Figure 4-3) where you can search for groups and view group suggestions that might fit your profile.

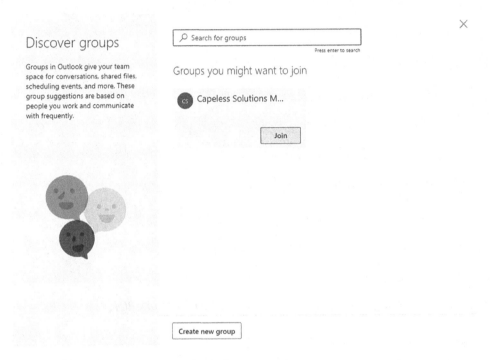

Figure 4-3. *The Discover groups interface*

On the right side of the "Discover groups" modal window, you can also search for groups.

Creating a Microsoft 365 Group

Creating a Microsoft 365 group can be done in multiple ways, some of which I will not cover in this book. The first and easiest way to create a Microsoft 365 group is by selecting the "New group" link (Figure 4-1) in Outlook Web Access. The link is located within the Groups section.

Clicking the link displays the "New group" interface to create your new Microsoft 365 group (Figure 4-4).

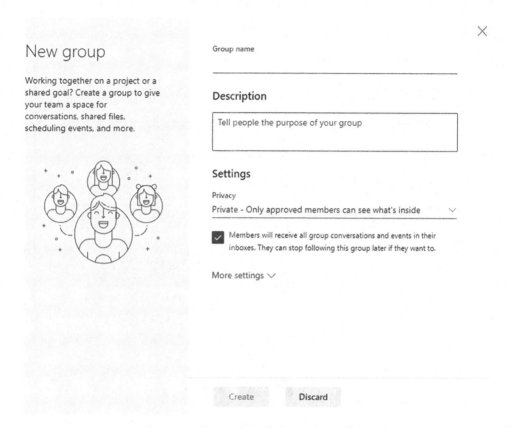

Figure 4-4. *Creating a Microsoft 365 group through Outlook (web version)*

The form contains the following fields:

- **Group name**: This will be the display name for the Microsoft 365 group.

- **Description**: Describe the main use of the Microsoft 365 group.

- **Privacy**: Choose public or private. I will discuss this in detail later.

- **"Members will receive all group conversations and events in their inboxes" checkbox**: Any conversation will also be sent to the member's inbox. Members will not have to check the Microsoft 365 group for communications because they will receive a copy in their own inbox.

- **Language for group-related notifications**: Choose the default language.

Once you are satisfied with the data you entered (Figure 4-5), click the Create button, and your new Microsoft 365 group will be created.

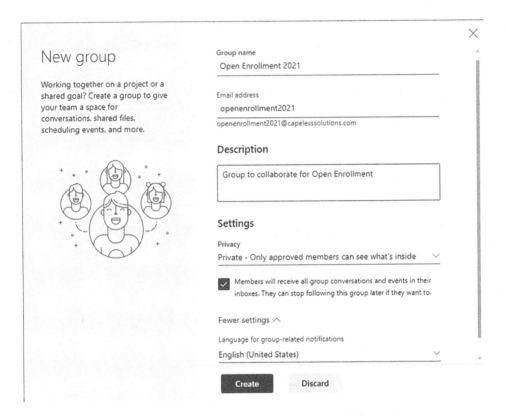

Figure 4-5.   *Creating your first Microsoft 365 group*

You also have the option to add members, or you can add them later. I will discuss member management in detail in the next section.

But first, I want to spend some time discussing the privacy settings available in Microsoft 365 Groups and what they mean within an organization. By default, all Microsoft 365 groups are accessible to your organization only and not available to outside guests. Thus, a colleague might find a Microsoft 365 group that they could contribute to, such as a software bug tracking. They could then submit or view the bugs and contribute in a collaborative way without formally being invited to the group.

On the other hand, you may want to set the privacy of the group to private and invite your colleagues to the Microsoft 365 group. For example, if your HR team is examining the current benefits it provides to employees and is making changes or reviewing them, a private group would be ideal. This way, only invited members can review and make recommendations for change without having confidential information available to all employees until the employee benefits are approved.

In either case, you can quickly change the privacy settings from public to private or vice versa. In Outlook 2019, select the group from the left-hand navigation. Once the group is selected, click Edit Group via the Group Settings icon (Figure 4-6) in the Outlook ribbon.

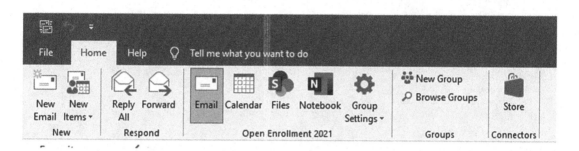

Figure 4-6. *Outlook 2019 ribbon, editing group permissions*

Once you click Edit Group, a new window will open, displaying the settings for the group (Figure 4-7). Choose either "Private" or "Public within organization" from the Privacy drop-down menu. Click the OK button when complete.

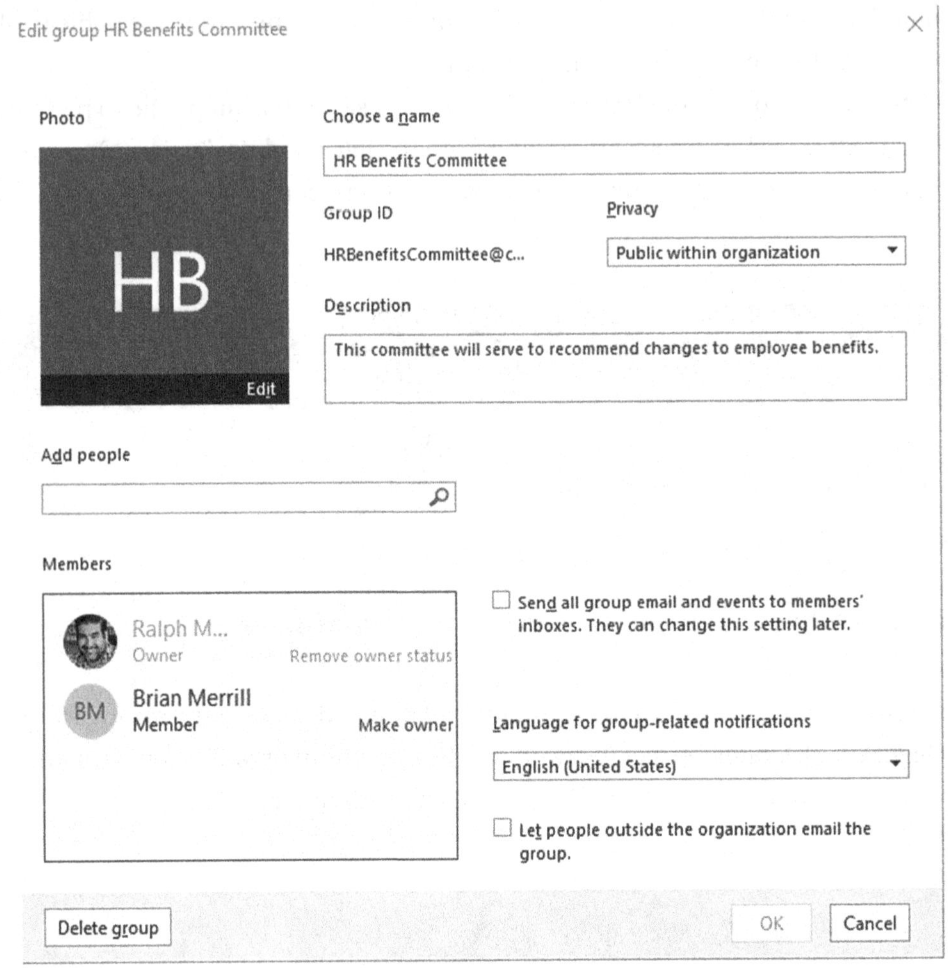

Figure 4-7. *Editing the settings of a Microsoft 365 group*

The process is similar using Outlook Web Access through Office.com. Select the group you want to edit under the Groups heading in the Outlook left-hand navigation. Once the group is selected, click the ellipsis and select "Settings" (Figure 4-8).

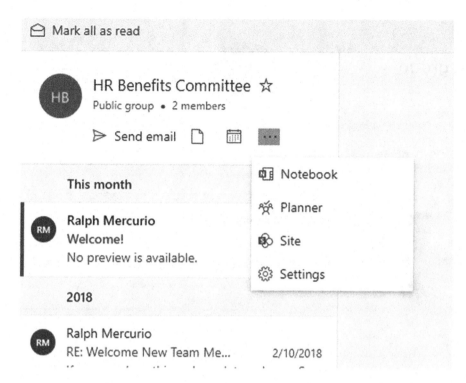

Figure 4-8. *Microsoft 365 group settings through Outlook Web Access*

Clicking "Edit group" opens a new menu (Figure 4-9), allowing you to change the privacy settings of the Microsoft 365 group.

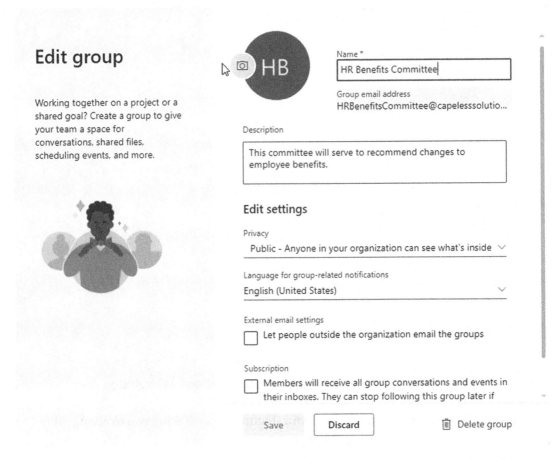

Figure 4-9. *Modifying a Microsoft 365 group privacy setting in Outlook Web Access*

Within the Privacy drop-down, you can select either "Public – Anyone in your organization can see what's inside" or "Private – Only approved members can see what's inside."

Microsoft 365 Groups Member Management

Microsoft 365 groups need members to converse, upload files, and perform other collaborative activities to ensure that the groups are used to the fullest. Microsoft has recognized this and has made adding members very easy and efficient. To add members to a group, you don't need the intervention of IT because adding members is a primary Microsoft 365 Groups function.

Adding Internal Members

To add users to a Microsoft 365 group within Outlook Web Access, select the group from the Groups heading and click the title of the group as seen in Figure 4-10.

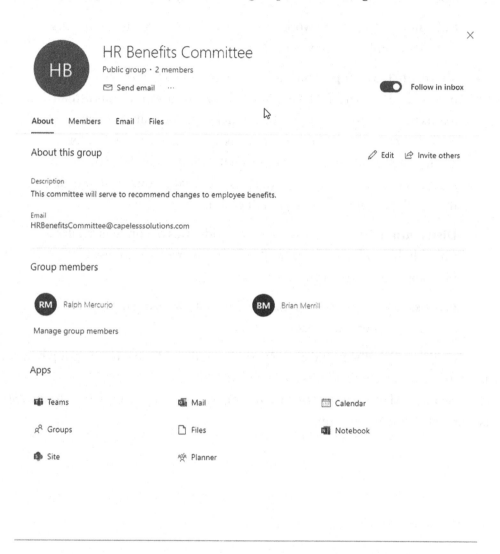

Figure 4-10. *Adding members to a Microsoft 365 group*

To add a new user, click the "Members" heading, shown in Figure 4-10. After which, click "Add members (Figure 4-11)"; you can add four types of members to any Microsoft 365 group: colleagues, Microsoft 365 groups, distribution lists, or guests. An easy way to distinguish between the different types of members accepted is the following:

- **Colleagues**: People you work with or within your organization. This includes members of any department.

- **Microsoft 365 groups**: You can add other groups to your group as members. This is useful if you decide to create groups around small teams that feed into a more substantial team. For example, you could have a group where all of HR has access and create smaller groups such as Retirement, Employee Relations, Benefits, HR Administration, and Training. In this model, you would just add all the smaller groups to the larger HR group.

- **Distribution lists**: Contains the email addresses of contacts available through the Global Address Book of Outlook. You cannot use a personal distribution list.

- **Guests**: Any user who is not part of the organization. This includes vendors, partners, and external users.

Simply begin to type the name of a user (colleague), a Microsoft 365 group name, a distribution list, or the email address of an external user.

Type the name of the user or distribution list, and it will appear in the window. Select the user and click the Add button.

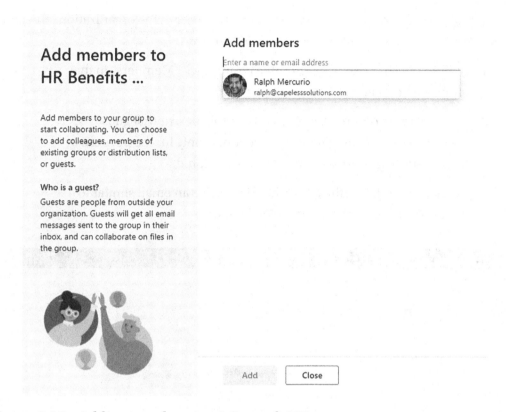

Figure 4-11. *Adding members to a Microsoft 365 group*

Guest Users

Guest users are considered users who are not part of your organization. These guest users can be vendors, partners, consultants, and so on. Please make every effort to be aware of the guest users and create a process to validate guest users to ensure that they are still needed and valid.

Adding External (Guests) Members

Adding internal colleagues, distribution lists, or Microsoft 365 groups will provide a seamless experience and login for users already on the Microsoft 365 platform. The process and experience for guest users is a little different. To demonstrate it, let's invite

Ralphmercurioapress@gmail.com, who is an external user of the organization, and add him to the HR Benefits Committee Microsoft 365 group:

1. Within the HR Benefits Committee group, click "Members" in the upper-left corner and then "Add members."

2. Enter Ralphmercurioapress@gmail.com as the external guest whom you will invite. This email account is only for the purpose of demonstrating guest access and is unmonitored.

3. Once he is added to the group, he will receive an email similar to that shown in Figure 4-12 in his Gmail inbox.

Figure 4-12. *Guest user invite after being added to a Microsoft 365 group*

At this point, Ralph (guest user) has the ability to start a conversation and even contribute or create a conversation within the group through the email client. He does not get access to the actual Microsoft 365 group via Outlook or Outlook Web Access.

Guest Experience Within Microsoft 365 Groups

Being an external user vs. an internal user is a slightly different experience. Internal users have access to all the features of a Microsoft 365 group in Outlook or Outlook Web Access.

The introduction email contains a link to access the files shared within the group. Clicking the link will ask the user to create an account in Microsoft 365, as shown in Figure 4-13.

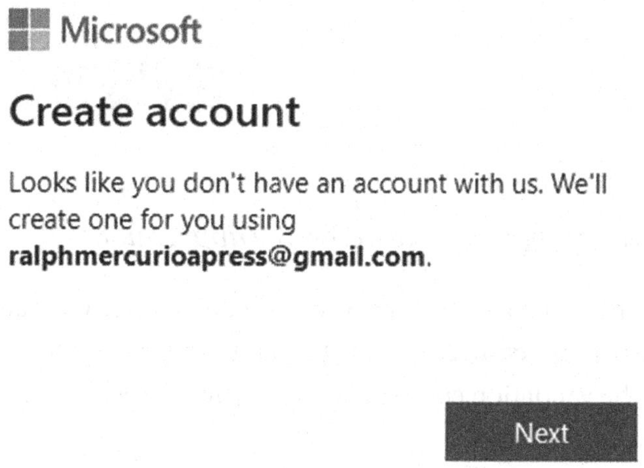

Create account

Looks like you don't have an account with us. We'll create one for you using **ralphmercurioapress@gmail.com**.

Next

Figure 4-13. *Creating a Microsoft account to access applications in the Capeless Solutions tenant*

Microsoft 365 will create an account for ralphmercurioapress@gmail.com and allow the user to create a password to access it, as depicted in Figure 4-14. Microsoft 365 will also ask about the region the user is connecting from and their current birthday for legal reasons.

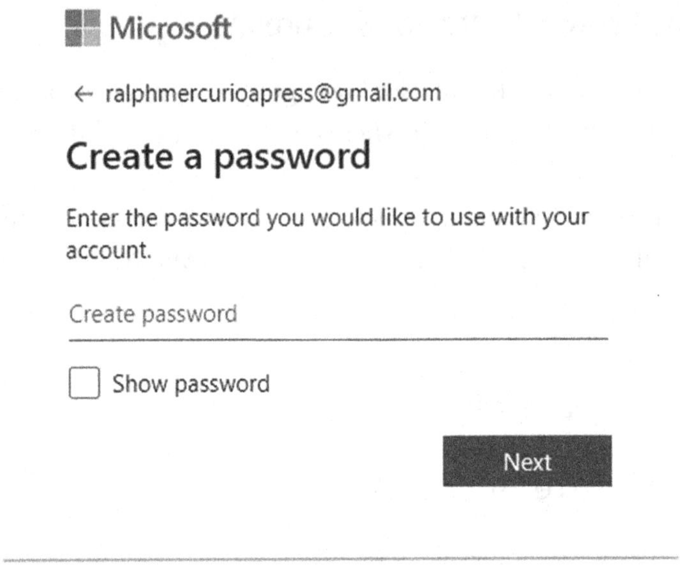

Microsoft

← ralphmercurioapress@gmail.com

Create a password

Enter the password you would like to use with your account.

Create password

☐ Show password

Next

Figure 4-14. *Creating a password to access the applications*

Once the user creates a password, the Microsoft 365 service will validate the user by emailing the user (in this case, `ralphmercurioapress@gmail.com`) a validation code. The user will enter the validation code that was sent by Microsoft; if the correct code is entered, the account is validated.

After the validation process, the user is granted access to the Microsoft 365 group through the web browser. The guest user will have access to the OneNote notebook, OneDrive, and the SharePoint site (Figure 4-15) associated with the group. The guest user will not have access to the conversation stream of the Microsoft 365 group.

Figure 4-15. *Microsoft 365 group SharePoint site logged in as a guest user*

Components of a Microsoft 365 Group

As mentioned, a Microsoft 365 group is a combination of a few familiar applications that bring people together to collaborate. In this next section, I will discuss each component and what it can do for the Microsoft 365 group.

Conversations (Outlook Inbox)

Conversations are essentially emails that can be viewed by all members of the Microsoft 365 group. These conversations remain in the group forever until they are deleted by someone. The foremost benefit of the conversations is that they are available from the day the Microsoft 365 group was originally created and any members who join after can see all the conversations. This avoids the task of forwarding important emails or copying all the pertinent emails and giving them to the new group member.

Conversations retain many of the same features of emails (Figure 4-16); a member can create a new conversation, reply to all, or forward the conversation.

Figure 4-16. *Available actions for a conversation*

Currently, all members can send, forward, and view messages, while external members cannot delete conversations.

Calendar

Every Microsoft 365 group contains a calendar where members can post events and have a single calendar to hold all the group appointments. The calendar also functions like the one in Outlook and can even be overlaid with other calendars to create a seamless calendar viewing experience.

To access the group calendar, click the Calendar link shown in Figure 4-16. The personal calendar is on the left, while the HR Benefits Committee group calendar is on the right and is shaded light blue, as shown in Figure 4-17 within Office 2019.

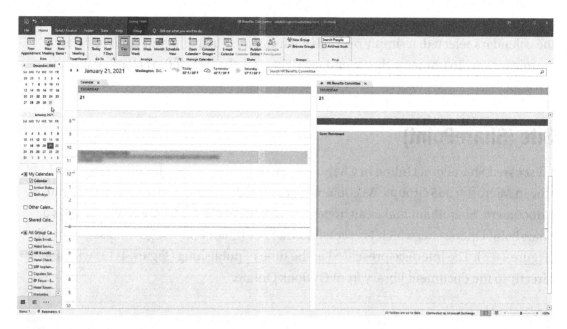

Figure 4-17. *Viewing a calendar in a group*

To overlay the calendars and create a single view of multiple calendars, click the calendar title and choose "Overlay"; see Figure 4-18.

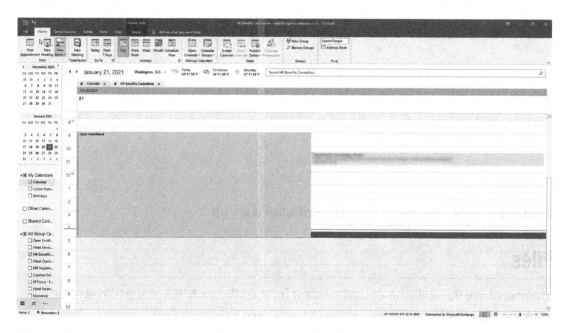

Figure 4-18. *Merging two Outlook calendars in Outlook 2019*

Merging two or more calendars does not create or move any appointments between the calendars selected; it simply overlays each calendar in a different color to create a seamless view. To unmerge the calendars, right-click the title of the calendar and choose "Overlay."

Site (SharePoint)

I discussed SharePoint Online in Chapter 2, and the same principles discussed also hold true in Microsoft 365 Groups. As content is generated or there is a need to collaborate on a document, SharePoint makes an appearance. Behind every Microsoft 365 group is a SharePoint Online site, which is accessible via Files (SharePoint Logo) and selecting Site (Figure 4-16). The interface presented at the time of publishing (Figure 4-19) will link directly to the document library from Outlook Online.

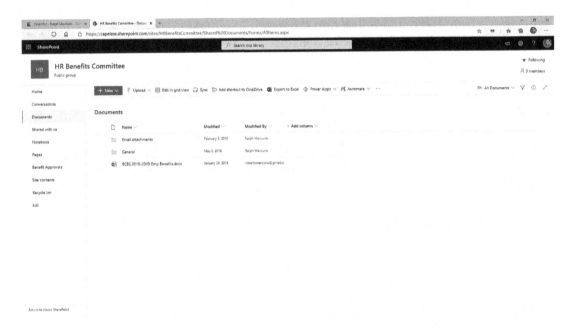

Figure 4-19. *SharePoint site associated with a group*

Files

Members have the ability to upload content for the Microsoft 365 group to consume. Click the Files link located between the Calendar and Notebook links, shown in Figure 4-16 within Outlook 2019.

Now there is a bit of trickery going on because "Files" is actually the SharePoint site document library presented in a different view. This view presents content with minimal options; for example, you cannot create views or add new columns. In this document library, you can click the following options (Figure 4-20):

- **New**: Create an Excel file, PowerPoint file, Word file, OneNote notebook, forms for Excel, or link. I further discuss the Office Online applications in Chapter 7.

- **Upload**: Upload content from your local workstation using the familiar Windows Explorer interface.

- **Edit in grid view**: Can edit the associated columns in an Excel-like interface.

- **Sync**: Will allow the OneDrive sync agent to sync the contents of the library to your local device.

- **Add shortcut to OneDrive**: Will add a shortcut to this library into OneDrive, so the user can access the library from within OneDrive.

- **Export to Excel**: Will export the items in the library into Excel as a spreadsheet.

- **Power Apps**: Allows to add, view, and edit forms to be customized.

- **Automate**: If configured, you will be able to select an Automate and execute it against the library. An Automate, which is discussed later in this book, could be an approval or a related workflow.

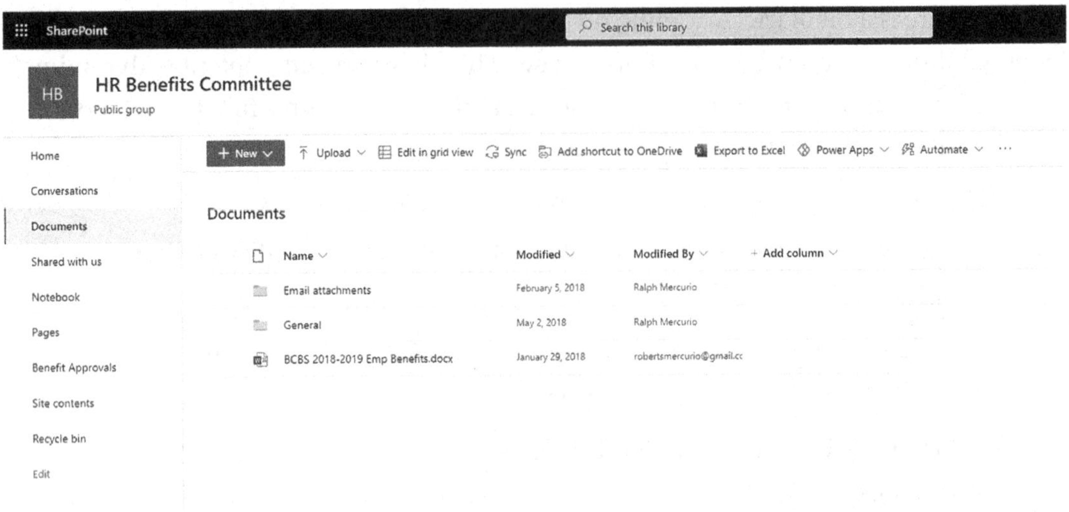

Figure 4-20. *The Files view*

Planner

Microsoft Planner is discussed in greater detail in Chapter 8, where I will detail the ins and outs of Planner and how to use it to manage any tasks. To open Planner in a Microsoft 365 group, click the title of the group within Outlook and then select the ellipsis (three dots) and select "Planner" from the drop-down list.

In this example, Planner can be used to keep track of which members are reviewing benefit proposals and when they are due. As you will see in Chapter 8, Planner offers a simple way to manage tasks and a basic reporting dashboard to view statuses quickly.

Notebook

A Microsoft 365 group also contains a OneNote notebook where all members can share their notes as they collaborate, which can serve as a repository for non-documentcentric or conversation content; access it by clicking the title of the group within Outlook and then selecting the ellipsis (three dots) and selecting "OneNote" from the drop-down list.

OneNote Online is discussed further in Chapter 7.

Deleting a Group

To delete a Microsoft 365 group from Outlook 2019, select the group from the left navigation of Outlook 2019, and in the Outlook ribbon, select "Group Settings" and then "Edit Group." In the Edit Group modal window, click "Delete group" in the lower-left corner.

Because Microsoft 365 believes in second chances, it will offer a confirmation window informing of the deletion and what happens to the data. When deleting a Microsoft 365 group, the entire conversation stream, SharePoint files, the shared OneNote notebook, and the associated Planner tasks are deleted. If you still wish to delete the group, check the checkbox confirming your understanding that the data will be deleted and click the Delete button.

The experience is similar if you are deleting the Microsoft 365 group from Outlook Web Access. From within Outlook Web Access, select the Microsoft 365 group you would like to delete from the Groups heading. Once the group displays, select the ellipsis and choose "Edit group" and then "Delete group" and confirm the deletion.

Note   If you accidentally delete a Microsoft 365 group, there is about a 30-day window where it can be restored. This is an IT administrator activity only and is done with the administrator sections of Microsoft 365.

Access Microsoft 365 Groups on Mobile Devices

Microsoft 365 allows users to access Microsoft 365 Groups from within the Outlook mobile app for either Google or Apple devices. More about the Outlook app and accessing groups is discussed in Chapter 7.

Retention Policies for Microsoft 365 Groups

A big gap in Microsoft 365 has been around preservation of content and recovery. Think about it for a moment: when systems were located within a company's data center, the company had the tools needed to back up data to ensure easy recovery and preservation. With the shift to IT as a service, the need has become less and less.

Recovery of email is no longer needed because it is the responsibility of the vendor (Microsoft) to ensure that it is available, and the same is true for the other systems. Did you ever lose the contents of your personal email account with Google or Yahoo? I caution that if backup of content is needed due to legal or company policies, then it should be backed up properly.

Back to the task at hand, IT administrators can set retention policies to ensure that data can be placed on legal hold or for eDiscovery cases. Microsoft 365 now includes preservation policies around Microsoft 365 Groups, where the data inside the group is preserved.

Microsoft has the ability and capability to offer retention policies around the majority of the content in Microsoft 365. These policies can only be created and activated by an IT administrator with appropriate access in Microsoft 365. The content of a Microsoft 365 group can be retained for a number of years and can be custom tailored to the specific needs of the organization.

Summary

Microsoft 365 Groups combines a SharePoint site, a OneDrive location, and a conversation stream (Outlook) into a convenient package. There is less focus on a document-centric approach, but it does include the ability to incorporate documents. In this example, an HR Benefits Committee can leverage the various components of a group. There are conversations between internal HR members, and the conversation log is viewable by everyone without the need to forward messages. There is a need to have the proposals be viewed or consumed by members of the group, which the SharePoint site allows. There is integration with Planner, allowing the team to assign and track tasks to meet their deadlines, which can also be added to the shared calendar.

In the next chapter, you will explore Microsoft Teams, which is another collaborative mash-up for teams to use. Microsoft Teams differs from Microsoft 365 Groups because Teams is based on the concept of chat, not email.

CHAPTER 5

Teams

Microsoft 365 presents different ways of working, each with a different set of capabilities. For example, SharePoint is best suited for document and item management and as a place to share information. Microsoft 365 Groups combines the familiar inbox with a SharePoint site. Teams works in a completely different way: it employs the concepts of chatting and collaboration.

This is one of the new ways to work and collaborate with users throughout the enterprise. It moves the team away from an email-centric approach to a fluid, chat-based approach where ideas can flourish and interactions can occur. This is especially important for users who are geographically dispersed and not located in the same office as their colleagues. Imagine for a moment that you are a user who works from home and thus you do not have the daily interaction that your colleagues do in the central office. Teams gives you the feeling of being connected to your colleagues and contributing to the work effort. (This sounds familiar as the majority of us have used Teams in the last year as the pandemic devastated the world.)

As this is a Microsoft flagship application within Microsoft 365, there are a lot of pieces and integrations. In this chapter, I want to take the approach from a high level and provide an overview of the critical features; I hope to disseminate enough information to make you feel comfortable with Microsoft Teams by the time you finish this chapter.

Using Microsoft Teams

In the Microsoft 365 tenant, click the app launcher in the upper-left corner and select Microsoft Teams, as shown in Figure 5-1.

© Ralph Mercurio and Brian Merrill 2021
R. Mercurio and B. Merrill, *Beginning Microsoft 365 Collaboration Apps*,
https://doi.org/10.1007/978-1-4842-6936-7_5

Teams

Figure 5-1. *Microsoft Teams application*

Once you click the application, you will be presented with the Microsoft Teams interface. The interface contains a few critical areas, as shown in Figure 5-2.

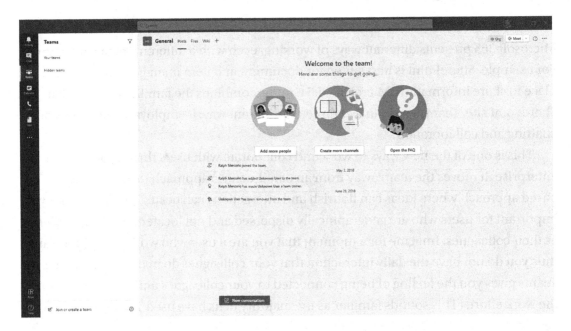

Figure 5-2. *Teams interface*

There are seven available menu options located on the left that allow you to do a variety of different functions. Let's review each of them before you explore Teams further:

- **Activity**: As the name suggests, the Activity dashboard displays recent unread chats, if you are mentioned, replies to chats, what items you are following, any likes of content, missed calls, and any voicemails. The latter two options are dependent on your organization's Microsoft 365 plan.

- **Chat**: The Chat dashboard shows chats you are a part of and allows you to either place a voice call or video call to a particular user.

- **Teams**: Clicking the Teams icon opens the Teams dashboard and allows you to create or join a team.

- **Calendar**: The power of Microsoft 365 is that there is substantial integration between all of the applications. You can see your Outlook Calendar in the Meetings view and any meetings that are scheduled.

- **Calls**: Any calls that are made to you via Teams will show here.

- **Files**: Clicking the Files icon condenses files you recently viewed, files in your OneDrive, and files shared among teams of which you are a member.

- **...**: The ellipsis when expanded will show some of the other MS Teams' applications including Shifts, Approvals, Help, OneNote, Stream, Tasks, and Wiki.

Now let's explore each area more to gain a broader sense of understanding. Teams is very different than any other Microsoft product you may have used as it's different from Office or any other application they have released.

Walking Through Teams

Teams is based on the fundamental concept of a team: a group of people working toward the same goal. These teams provide the building blocks that allow channels to be created and utilize Microsoft Teams to the fullest.

Creating Your First Team

To create your first team, click the Teams icon located on the left in the Microsoft Teams application. You'll see the Teams dashboard open, as shown in Figure 5-3.

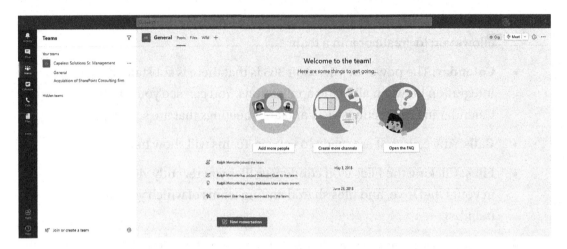

Figure 5-3. *Creating your first team within Microsoft Teams*

Click "Join or create a team" from the lower-left corner; this initiates the creation of a team. You will be presented with a choice to "Create a team" or "Join a team with a code." Select "Create a team," as depicted in Figure 5-4.

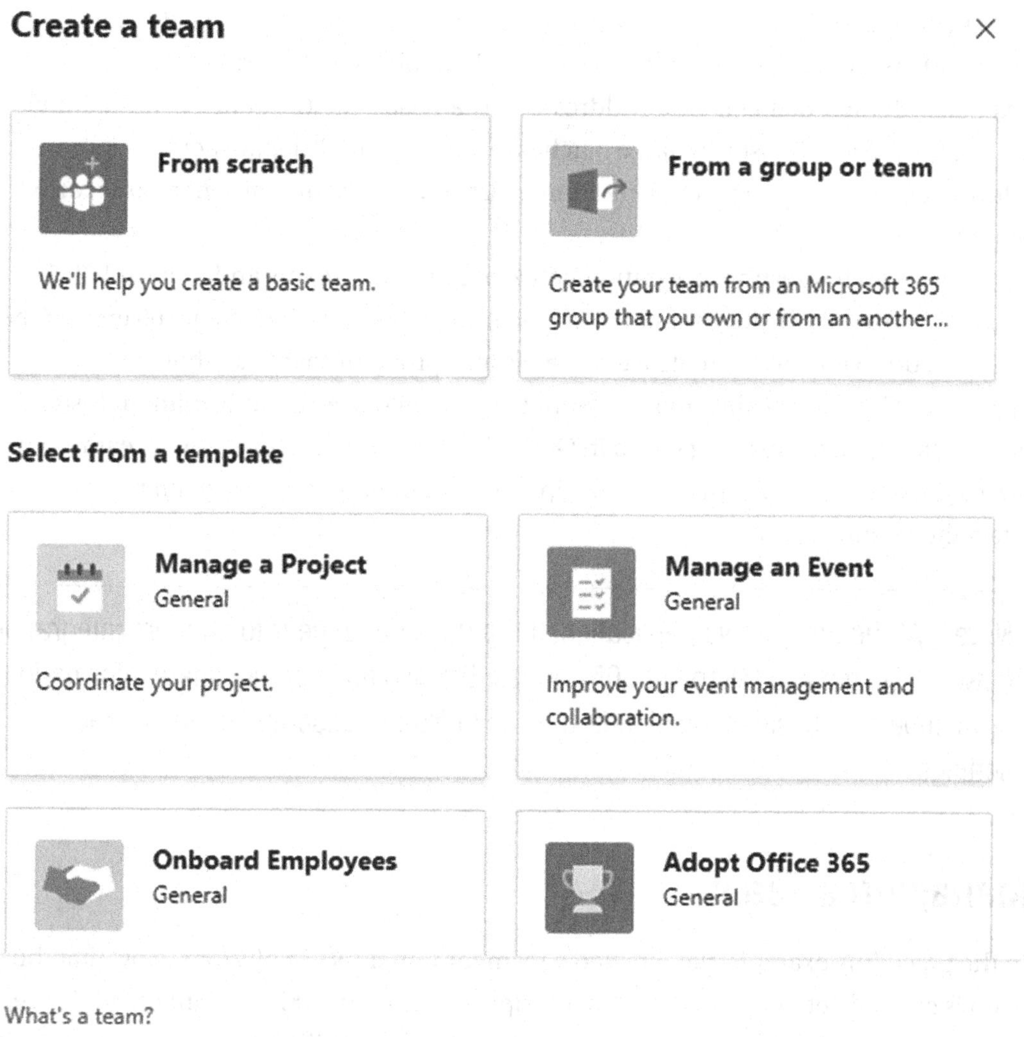

Create a team   ✕

 From scratch

We'll help you create a basic team.

 From a group or team

Create your team from an Microsoft 365 group that you own or from an another...

Select from a template

 Manage a Project
General

Coordinate your project.

 Manage an Event
General

Improve your event management and collaboration.

 Onboard Employees
General

 **Adopt Office 365**
General

What's a team?

Figure 5-4. *Create a team settings*

MS Teams offers multiple templates, which will create the appropriate teams and channels. Some templates are Manage a project, Onboard Employees, Organize Help Desk, and a whole bunch more. For this example, select "From scratch."

The first option you will be presented with is to determine what kind of team to create. As we discussed earlier and throughout this book, Microsoft 365 has a notion of Private or Public. Private teams are teams where users will need to be granted permission, while public teams are open to all. Go ahead and select Public for now. Populate the fields as needed. This includes a team name and a description. Click "Create" when ready.

After clicking Create, you can add any members you want. You'll be directed back to your MS team. This screen allows you to add members to the team by populating the text box with their name or email address. You can use a distribution list or mail-enabled security group to add users in large batches. Contact your IT department for more information to see if you can benefit from a distribution list or mail-enabled security group.

There is an interesting integration between Microsoft Teams and Microsoft 365 Groups. Teams allows the creation of a team from an existing Microsoft 365 group. The option to do so is called "Create a team ➤ From a group or team," as shown in Figure 5-4. Clicking the link allows a team to be created from a group without losing data or changing the existing group in Outlook. Also, you can create a new team from an existing team. This will copy settings, apps, and channels to the new team but will not affect the existing team.

Note   At the time of this publication, there does not appear to be more integration between Teams and Microsoft 365 Groups; the two apps do not share information or membership besides the standard fields of Name, Description, and Privacy settings.

Managing a Team

In the preceding example, you created a team for Capeless IT Solutions. Now that the team is created, let's explore the available options. Similar to SharePoint or OneDrive, click the ellipsis (…) next to the Microsoft team. Doing so will open a context menu with different options, as shown in Figure 5-5.

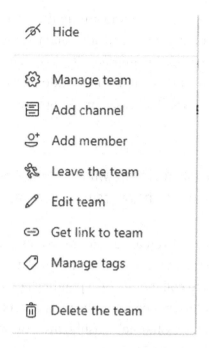

Figure 5-5. *Available menu options for managing a team*

The first available option within the context menu is "Hide." Clicking it removes the team from the Your teams menu and moves the team to Hidden teams. Don't worry; it does not delete the team. To add the team back, click "Show" via the context menu within Hidden teams.

The second available context menu item is "Manage team" and is depicted in Figure 5-6.

Figure 5-6. *Managing members, channels, and settings*

Clicking "Manage team" allows you to manage memberships and modify settings, analytics, apps, and channel information. The Members tab allows you to search for members and view members and their associated permission and offers the ability to remove or add a member. To remove a member from the team, click the X all the way to the right of the row you want to remove. To add a member to the team, click "Add member." Adding a member opens the interface. Begin to type the user's name or email address or, as mentioned, you can also add a distribution list or mail-enabled security group. Once the user or group is added, assign it an appropriate permission level through the interface.

Note   You cannot remove any members who have the "Owner" right assigned. You must change their permission before removing them.

The Channels tab allows you to create a channel, which is a way to organize a project, discussion, or content and is a logical container. An example is to create a channel for senior managers to collaborate on a pending acquisition or to create a collaborative environment to discuss confidential matters. Let's create a channel by clicking "Add channel" within the Channels dashboard. This will open the interface for channel creation, as shown in Figure 5-7.

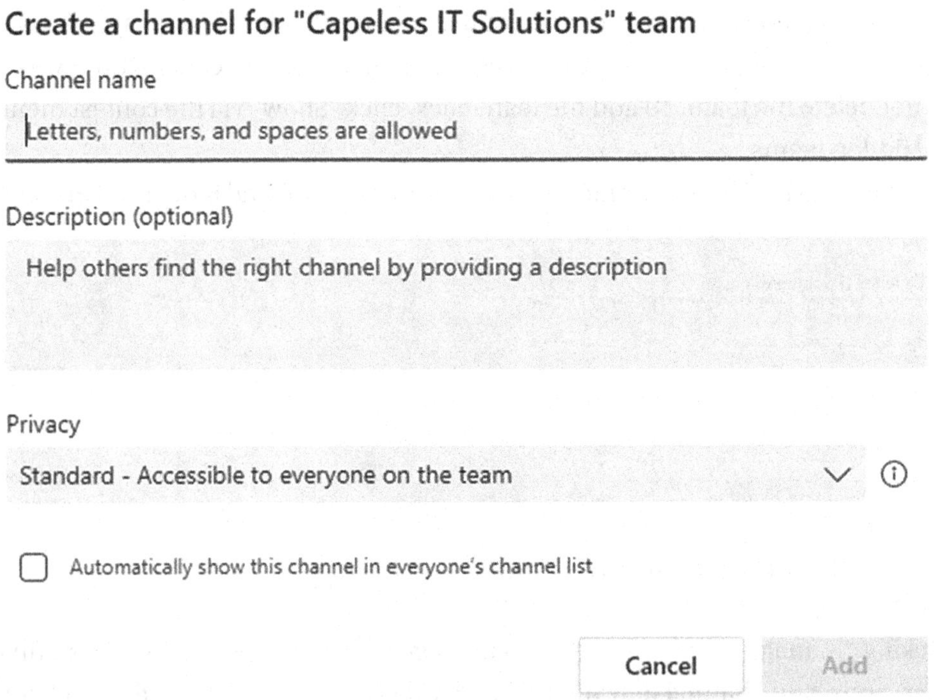

Create a channel for "Capeless IT Solutions" team

Channel name

Letters, numbers, and spaces are allowed

Description (optional)

Help others find the right channel by providing a description

Privacy

Standard - Accessible to everyone on the team   ∨   ⓘ

☐   Automatically show this channel in everyone's channel list

Cancel   Add

Figure 5-7. Creating your first channel within Microsoft Teams

The first step is to name the channel appropriately and give it a description (if desired but not required). You also have the ability to make the channel show for all members of the team. With recent updates, channels can now also be public or private to the team. This is important as it allows a team to be public but have private channels for confidential teams. Click the Add button when complete. You will explore channels in their entirety in the next section.

Still within the Manage team options, "Settings" allows you to configure the team picture; permissions of members; if guests are allowed; who can use @mentions; team code; fun stuff including emojis, gifs, and stickers; and who can manage tags.

The last two settings of Manage team are Analytics and Apps. Analytics will show statistics of number of users, active users, inactive channels, and engagement of the team in different time periods. Apps are components that provide functionality and integration. Apps are also available via the "More apps" link and will bring you to the app store. Some apps are free and some are not. Be cautious when installing apps, as some apps are not free or may not be suitable for your business problem.

The fourth and fifth options from the context menu are "Add member" and "Leave the team." Clicking "Add member" allows users or groups to be added. Clicking "Leave the team" allows a member to leave the team and stop receiving updates or being included. Prior to removal, the user will receive a warning confirming the selection.

The last four options from the context menu are "Edit team," "Get link to team," "Manage tags," and "Delete the team." Clicking "Edit team" allows you to modify the team name, description, and privacy setting. The "Get link to team" option generates a URL that can be copied into an email or shared via another method such as chat. The party will still need access if it is a private team. "Manage tags" is an interesting feature and allows a tag to be created and users assigned to the tag. That tag can then be used in a chat using @mention within Teams, notifying the users assigned to it. "Delete the team" allows the owner to delete the team and the data behind it. The owner needs to confirm the request for deletion.

Exploring Channels

You created your first channel in the previous section (if not, please go ahead and create one), and now you will take an in-depth look at the components of a channel within a team. In the Teams dashboard, you will see the team and channel. The first thing you will notice is that there are two channels: General and Microsoft 365, as shown in Figure 5-8.

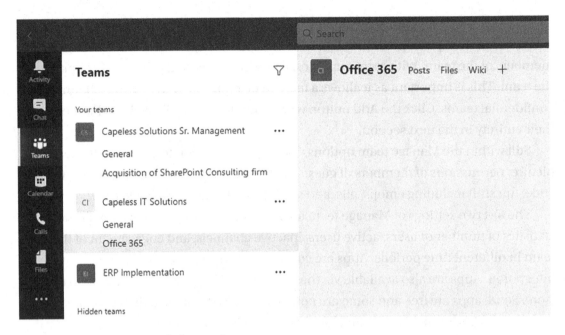

Figure 5-8. *Teams and channels*

The General channel is created by Microsoft 365 as the default channel. This default channel contains and catalogs all the activity in a team and displays it on the homepage of the channel. The default General channel and any channel you create will share the following options via the ellipsis to the right of the channel: "Channel notifications," "Pin," "Manage channel," "Get email address," "Get a link to the channel," and "Connectors."

The "Channel notifications" is a welcome addition to the age of constant notifications through email, text, alerts, and so on. These notifications can be tailored to show all activity, which will notify you on posts, replies, and mentions. Toggling the notification setting to off will limit the notifications. You can also create a custom notification setting if desired. I would recommend leaving the default notification settings to fully understand and then tweak them as needed.

The "Pin" option allows the channel to be pinned to the very top of the application. This is useful as it will keep track and always show the pinned channels for easy access. The opposite setting "Hide" will hide the channel in place so it is not displayed.

The "Manage channel" setting will allow one to set who can start posts in the conversation stream of a channel, and if enabled, channel moderation will allow a finer set of permissions on what channel members are able to do.

The "Get email address" allows mail to be sent to the channel. Clicking the "Get email address" option within the context menu reveals an email address. Any mail sent to the address will show in the Conversations tab of the channel. You also have the option to download the original email if desired. The "Get a link to the channel" allows you to generate a URL to share with colleagues. "Edit this channel" will allow you to set the name and description; however, you cannot change the privacy setting of a channel.

The Connectors option allows you to connect the channel to a variety of sources. Connectors exist to connect Microsoft Forms, Bing News, Dynamics 365, or other sources with the team. As Teams is adopted by more and more companies, the list of connectors will grow, and the integration will grow as well.

The final option, "Delete this channel," will delete the channel permanently. This includes all conversations and currently cannot be undone.

Now that you know the basics of creating and maintaining teams and channels, let's take a ride through the components of a channel and how they work together to provide a seamless experience.

Clicking any channel opens the channel within Microsoft Teams. For this example, let's use the channel you created earlier in this chapter. When the channel opens, you'll see four options along the top: Posts, Files, Wiki, and the (+) sign.

The Conversations section contains the chat stream for the team. A conversation can be started by typing into the conversation text box located at the bottom of the channel, as shown in Figure 5-9.

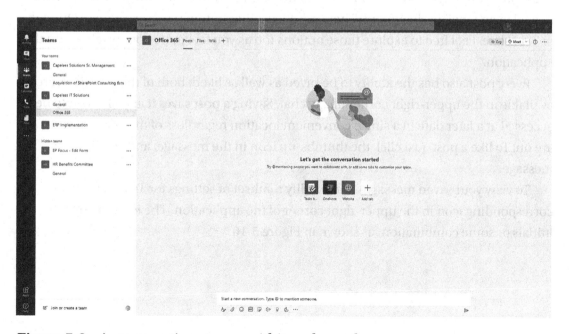

Figure 5-9. *A conversation stream within a channel*

A chat or post can be edited by clicking the corresponding icon underneath the text box: formatting text, attaching an item, emojis, gifs, stickers, scheduling a meeting, and the option to meet now. Recent updates to Microsoft Teams now include links and integrations into other apps, Stream, and showing praise. Once a post is posted, it is viewable by all members of the team in the conversation stream, and members can reply back to the post.

First and foremost, if you posted a chat and decided it shouldn't have been posted, the chat can be deleted from the conversation stream by choosing the Delete option from the ellipsis when you hover over your post. When deleting a post, it does not delete the replies to the post and will display a "This message has been deleted" message in the conversation stream. You also have the ability to undo the deletion by clicking "Undo" within the deleted chat.

Your chats can also be edited by selecting Edit from the context menu. Clicking "Edit" allows you to edit the post with the same tools when you originally posted the post with the exception of the "Meet now" option. Editing any post will mark the post with an "Edited" message, indicating it is not the original post.

The final two options for discussion via the context menu of a post are "Mark as unread" and "Copy link." Marking a post as unread will not separate the post but will separate all the posts that were created after the post you are marking as unread. The "Copy link" option generates a link back to the channel and copies the post so it can be posted in an email or document. There are a few other options such as Share to Outlook or Translate. Feel free to explore those options too as you feel more comfortable with the application.

Every post also has the ability to be saved as well as liked; both of these options are available in the upper-right corner of any chat. Saving a post saves it and allows it to be accessed at a later date in a single convenient location regardless of the channel you are on. To like a post, just click the thumbs-up icon in the message, and you liked the message.

To view your saved messages and modify a subset of settings for Teams, click the corresponding icon in the upper-right corner of the application. The icon will be your initials or some combination, as shown in Figure 5-10.

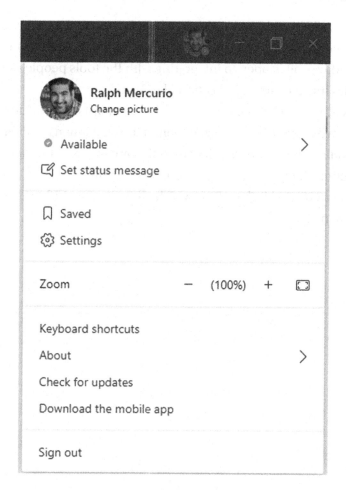

Figure 5-10. *Accessing a subset of settings*

The first option is Available, and it relates to what is known as presence, which can be Available, Busy, Do not disturb, and Away. Each presence status relates to a particular color, and this indicator is used throughout the Microsoft 365 applications. Next is the Saved option; clicking it loads all of the posts you have saved.

The Settings menu allows you to change the color scheme of Teams from the default interface to Dark and High contrast. You can also modify the notifications from Mentions, Messages, and Other categories. To begin, I would leave these as is until you feel comfortable with Teams and know what information you want to see in the activity stream, banner, and email notifications.

Within the channel, there is also the Files link. The Files link allows members to upload files into a SharePoint document library, as discussed in Chapter 2. A surprising option that Microsoft has released is the ability to add cloud storage that is not part of

Microsoft 365. You have the ability to add Dropbox, Box, ShareFile, Egnyte, and Google Drive. You will need a subscription (paid or free) to use these cloud storage providers, but it shows that Microsoft is open to integrating with the tools people use and to bring those technologies into a central application like Teams.

The Wiki link allows a wiki to be created and have members of the team add content. I have never liked wikis and always viewed them to be challenging to create and manage. However, you should explore the wiki. If you don't want that functionality, remove the Wiki link by selecting "Remove" from the drop-down arrow.

The last link in a channel is the + link, which allows you to add a tab from a variety of sources, as shown in Figure 5-11.

Figure 5-11. Adding one of many integrations to a channel

For example, I discuss Planner in detail in Chapter 8, but the primary purpose of Planner is task management. You can create a plan from the channel and have the ability to add tasks, assign them to members, and view it all in a dashboard that shows the tasks and their status. Not only will you have a conversation stream and any supporting files but also the tasks that need to be completed. This allows for a 360-degree experience without ever leaving the Microsoft 365 applications or purchasing additional applications or signing in multiple times.

Activity

The Activity feed catalogs the activity on the channels you follow and offers an audit trail of what you have been doing in Teams, as shown in Figure 5-12.

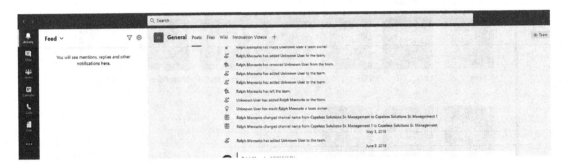

Figure 5-12. *Activity dashboard*

Clicking the Activity icon on the left-hand side of the application opens the Activity dashboard. You can switch from Feed to My Activity. You also can filter the Activity feed to show only specific items as noted:

- **Unread**: Displays unread messages (chats).

- **Mentions**: Displays when you are mentioned in a post. Mentions are formatted as @username.

- **Replies**: Displays all replies to your posts.

- **Following**: Displays users that are following your posts.

- **Likes**: Displays posts that you have liked.

- **Missed call**: Displays all missed calls.

- **Voicemail**: Displays all voicemails (pending licensing and setup).

- **Apps**: Displays updates from integrated apps.

However, you can't filter the My Activity feed and instead will see all of the activities you have made in Microsoft Teams.

Chat

As described earlier, Teams is based on the concept of chatting, not emailing, so it only makes sense that chat is integrated into the Teams platform without the need to open another application. Figure 5-13 shows the Chat dashboard.

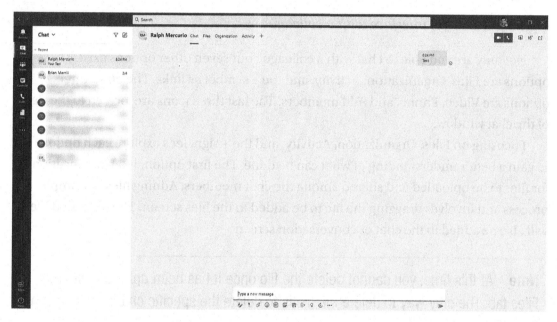

Figure 5-13. _Chat dashboard_

Access the Chat dashboard via the Chat icon located below Activity on the left-hand side of Teams. Once the screen refreshes, you will be able to chat with your colleagues, see past chats, and also have the ability to call others from within a chat.

To start a chat, click the new chat icon in the upper-right corner of the chat stream next to the filter icon. Clicking this icon allows you to type the name of your colleague and send a message via the same interface you explored in the Conversations section of channels, as shown in Figure 5-14.

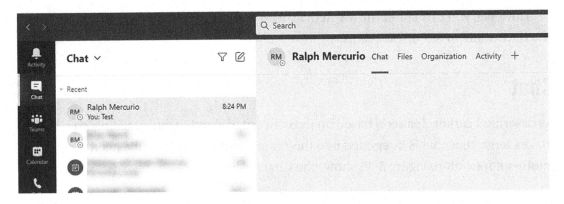

Figure 5-14. *Chat interface with a colleague*

Not only are you able to chat with a colleague but seven other options exist. These options are Files, Organization, Activity, and the + symbol as links. The other three options are Video, Phone, and Add members. The last three icons are located to the right of the chat window.

Focusing on Files, Organization, Activity, and the + sign, let's explore each option to gain a better understanding of what can be done. The first option, Files, is a location for files to be uploaded and shared among the chat members. Adding files is a simple process and involves dragging the file to be added to the files screen. The uploaded file will also be added to the chat or conversation screen.

Note   At this time, you cannot delete the file once it has been uploaded via the Files tab. The only way to delete the file is to delete the specific chat post in which the file was uploaded.

The next option, Organization, displays the organizational hierarchy, if the appropriate fields are populated within Active Directory.

Active Directory is a system that contains all the users and their properties in a central location. These properties include name, phone number, manager, and a variety of other fields to identify and catalog users. The organization hierarchy depends on the Manager field being populated. Hovering over a contact will also allow you to chat, email, call, or video call with them. This is not available if you are chatting with more than one person.

The Activity link is slightly different than the Activity dashboard I described earlier. This Activity link displays updates based on the teams that are common between you and a singular chat participant. This is not available if you are chatting with more than one person.

The + sign link to the left of Activity allows you to add a tab to the chat window. This is very similar to how it works within channels, as described earlier.

Within a chat, in the right corner of the Teams app, there is a share icon (square box with an arrow). This is one of the best features of Teams and allows one to share their screen or application.

Calendar

The Calendar icon, located under the Teams icon on the left-hand side of the application, allows meetings to be scheduled in a variety of ways to have the most significant impact on communicating. Depending on the situation, a scheduled meeting might be the best route, or maybe you want ad hoc meetings, keeping the team more fluid and adapting to day-to-day operations.

Meetings can be scheduled within a channel or with a particular colleague. Figure 5-15 depicts the "New meeting" interface, which is available when clicking "Schedule a meeting" within the Meetings dashboard.

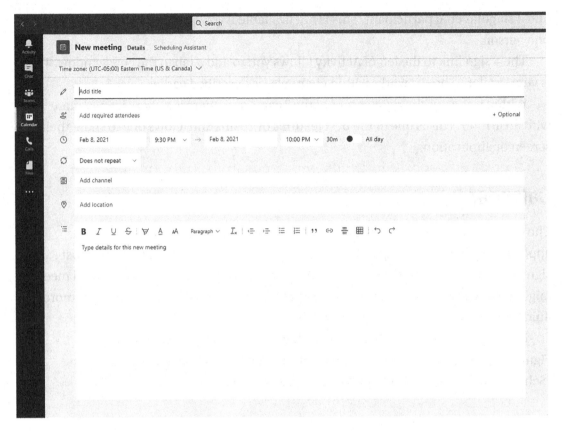

Figure 5-15. *The "New meeting" interface*

To schedule a meeting, the fields must be filled in to ensure the accuracy of the invite. Picking the "Select a channel to meet in" option and choosing the appropriate team allows the meeting to take place and be open to anyone who has access to that specific channel. You can also "Select a channel to meet in" and invite a small subset of users. This creates an openness of communication and transparency with the team. Members of the team will also be able to join if needed.

Video and phone meetings can also be started from within a chat conversation by selecting the video or phone icon from the chat area. These meetings are referred to as ad hoc because they are generally not scheduled and also are private.

Calls

Calls allow users to communicate via the Microsoft Teams app to make calls within the application to other users and choose to display video or just voice and the ability to leave a voicemail if the user does not answer the call.

One to thing to note is this does not mean you can call non-Teams users who are not using Microsoft Teams. If you wish to call non-Teams users, certain Microsoft 365 licensing, software, and IT administrative setup are needed.

Files

The last area to discuss with Microsoft Teams is the Files icon located on the left-hand side of the application. The Files icon, when clicked, opens the Files dashboard and allows you to see recent files, Microsoft Teams, and OneDrive files. Also, if any cloud storage was added previously, it will be accessible through the Files dashboard. Figure 5-16 shows the Files dashboard of Teams.

Figure 5-16. *Storing files within teams*

The files, if supported by Microsoft 365, can be edited by clicking the ellipsis in the rightmost column. Editing files is a similar experience in almost every Microsoft 365 application; for reference, I discuss Office and Office Online in Chapter 7.

Microsoft Teams Mobile App

Microsoft maintains a mobile version of Microsoft Teams, as it does for almost every one of its core products (SharePoint, Planner, OneDrive, etc.). The mobile application is supported on both Android and Apple platforms and is available from the respective app stores.

To install your specific version, download the mobile app from the correct app store. Once the app is downloaded and installed on your mobile device, open it and specify your Microsoft 365 credentials. Once Microsoft 365 authenticates you, you will be presented with a very similar interface to the web version. Figure 5-17 shows the mobile view and the associated icons available.

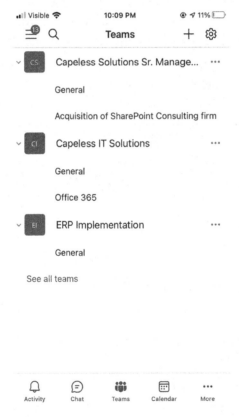

Figure 5-17. *Microsoft Teams on an Apple iPhone*

The mobile application aligns really well to the actual Teams client (preferred) or the web browser version of Teams. For this reason, I am not going to go through each of the icons and capabilities.

Summary

Microsoft Teams is a significant collaborative tool for teams. It couples the power of SharePoint and OneDrive plus the ability to make video/phone calls without the need to use multiple applications.

By shedding email, the collaborative experience can now take place in teams and channels. These areas allow for a fluid, collaborative effort centered around documents, conversations, and integrations with the Microsoft 365 stack of applications for now. In the future, the integration will grow, and Microsoft Teams will be able to interface with a whole new bunch of third-party applications.

The next chapter will focus on Yammer, which enables enterprises to create a social site to share information.

CHAPTER 6

Yammer

In the last chapter on Microsoft Teams, we discussed an application that allows collaboration in an email-less environment. In this chapter, we will explore Yammer, which is similar to but different from Teams.

Microsoft Yammer is very similar to an enterprise social network application that allows colleagues to find relevant information or people, find and use content, and collaborate and join the conversation. This is where the differences become apparent, in my opinion. Yammer is designed for the entire enterprise, while Teams is designed for smaller groups of users who collaborate on specific projects or work efforts, as you explored in the previous chapter.

The story behind Yammer is that it was acquired in the late 2000s and has been around since then in a variety of versions. What is different this time is that it is an integrated, featured application within Microsoft 365, which allows Microsoft to provide value to it, whereas before it was always considered a sort of bolt-on application within SharePoint and didn't really fit into the SharePoint platform.

Using Microsoft Yammer

In Microsoft 365, click the app launcher in the upper-left corner and select Microsoft Yammer, as shown in Figure 6-1.

Figure 6-1. *Microsoft Yammer*

Once you click the application, you will be presented with the Microsoft Yammer interface. The interface contains a few critical areas, shown in Figure 6-2.

© Ralph Mercurio and Brian Merrill 2021
R. Mercurio and B. Merrill, *Beginning Microsoft 365 Collaboration Apps*,
https://doi.org/10.1007/978-1-4842-6936-7_6

Figure 6-2. *The Yammer Home Feed interface*

On launch, you will be presented with a Home Feed screen. This screen will display any updates that occurred in the communities you are a part of. You will also see a listing of communities that you are a part of as well as the option to start a discussion.

Walking Through Yammer

Yammer looks intimidating upon logging in, but once you're familiar with its interface, it is quite simple. The first area I will discuss is around groups. Communities in Yammer are not the same as Microsoft 365 groups. Yammer groups do not contain an inbox or a SharePoint site or some of the other Microsoft 365 Groups functions you explored in Chapter 4. Yammer communities are like a team in Microsoft Teams; but, as discussed, Yammer communities are meant for the enterprise, where Teams is more suited toward smaller groups of people.

Creating a Yammer Community

In the lower-left corner of the Yammer application, you will see the current communities in Yammer as well as the ability to create or discover communities. Your first objective is to create a community. To begin the process, click "+ Create a Community," which opens a modal window titled "Create a New Community." See Figure 6-3.

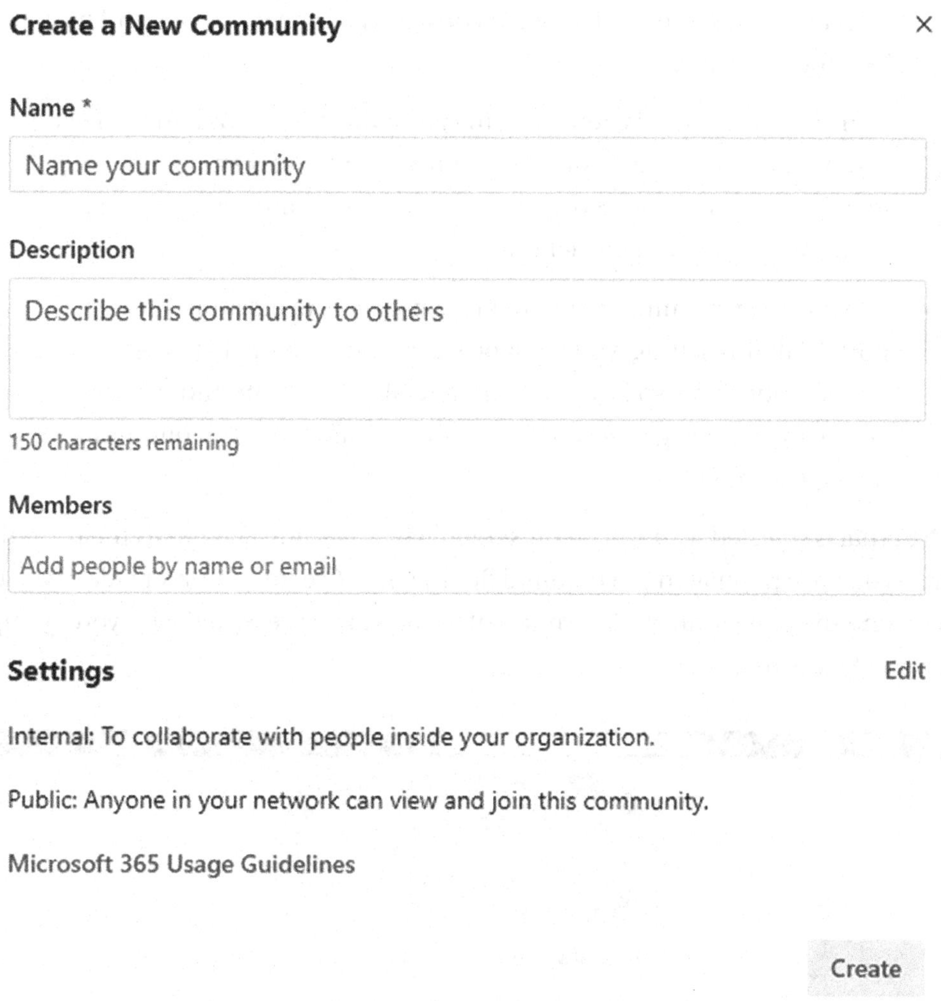

Create a New Community   ✕

Name *

> Name your community

Description

> Describe this community to others

150 characters remaining

Members

> Add people by name or email

Settings   Edit

Internal: To collaborate with people inside your organization.

Public: Anyone in your network can view and join this community.

Microsoft 365 Usage Guidelines

Create

Figure 6-3. *Creating a new Yammer internal or external community*

The first thing you will notice is that you have the ability to create two types of communities: an internal community or an external community. Internal communities allow your colleagues to communicate and belong to a community; an external community allows external members to join.

Both communities share a few common fields. The first is "Name," and it is used to identify and title the Yammer community. The second field is "Description," and this field gives you the ability to describe the community. The third option is "Members," where you would add members. The fourth option is "Internal or External."

If you select Internal, your choices for "Who can view conversations and post messages" are the following:

- **Public**: Anyone in this network can view conversations and post. This setting allows anyone to join the Yammer community and participate in it. With Yammer, once you have access to the community, you can perform a majority of the actions.

- **Private**: Only community members can view conversations and post. With this setting, you must be sure to add members to the community. You also have the option to allow the community to be visible to all colleagues even though they cannot join the community unless specified.

If External is selected, you will be presented with the same choices as the preceding.

Once you have populated the required fields, click "Create." Yammer will create the group behind the scenes; after a few moments, you will be presented with your group, as shown in Figure 6-4.

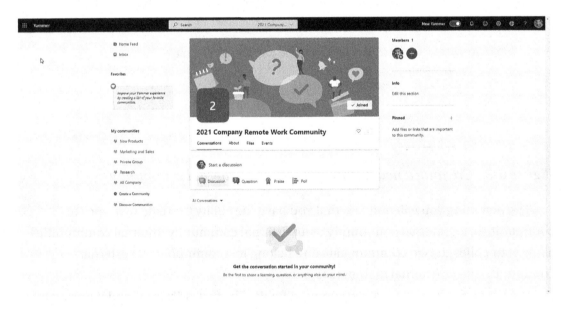

Figure 6-4. *Viewing a Yammer community*

Basics of a Yammer Community

A Yammer community allows you to view "Conversations," "About," and "Files" and "Events." You also have the ability to search within the Yammer community. These options are located below the title of the community, as shown in Figure 6-5. I will discuss each one as many of the options have shifted around within the new Yammer interface. The first edition of this book was focused on the classic Yammer interface.

Figure 6-5. Yammer community options

Conversations: These types of communication (discussions, questions, praise, and polls) are used to facilitate dialog within the group. We will discuss the different types further in this chapter.

About: Since the inception of Yammer within Microsoft 365, the classic interface filled the screen with options and configurations for the user. In the new Yammer interface, a lot of those settings had been moved to the "About" of a community:

- **Community Insights**: This will show data statistics of how many active users have visited the community in the last 28 days and the total number of conversations posted within 28 days. Clicking "See More" will take you to more in-depth statistics about your community.

- **Members**: Will show the members of the community as well as allow you to add more members.

- **Community Info**: Will display the information about the community.

- **Related Communities**: Manually add other communities that are related to the current community.

Files: Allows the members of the community to upload or create new files (Figure 6-6). Once these files are part of the community, users can view, edit, delete, or download them. There is also the ability to make the item official, so no changes are allowed.

Figure 6-6. New file options in a Yammer group

Events: These are not calendar events or similar to the calendar of a Microsoft 365 group. This is specifically for live events, which are out of scope for this book. More information can be found on the Microsoft Support site.

> **Info**: Gives the community owner the ability to add more information about the community. The owner can add rules on postings or files. To add info about a Yammer community, click the link and then the Edit link to provide information. Be sure to save your changes after.

Pinned: You can "pin" links that are relevant to the community in an easily accessible location. Links can also be posted. See Figure 6-7 for more details.

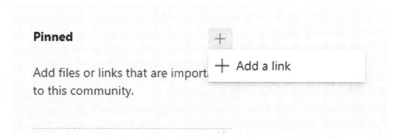

Figure 6-7. *Adding a link to the Pinned section of a Yammer community*

Posting to a Yammer Community

The second area that I will discuss is the ability to start a discussion, question, praise, or poll, as shown in Figure 6-8, in a Yammer community.

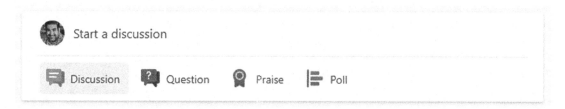

Figure 6-8. *Posting to a Yammer community*

There are four types of posts that can be made in a Yammer group. Each of these posts has a unique purpose, and you will explore them in the following in further detail:

- **Discussion**: A conversation post to a Yammer community is the simplest of all posts. Type your message in the text box; and if you want, you can also add a gif or a file from Yammer or SharePoint or upload directly from your computer. You also have the ability to notify people of the update by specifying their name in the "Add people" text box. See Figure 6-9 for more details.

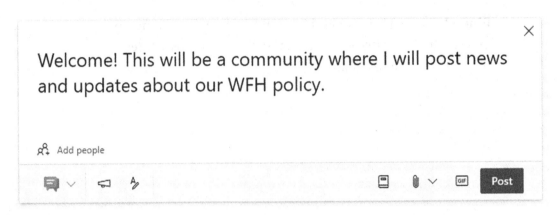

Figure 6-9. *Posting a discussion to a Yammer community*

- **Poll**: A poll is akin to a single-question survey (Figure 6-10). For now, you can only post a single question. No other data types are available. It's similar to an update post because you can also attach a file or notify a person.

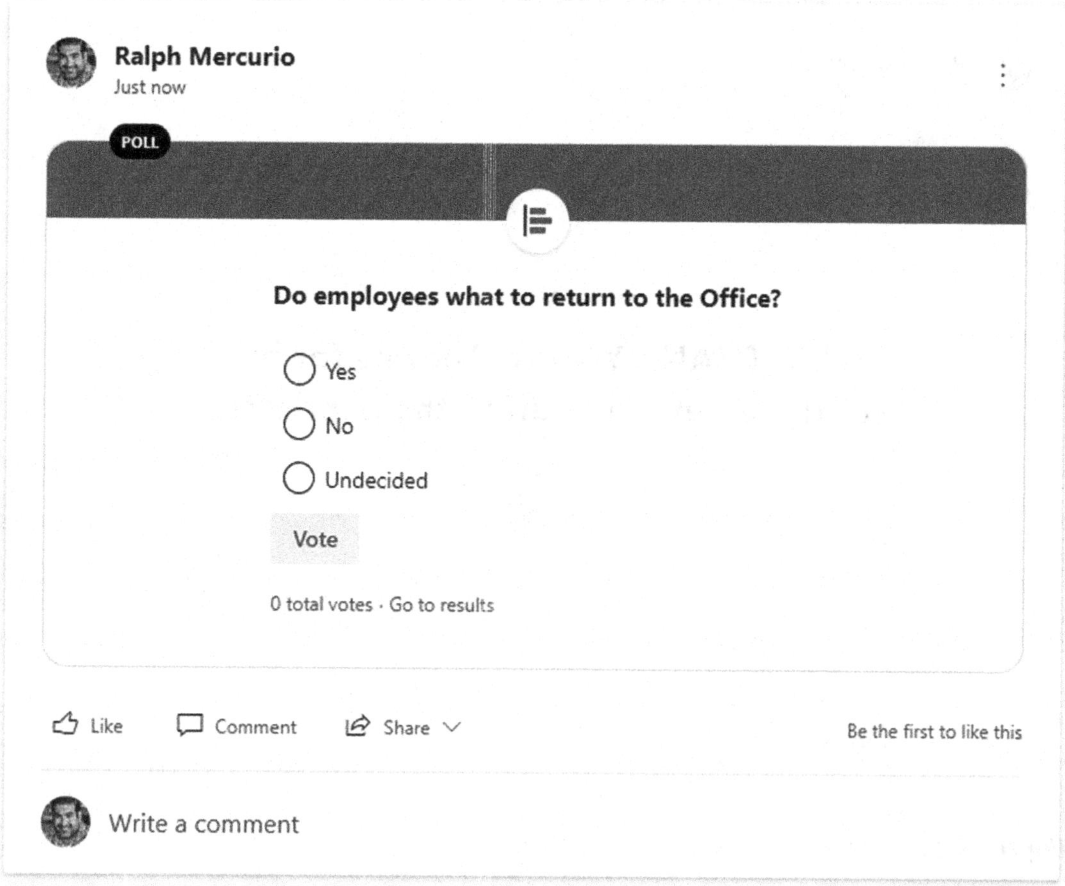

Ralph Mercurio
Just now

POLL

Do employees what to return to the Office?

◯ Yes

◯ No

◯ Undecided

Vote

0 total votes · Go to results

👍 Like   💬 Comment   ↪ Share ∨   Be the first to like this

Write a comment

Figure 6-10. *Creating a poll for a Yammer group*

The poll isn't as robust as Microsoft Forms, which is discussed in Chapter 10. In this scenario, a Microsoft form can be created, and the link to the form can be pasted into an update post.

- **Praise:** Built upon the update post, but gives you the ability to give your post a little more detail, as shown in Figure 6-11.

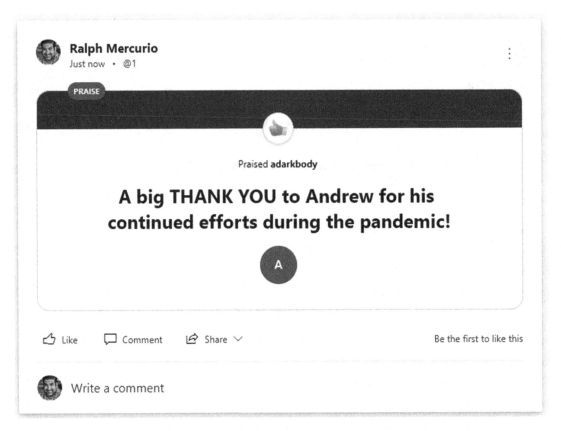

Figure 6-11. Creating a praise post in Yammer

A praise post contains two parts: "Who do you want to praise?" and "Share what they've done." You also have the same ability as the previous post types to notify people or add files.

- **Question**: The final post type is a question, as shown in Figure 6-12.

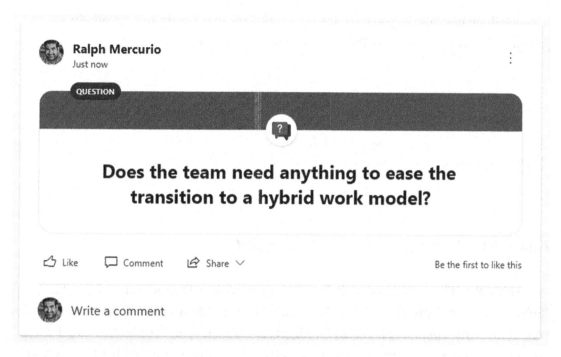

Figure 6-12. *Creating an question post in Yammer*

Interacting with Yammer Posts

Similar to Microsoft Teams, which was discussed in Chapter 5, Yammer is also a chat-based collaboration tool. Every post (conversation, question, praise, and poll) can be liked, commented on, or shared as shown in Figure 6-13.

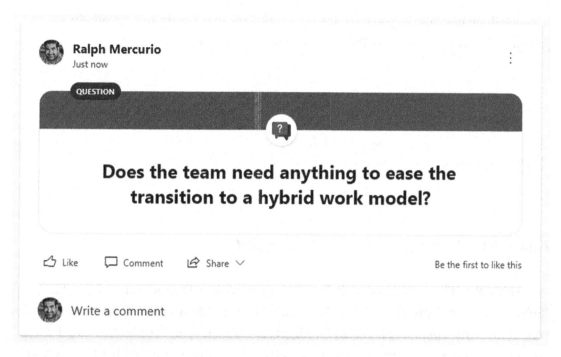

Figure 6-13. *Options for interacting with posts*

To like any of the posts, select the Like icon located under the post. Clicking the icon will change the icon name from Like to Unlike. If you choose to unlike a post at a later date, click the Unlike icon. Commenting on a post is a similar action to liking a post. Click the Comment icon, and a text box will appear underneath the original post. Type your message and choose to notify others, add a file, or post text.

The Share icon allows you to share a post with another community or within a private message or to copy the link as shown in Figure 6-14.

Figure 6-14. *Sharing options for a Yammer post*

Within the "Share to Community" modal window, select a community from the "Select a community to post to" link. You can add context to sharing a post by adding your comments, uploading a file, and notifying specific people. In order to share the conversation directly in a private message, select the "Share to Private Message" option. This option requires you to add specific participants because you are sending a private message. You also have the ability to add a gif or upload a file. When you are satisfied with your selections, click "Share" in the lower-right corner to post to a group or send a private message.

If you are the creator of the post, you will also see the vertical ellipsis in the upper-right corner of the post. Clicking the ellipsis allows you to edit your post and correct context or spelling. All edited posts are labeled as edited. You can't edit a poll post.

The ellipsis menu of a post, shown in Figure 6-15, displays the other actions one can take on their post.

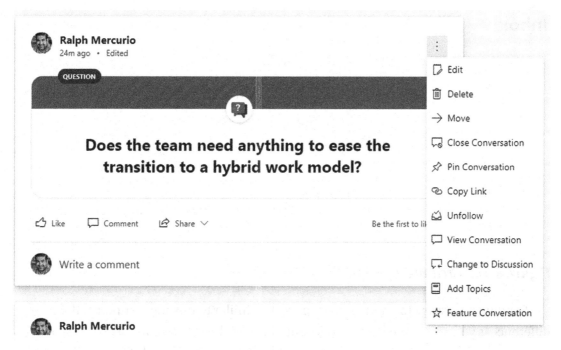

Figure 6-15. *Accessing advanced-level control of a post*

Inbox

The inbox, located in the upper-left corner, allows you to send private messages as well as receive notifications. To create a private message, select "New Private Message" in the upper-right corner of the inbox.

The familiar dialog of posts is shown (Figure 6-16), and you are able to craft your message and add people to send it to.

Figure 6-16. *Creating a private message*

Sending a message to another colleague(s) is similar to posting an update; the difference is you need to select the colleagues to send the message to. Once you select the colleague(s), type your message, attach any items if needed, and click "Post."

An interesting feature with private messaging on the Yammer platform is that a conversation can be moved to a private or public community if deemed appropriate. To move a private message to a group, select "Move" from the available options within a private message, as depicted in Figure 6-17.

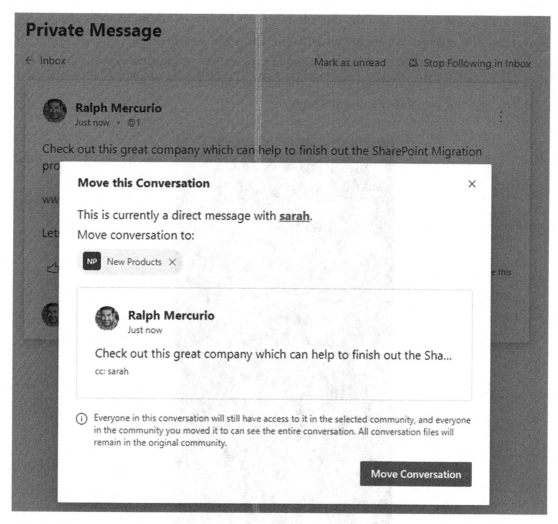

Figure 6-17. *Moving a private message to a community*

Once the message is moved, it cannot be undone. Also be aware if your message contains sensitive or confidential information; it will be visible to all members of the group.

Yammer Mobile App

Microsoft released a mobile version of Microsoft Yammer, as it did for almost every one of its core products (SharePoint, Planner, OneDrive, Teams, etc.). The mobile application is supported on both Android and Apple platforms and is available from the respective app stores.

To install your specific version, download the mobile app from the correct app store. Once the app is downloaded and installed on your mobile device, open it, and specify your Microsoft 365 credentials. Once Microsoft 365 authenticates you, you will be presented with a very similar interface to the web version. Figure 6-18 shows the mobile feed view and the associated icons available.

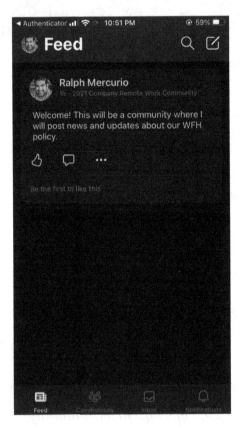

Figure 6-18. *Accessing the Yammer mobile application*

On the Yammer mobile app, you will see a list of your communities; you also have the ability to add and discover more groups. Along the bottom of the application, you can navigate to the Feed, Inbox, and Notifications.

The functionality of the Yammer mobile application is well thought out and compliments the web version of Yammer. As depicted in Figure 6-19, viewing a community allows a colleague to view the feed of updates and be able to post an update, announcement, or praise.

Figure 6-19. *Posting to a Yammer group in the mobile app*

To post to a Yammer group, click the "Create Post" icon in the upper-right corner when viewing a community. Similar to the web version of Yammer, you can add a photo, take a photo, or upload a file via the interface. To change to a different posting type, select the icon in the lower-right corner of the new post text box displayed in Figure 6-20.

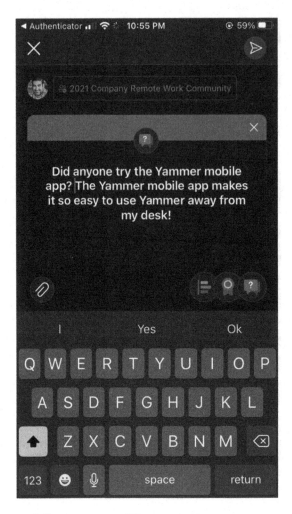

Figure 6-20. *Create a different type of Yammer postp*

Business Retrospective

I want to touch base on a past experience concerning Yammer and a business problem that the executives wanted to solve. The company was dinged by their employees on the yearly employee survey for not being transparent with information, so the company wanted to create a culture of employee empowerment. After a discussion with them, they agreed to green-light Yammer as a PoC (Proof of Concept). Part of winning them over was to show that Yammer had the features needed to solve the issues and increase employee engagement.

Part of the success of the project was to ensure that the executives would be responsible and willing to post updates and engage with employees. I would love to tell you that once we configured Yammer in the enterprise, created a public community, and had the executives begin posting short updates about what the company was going through, user adoption shot through the roof and employees felt they were informed.

That didn't happen, and it would appear on the surface that we failed. However, we noticed something odd: we engaged at the wrong level in the organization. Having executive buy-in was needed, but employees felt they couldn't relate or shouldn't respond to upper management.

Because of this, we started to engage other managers, and Yammer became a more widely used platform. A year later, the yearly employee satisfaction survey showed that they were moving toward their goals of disseminating information and engaging employees.

Summary

A common thread throughout this book is that Microsoft has shifted from providing a single application to solve the many collaboration challenges we face to building applications that allow us to choose the best ones for our needs.

Yammer is similar in many ways to Microsoft Teams but is geared toward connecting colleagues at the enterprise level and not on the project or team level. The key to Yammer is to create communities, public or private, and to ensure that all users have access to the Yammer network. For this to happen, users can be imported directly from Microsoft 365 with the aid of a Yammer administrator.

The key to working with Yammer is to ensure that posts are made, whether they are updates, polls, praises, or announcements, and that those posts are replied to. This is important because without any content or current updates, users won't see the value in contributing to or using Yammer.

In this chapter, I covered the basics of Yammer including communities, users, interacting with posts, and the Yammer mobile application. In the next chapter, I will discuss another cornerstone of Microsoft 365, the Office 2019 suite including Outlook, Word, Excel, OneNote, and PowerPoint.

CHAPTER 7

Office

In the last chapter, you explored Microsoft Yammer and its ability to deliver communication for the entire enterprise. In this chapter, you will explore Microsoft 365 Apps, Microsoft's flagship productivity end user application, which is available with most subscriptions to Microsoft 365. It includes Outlook, PowerPoint, Word, Excel, OneNote, Publisher, OneDrive for Business, Teams, Access, and Sway (web version only). I will highlight the key applications in the suite and provide a quick overview and some functionality of each.

There is no separate cost or buying the Office DVD from your favorite retailer because it is included in your SaaS (Software as a Service) monthly cost. Your user license to Microsoft 365 allows for five installations of the product on a variety of devices: PCs, Macs, and tablets (iPad and Android). The software is also supported on mobile device platforms.

The difference between purchasing the DVD from a retailer and using it as part of the Microsoft 365 subscription is that you are allowed five installs across any devices that support it. There is a product key that will not allow you to install more than five times, and each install is cataloged by Microsoft 365 during product activation. Companies that use Microsoft 365 may choose not to use Office 365 Apps from the Microsoft 365 portal but rather the more traditional Office 2019 license available depending on their license agreement.

Not only do you get access to download and use the Microsoft Office 365 Apps client applications but you can also use the Office Online versions of Outlook, PowerPoint, Word, Excel, and OneNote in any modern supported browser. These Office Online versions of the popular client applications allow for most tasks to be completed in the browser version. However, certain tasks aren't possible with the Office Online versions.

© Ralph Mercurio and Brian Merrill 2021
R. Mercurio and B. Merrill, *Beginning Microsoft 365 Collaboration Apps*,
https://doi.org/10.1007/978-1-4842-6936-7_7

Installing Office 365 Apps from Microsoft 365

Log into Office.com with your credentials. On the main page, you will notice an "Install Office" link; see Figure 7-1.

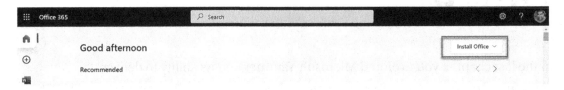

Figure 7-1. *The Install Office link in Microsoft 365*

Click the link, and two options (Figure 7-2) will be presented to you. One option is to download and install Office 365 Apps, while the other option is "Other install options."

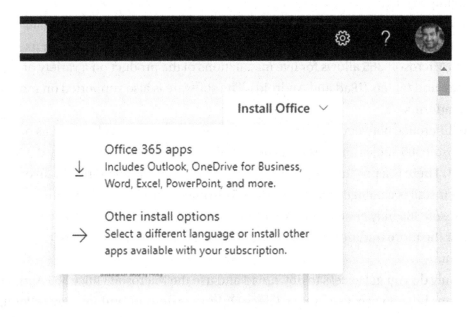

Figure 7-2. *Microsoft 365 Apps install options*

Microsoft 365 Apps

There are two variants of Office: 32-bit and 64-bit. There are some differences between the two variants; one notable difference is that Excel 64-bit offers support for many more rows then Excel 32-bit. You can't install the Office 32-bit version in conjunction with Office 64-bit products; all Office applications must be the same version. Most users choose to install the 32-bit version, which is what Microsoft 365 defaults to.

If you currently have Office installed on your device, it is considered a good practice to uninstall that version and install the latest version. However, please check with your IT department because there may be business reasons to use a version of Office specified by a company's IT department.

To install the 32-bit version of Office 365 Apps, click "Office 2016" from the context menu (Figure 7-2). This will launch the click-to-run version, which is automatically updated from Microsoft (Figure 7-3).

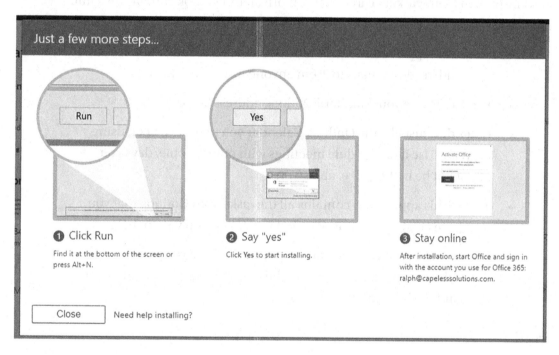

Figure 7-3. *Office 365 Apps 32-bit click-to-run installer*

In the web browser, it will download a small program (Figure 7-3). It will offer the following download options: Run, Save/Save as, or Cancel. Choose Run and allow the installer to begin the install process. It may prompt for permission to make changes, but that is dependent on your specific security settings. Once the installer proceeds, follow the on-screen prompts to finish the install.

Office 365 Apps Application Overview

My intention with the next sections is not to provide an in-depth guide to each application but rather to give a brief overview of each application in the Office 365 Apps suite and some of the improvements that will make your life a little easier.

Outlook

Outlook is the most well-known mail client in the world and is used by most people at some time in their working career or even privately. Outlook contains five mini-applications that together provide a seamless experience:

- **Mail**: This application is your inbox for email communication. You can send/receive emails to/from anyone just as you do now.

- **People**: This is your standard Outlook address book.

- **Calendar**: Just like the Outlook Calendar you may have been using for years. Use it to schedule meetings with other people, days you might not be in the office, and so on.

- **Tasks**: This application contains all the tasks from Outlook that you may have created or the application has created on your behalf.

- **Notes**: A virtual sticky note–like application where you can keep notes about anything, just the like the ones that currently clutter your desk and the bottom of your monitor.

Mail

Launch the Outlook client from your device by going to Start and opening Outlook if you're on a version of Windows. If Outlook is already configured, you will be presented with the Outlook interface (Figure 7-4).

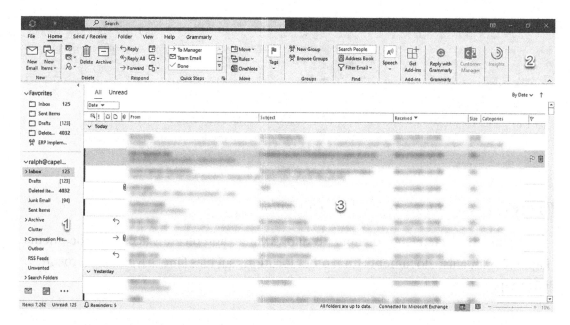

Figure 7-4. *Outlook app*

Don't worry; your eyes are working fine. I intentionally blurred the preceding image because it contains sensitive information I do not wish to disclose.

The application contains three main areas:

- **Area 1**: The leftmost area is known as the Folder pane and contains the Outlook email account (Inbox). This is where you will find not only the Inbox but also sent and deleted items.

- **Area 2**: The Outlook ribbon contains actions such as creating a new email, replying to all, or forwarding. You can also access the Outlook address book or install Office add-ins from the Microsoft Office store.

- **Area 3**: The main window of the Mail application, it contains the mail items dependent on the folder chosen in the Folder pane.

Microsoft listened to customer feedback, and one of the most notable improvements for me is the ability to add recently accessed documents to emails. There is no need to search for the file you just saved to an unknown location on your device. To add a recent file, select "Attach File" from the Include section of the Office Outlook ribbon in a new email, as shown in Figure 7-5.

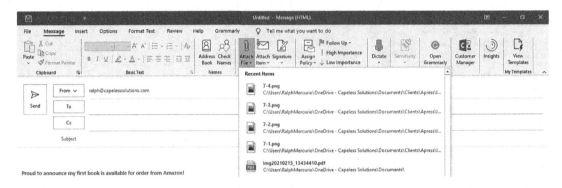

Figure 7-5. *Attaching a recent file to an email*

Clicking the Attach File icon not only allows you to add recently accessed documents (Figure 7-6) but also documents from other locations such as OneDrive or a Microsoft 365 group.

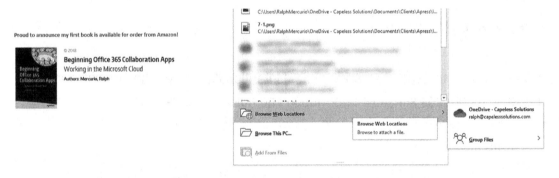

Figure 7-6. *Attach File options in Outlook 2016*

Of course, you can still access your documents locally by clicking "Browse This PC." You will see the familiar Windows Explorer interface to find and attach your files. Microsoft also included a way to attach files from Microsoft OneDrive and Microsoft 365 Groups. This creates seamless integration between Outlook and where you store your files in the other applications.

Attaching a File from OneDrive

Attaching a file from OneDrive is straightforward and simple. To attach a file, follow these steps:

1. In a new mail message in Outlook, select "Attach File" (Figure 7-6) from the Outlook ribbon.

2. Select "Browse Web Locations" from the menu and choose "OneDrive" (Figure 7-7).

Figure 7-7. *File attachment options*

It will be named slightly differently in your Outlook.

3. Selecting the OneDrive link opens Microsoft OneDrive via File Explorer. It may seem like it is the local copy of OneDrive, but it is the Microsoft 365 storage location.

4. Select your file. You will be presented with two options. The first option, "Share link," shares the file directly from your OneDrive. This adds the user as a reader and allows them to see and access the file. The other option, "Attach as copy," sends the recipient a copy of the file. The second method is the traditional method of sending files as attachments.

5. Compose the remainder of the message and send the email to the recipient.

Attaching a File from Microsoft 365 Groups

The process is similar to attaching files from OneDrive. Follow these steps to attach a file from Microsoft 365 Groups:

1. In a new mail message in Outlook, select "Attach File" (Figure 7-6) from the Outlook ribbon.

2. Select "Browse Web Locations" from the menu and choose "Group Files" (Figure 7-8).

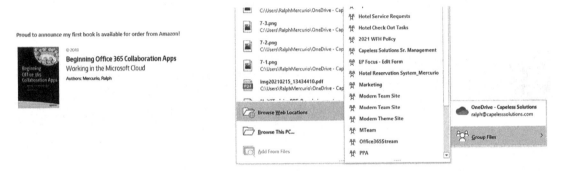

Figure 7-8. *Selecting the Group Files link lists all the Microsoft 365 groups of which you are a member*

3. Select the Microsoft 365 group and select the file you want to attach. You will be presented with two options. The first option, "Share link," shares the file directly from your Microsoft 365 group. It adds the user as a reader and allows them to see and access the file. The other option, "Attach as copy," sends the recipient a copy of the file.

4. Compose the remainder of the mail message and send the email to the recipient.

People

Connecting with others is the cornerstone of Microsoft Outlook. The Outlook address book allows you to connect to and remember the people you are connected to.

The Outlook address book (Figure 7-9) keeps track of contacts and their associated details. These details include multiple email addresses, phone numbers, or any other details you deem important.

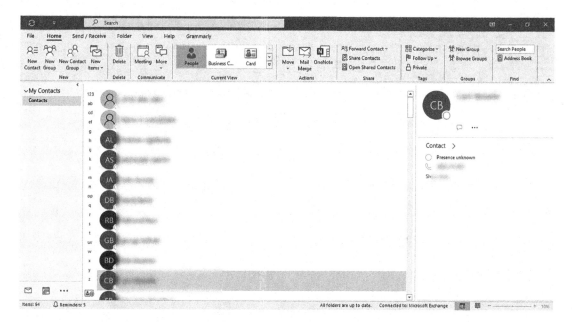

Figure 7-9. *Outlook address book (People)*

In my opinion, Outlook's address book hasn't evolved through the Office product lifecycle.

Calendar

The infamous Outlook Calendar: keeping track of our meetings, events, doctor's appointments, and when we are not in the office. Outlook has introduced incremental changes over the years to include calendar overlays (superimposing calendars on top of each of other), but the calendar has remained roughly the same throughout the Office iterations. The current interface of the Outlook Calendar is shown in Figure 7-10.

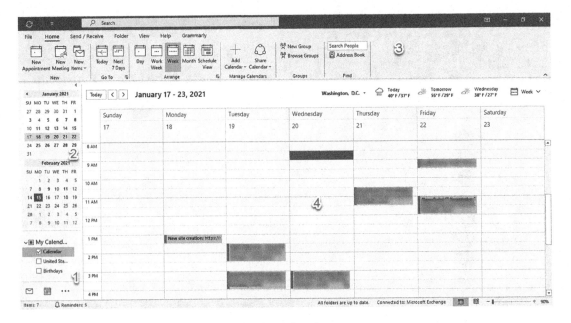

Figure 7-10. *Monthly view of Outlook Calendar*

The Calendar application contains four main areas:

- **Area 1**: This area displays your Outlook Calendar as well as any Exchange group calendars and any other calendars that may have been shared with you.

- **Area 2**: This area will always show the current month as well as the next month. It quickly lets you pinpoint a date and will update Area 4.

- **Area 3**: The Outlook ribbon contains actions such as creating a new appointment and various views of the calendars such as Day, Work Week, and Month.

- **Area 4**: This view reflects the view chosen from the Outlook ribbon.

Tasks

Outlook also can manage tasks from flagged emails, create new tasks directly from emails, or create new tasks. Tasks created from flagged emails are known as To-Do items, and tasks created from emails are tasks. These tasks are different than tasks created in Planner or SharePoint and are not integrated with those products. I will discuss Planner tasks in Chapter 8; SharePoint tasks were described in Chapter 2. I will explain Outlook To-Do items and tasks and their slight nuances next.

To-Do Items

To-Do items are generated when an email is marked for follow-up. An email can be marked for follow-up by right-clicking the email and choosing "Follow Up." This will not only mark the email with a colored flag but will also create a To-Do item in Outlook Tasks. Be aware that when a To-Do item is deleted, the email is deleted as well.

Tasks

Creating a task can be done in two ways: either through the Outlook ribbon (Figure 7-11) or within Outlook Tasks.

Figure 7-11. *Create a task from the Outlook ribbon*

When creating a new task, you need to specify the values such as subject, start date, end date, status, and so on. Tasks can be assigned to others in the organization by selecting "Assign Task" in the Outlook ribbon (Figure 7-12).

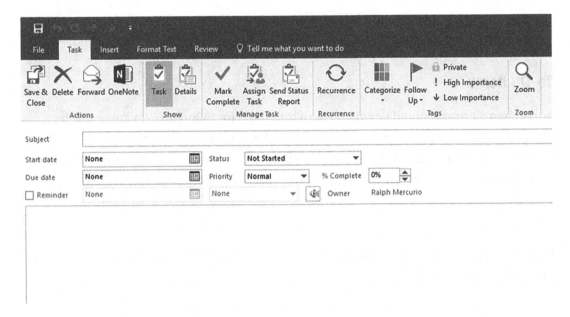

Figure 7-12. *Assign Task settings*

Tasks from Emails

Another way tasks are generated is by dragging an email directly onto the Tasks icon
in Outlook Quick Launch in the lower-left corner of Outlook. Dragging the email to
the Tasks icon opens a new task window with the subject and the contents of the email
added to the task (Figure 7-13). You can then set the other details of the task and save it
to Outlook.

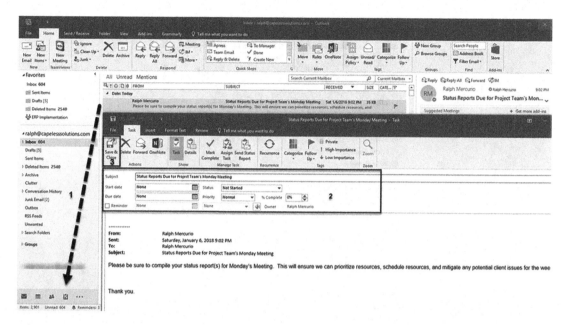

Figure 7-13. *Creating a task from an email*

Notes

Notes in Outlook was introduced in the early 2000s and hasn't received a major redesign since. The purpose of Notes is to give users a place to take and store notes about a project, meeting, or even passwords. Outlook Notes and Microsoft OneNote are not the same product, but OneNote is far superior to Notes and is my preferred editor for notes in the Microsoft stack. I am not going to explore Notes in too much detail, but I will give a basic introduction.

To access Notes, click the ellipsis located in the lower-left corner of Outlook (Figure 7-14) and select the Notes application from the pop-up menu.

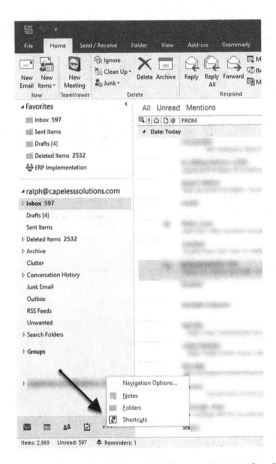

Figure 7-14. *Accessing the Notes application from the Outlook bar*

Accessing the application opens the Notes interface (Figure 7-15). You will notice the interface is like the other applications: Email, People, Calendar, and Tasks.

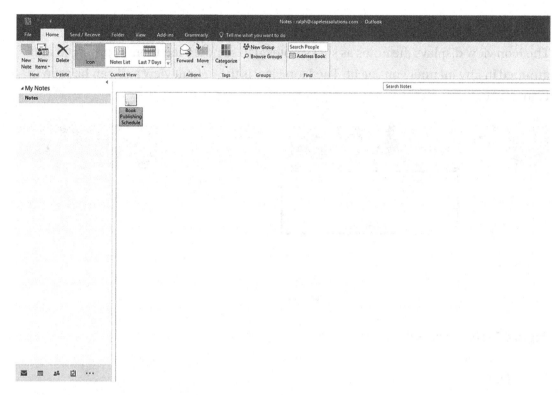

Figure 7-15. *The Notes application within Outlook*

The interface contains the Outlook ribbon with the appropriate actions just for Notes, the Notes window, and a My Notes navigation control.

Creating a Note

From the Outlook ribbon or by right-clicking the main Notes window, select "New Note." A yellow sticky note will appear, and you can add text to it. You can only add text to the note. The note is time-stamped, and once you click out of the note, it is automatically saved.

Viewing and Sorting Notes

Notes can be sorted and viewed in three distinct views to quickly access and find them. The views include Icon, Notes List, and Last 7 Days. Currently, you cannot customize the views further.

Icon

The Icon view displays the notes as sticky notes. These notes can then be arranged and grouped in any manner you see fit. The Icon view is the default view and can be seen in Figure 7-16.

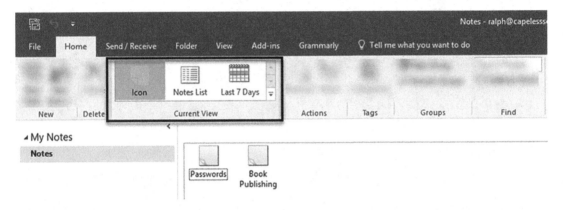

Figure 7-16. *Available views*

Notes List

The Notes List view simply lists the notes in a list (Figure 7-17). You can sort by either the subject or created columns.

Figure 7-17. *Notes List view*

Last 7 Days

This view shows the notes that have been created in the last seven days. In this view, you can also sort through a variety of fields.

Deleting a Note

To delete a note, simply highlight the note and choose Delete from the Outlook ribbon or right-click the note and choose "Delete Note" from the menu.

PowerPoint App

Microsoft PowerPoint is arguably the most-used software to craft presentations for business, educational, or personal use. PowerPoint allows the user to create presentations with numerous slides. The trick to creating an amazing and well-thought presentation is to keep the content of each slide concise and to ensure that the presentation stays on track and delivers a clear message.

The PowerPoint layout contains three main areas: the Office ribbon, the current slide being edited, and a list of slides (Slide Sorter) in the presentation (Figure 7-18). When editing a slide, the Office ribbon changes, allowing only the appropriate commands.

Edit the slide as needed, adding text or images. When complete, click "New Slide" from the Insert tab of the Office ribbon or right-click in the Slide Sorter (leftmost) and choose "New Slide."

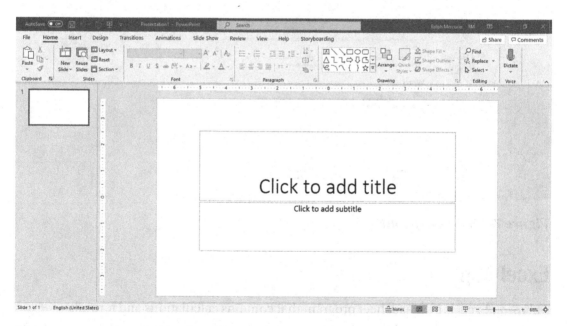

Figure 7-18. *PowerPoint layout*

To view your presentation as if you were presenting to an audience, press F5 on your keyboard; to end your presentation, press the Escape key. Continue to customize it as needed by adding slides and content.

Word App

Microsoft Word is used throughout to world to write and edit essays, resumes, business documents, and a whole host of other types of documents. Word is simple to use but at times can be frustrating when trying to line up text with the correct margins or when trying to make a document to look perfect. The Microsoft Word layout shares some commonalities with the PowerPoint layout; the Word layout is shown in Figure 7-19. The Word layout contains the Office ribbon and the document area.

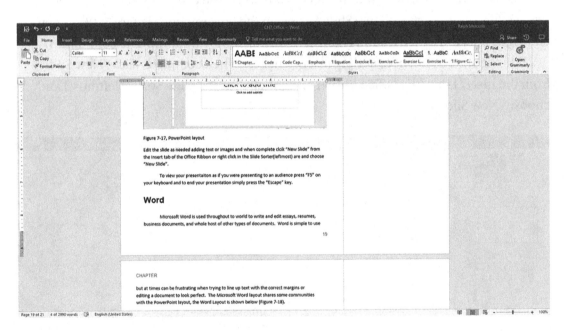

Figure 7-19. *Word layout*

Excel App

Microsoft Excel is a spreadsheet program that contains calculations and formulas, graphing capabilities, and even the ability to track a household budget. The Excel layout contains the Office ribbon (a common theme in both client and web apps) and the spreadsheet (Figure 7-20).

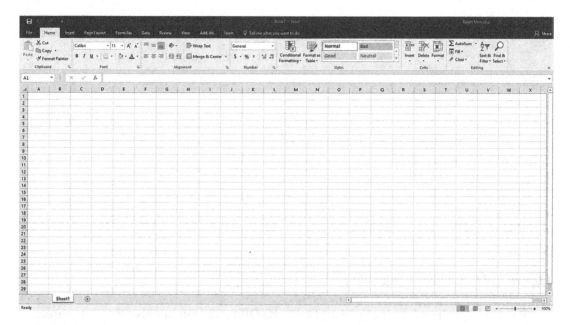

Figure 7-20. *Microsoft Excel 2016 layout*

OneNote App

Microsoft OneNote is like Outlook Notes' foreign cousin. In OneNote, you can keep "sticky notes," mark up your notes in color, insert images and other content, and easily share them across multiple devices or with other users. The OneNote interface (Figure 7-21) is intuitive if you're familiar with the Office layouts of Outlook, PowerPoint, Excel, and Word.

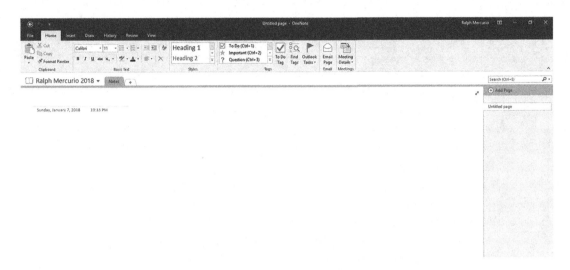

Figure 7-21. *OneNote interface*

The OneNote interface includes not only the Office ribbon but also the Notes area. To add a note, simply add the text or content directly onto the note.

With OneNote, you can mark up your notes with color or markings, which is truly different from Outlook Notes. This flexibility of marking up your notes translates really well to tablets and touchable-screen laptops. To access the markup features of OneNote, simply select "Draw" in the Office ribbon.

Publisher App

Microsoft Publisher is an Office product for creating and publishing books, newsletters, and other publication materials. It has been an Office staple since 1991 and is only available on the PC platform; it is not available on the Apple or tablet platform at this moment.

Launching Publisher opens the interface (Figure 7-22), which is similar to other layout and publication software such as products from Adobe or Quark.

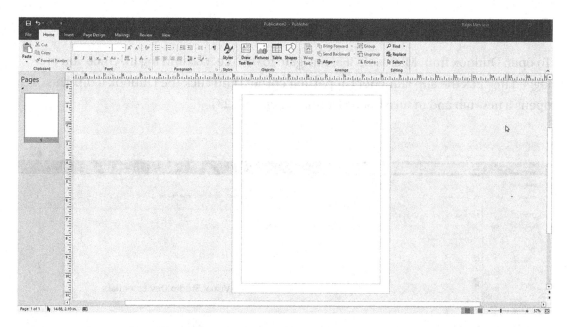

Figure 7-22. *Microsoft Publisher layout*

I hope these quick blurbs about the key Office products did provide enough of a background to get you started and to understand the purpose of each application. Learning Microsoft Office isn't easy, and it doesn't come overnight, but there is a wealth of resources in books, videos, and training to help you succeed.

Office Online Overview

With Microsoft 365, Microsoft made Microsoft Word, Outlook, Excel, PowerPoint, and Sway available within any modern supported browser. This also allows tight integration with the other SaaS applications within the Microsoft 365 suite.

The Office Online applications do not have a one-to-one relationship with the client applications discussed in the previous sections. Part of the reason for this is that developing an application to be installed and run from within a browser is extremely complex, and there are limitations and security concerns that Microsoft can't change and must comply with.

Outlook

To open Outlook from Microsoft 365, navigate to `Office.com` and log in. Once you are logged in, click the app launcher (upper-left corner) and click the Outlook icon. This opens a new tab and in turn opens Outlook (Figure 7-23).

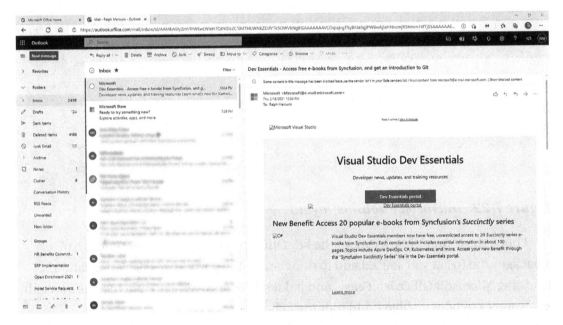

Figure 7-23. *Outlook interface viewed in a web browser*

Viewing Outlook in the web browser is quite similar to the installed Outlook ProPlus version; each contains Mail, Calendar, People, Files, and Tasks icons, but the web version of Outlook has Notes removed.

Files is an interesting module within Outlook Online. Files allows you to view the attachments of emails in a single view for easy access.

Word Online

To launch Word Online, launch the Word application from the Microsoft 365 app launcher. Opening Word Online presents an interface (Figure 7-24) where you can open a recent document, create a new, blank document, or view recent documents.

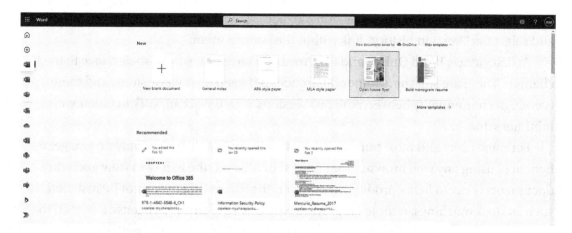

Figure 7-24. *Word Online start-up layout*

Let's create a new, blank document by selecting the document type from the list of available templates. Word Online prepares and creates the document and presents an interface similar to the Word app we discussed earlier in this chapter. The interface contains the Office ribbon, the document, and the ability to edit in Word if the Word Online version becomes unwieldy or you need to perform an advanced function not available in Word Online.

An interesting function of Word Online is that there is no Save button. Word Online continuously saves the document back to your OneDrive as you work on it. You can see the status in the header of Word Online; see Figure 7-25.

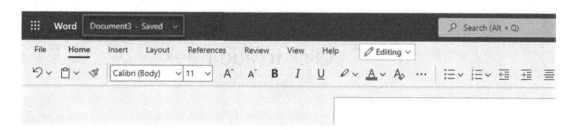

Figure 7-25. *Word Online's saving feature*

Since OneDrive is the default location to save Word Online files within Microsoft 365, you can view the versions within the OneDrive application. Word Online saves major versions of the document you are working on but not every single change. Because of this, you will not have access to all versions of the document you were working on, but you will have access to all major versions. To access the versions, navigate to OneDrive and select the "Version history" link within the context menu.

At first glance, Word Online and the Word app are similar, from spell-check to track changes. There are still some minor differences between the two versions, and there is enough commonality between the two versions where you can work in either with minimal setback.

For most users and most purposes, Word Online will suffice. Not only do you get the benefit of using any web browser from any PC or Mac but the ability to view and edit documents is key to being productive in situations where Office may not be installed, such as kiosk machines, remote employees who can't get an Office license assigned to them, or underpowered devices where the client software can't be installed.

PowerPoint Online

PowerPoint Online is similar to Word Online, and they share a common layout, much the same way the Office ProPlus products feel. With PowerPoint Online (Figure 7-26), you can create presentations and work on them completely in the browser.

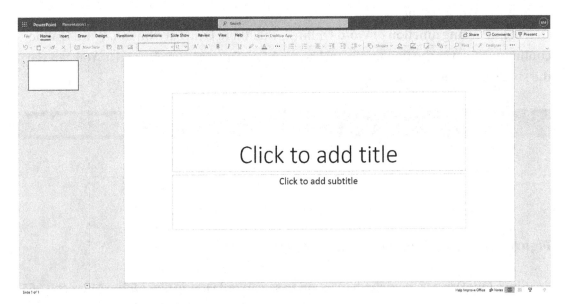

Figure 7-26. *PowerPoint Online interface*

PowerPoint Online contains the same Office Online ribbon, the ability to open PowerPoint Online documents in the PowerPoint app, auto-saving, and most of the functionality of its older brother, the PowerPoint app. There are gaps, however, much like Word Online vs. Word app. I believe those gaps are quite minimal for most presentation creators.

Using PowerPoint Online does have advantages over the PowerPoint app, and the traveling workers come to mind. Years ago I would have argued that PowerPoint Online, if existed, wouldn't be very good, simply because of the reliance on having an Internet connection. However, as time has passed, Internet connections are abundant either through cell devices, public access hotspots, or your home Internet provider.

Think of a traveling salesman whose PowerPoint app continues to crash and won't start. Having access to PowerPoint Online alleviates that frustration and still allows for the presentation to be consumed or collaborated on. There have been situations where I have gone to a client's location only to be told that that Office wasn't installed on the conference room PC or I forgot my converters to connect to their system. With Microsoft 365 and PowerPoint Online, I can present directly from the browser.

Excel Online

Excel Online (Figure 7-27), like the other online versions of Office, offers the same layout and feel as Excel. For most users, Excel Online will suffice to create and view content.

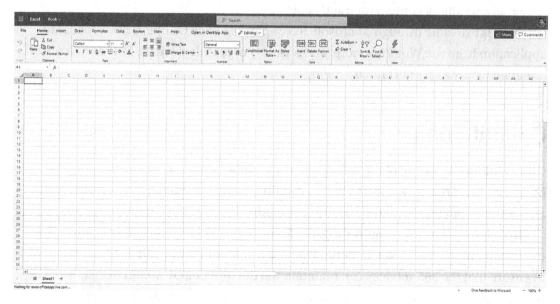

Figure 7-27. *Excel Online layout*

Once you require features such as macros, Power Pivot, Power Query, and data tools ("Text to Columns," "Remove Duplicates," and the other features), you will need to use the Excel app.

OneNote Online

OneNote Online is a great companion to Office Online. It shares a similar look and feel to the OneNote app and for the most part will suffice as an excellent application to create and store notes.

Like the other Office Online products, there are some limitations and features that have been removed to make it work within the confines of a web browser. However, I feel that those limitations should not hinder the ability to create and mark up notes.

Sway

Microsoft Sway, available from the app launcher in Microsoft 365, is aimed at storytelling and is not necessarily a presentation slide deck like PowerPoint. PowerPoint will always have its place in the business world because it is an excellent way to communicate an idea or slide deck to an audience.

Sway tries to shift the consumption from an audience to a single user. It does this by introducing "Sways" and forces the end user creating a Sway to focus on the message rather on generating content for a slide deck.

Sway is available through Microsoft 365 as part of Office Online, a downloadable application from the Windows store, and a variety of mobile devices. Microsoft has not integrated Sway as part of Office ProPlus.

Co-authoring

Office Online allows one of the most powerful collaborative features ever released in Microsoft 365. True co-authoring allows multiple people to edit and view a document and see the changes in real time as they are made, regardless of location.

In order to allow for co-authoring, the following two conditions must be met: First, the document must be saved in either OneDrive or SharePoint Online. This is required to ensure that the 365 services can maintain the document and stream of changes. The second condition is that users must be invited to collaborate on the document.

Co-authoring in Office Online

Each Office Online application (Word, PowerPoint, and Excel) does have certain co-authoring rules that dictate what and how things can be edited. For instance, only one user can edit a cell at the same time in Excel Online, while the other two Office Online applications are more lenient. Without these rules, the stream of changes would simply override the others, and co-authoring would fall flat.

Excel Online

From your specific OneDrive, select "New" and choose "Excel workbook." This will create a new Excel Online document and will serve as the example to show co-authoring in Excel Online.

From the Office Online ribbon, choose File ➤ Share ➤ Share with people (Figure 7-28). Opening the "Share with people" dialog allows you to invite either users from inside your organization, specific people, people with existing permissions, or anyone. For the Anyone permission level to be enabled, your IT administrators must enable certain settings with Microsoft 365 to make it work.

Choose "Users from inside your organization." Your screen will be different from what you see in Figure 7-28 because these images are based on my organizational name and settings.

Figure 7-28. *Excel Online sharing a document*

In the Share dialog box, enter a name or email address of a user within your organization. I am going to share the Excel Online document with Sarah Mercurio, a user in my organization. Simply type the user's name in the "Enter a name or email address" text box. Once the user is entered and recognized by Microsoft 365, you can share the link either by creating a shareable link or sending it via Outlook.

Sarah will receive an email with a link to the document to edit it. When she clicks the link specified in the email, it will open the Excel Online workbook in read-only mode. At this point, the document is just being viewed; once she selects to edit the workbook with Excel Online, the workbook will go into co-authoring mode (Figure 7-29).

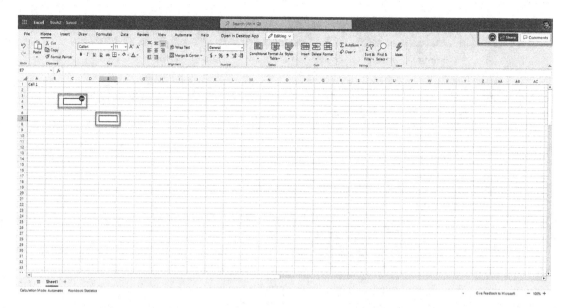

Figure 7-29. *Co-authoring an Excel Online workbook*

When the workbook is in co-authoring mode, you will notice two things: a green box around a cell (in this case E7) and who is editing the document. User Ralph Mercurio was assigned a green editing color by Microsoft 365, and he is currently editing cell E7. If you hover over "Ralph Mercurio is also editing," you will notice that it shows exactly what cell he is editing.

From my perspective (Figure 7-30), I can see that Sarah Merrill is editing cell C4 and was assigned a purple color.

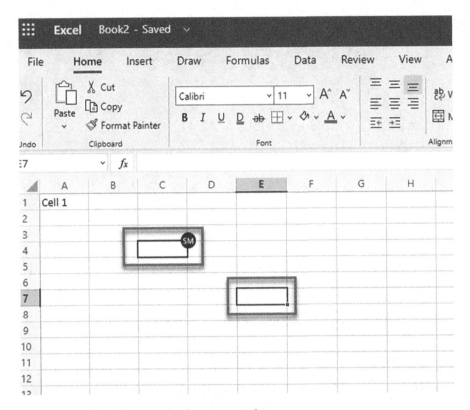

Figure 7-30. *Excel Online co-authoring with a user*

As I add content to the workbook, it will display in the workbook, and Sarah will be able to see the edits I make without delay.

With co-authoring, only one user can edit a cell at a time, and a user will not be able to edit the cell until the other user selects a different cell. The two users may continue to edit the workbook, and once the editing is complete, the document will be saved back to my OneDrive.

Word Online

Like co-authoring in Excel Online, the experience is similar in Word Online. You still need to ensure the document is located in OneDrive or SharePoint Online and the user you want to share with also has a valid Microsoft 365 license. In most cases, this won't be an issue because an entire organization will be on Microsoft 365, but if Microsoft 365 is being rolled out to an organization in a slow manner, it's possible that not all users will have the appropriate license.

To co-author a Word Online document, the process is similar to co-authoring in Excel Online. Once the document is saved in OneDrive or SharePoint Online, go ahead and share the document via File ➤ Share in the Office Online ribbon.

In Word Online, the co-authoring restrictions are relaxed compared to Excel Online. In Word Online, you can edit the same cursor location, whereas Excel Online will not allow you to edit the same cell. Figure 7-31 shows the experience in Word Online.

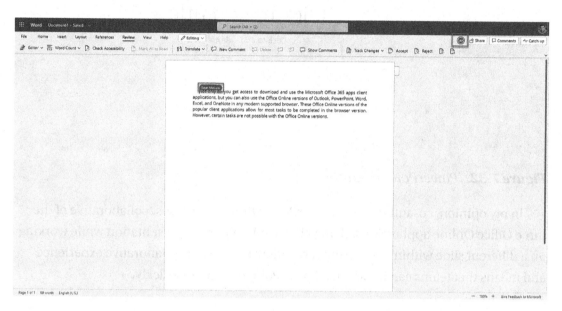

Figure 7-31. *Word Online co-authoring*

PowerPoint Online Co-Authoring

Like Excel and Word Online, PowerPoint Online co-authoring shares the same common functionality and experience. This is to ensure that the experience from an end user perspective is as unified and seamless as possible in Office Online.

To share a presentation for co-authoring, follow the same steps as in Excel and Word Online to invite a user to the PowerPoint document. Another way to share a document (PowerPoint, Word, Excel) is to click the Share button in the upper-right corner of the PowerPoint document. It will direct you to the same sharing interface as the previous method.

In Figure 7-32, Sarah and I are both editing the same PowerPoint document. I am working on Slide 2, while Sarah is currently editing Slide 1 of the presentation.

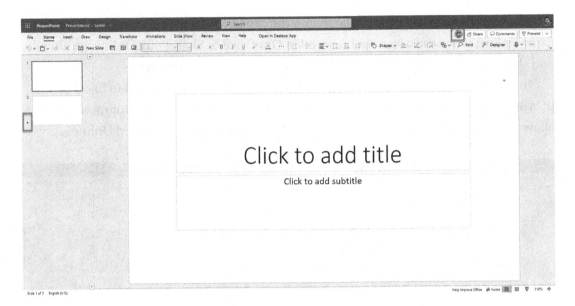

Figure 7-32. *PowerPoint co-authoring*

In my opinion, co-authoring in PowerPoint Online is the most collaborative of the three Office Online applications. Being able to edit the same presentation while working on a different slide within the presentation offers a powerful collaborative experience and means that teams can build out a PowerPoint document quickly.

Summary

Office Online and Office ProPlus offer the best tools for collaborating, creating and editing content, and creating effective documents to convey the appropriate message. For most users, Office Online will be sufficient enough, but some power users will need to use the Office ProPlus applications for the advanced features.

However, the ability to create content with Office Online is very powerful because you do not need the Office client installed locally on the device you are using. For Office Online, you only need a working Internet connection, a Microsoft 365 license, and a supported web browser. This makes it possible to work from most locations and have access to your documents in OneDrive or SharePoint Online.

When you need to do advanced data exploration in Excel or track changes within a Word document, you must use Office ProPlus. As an Office 365 subscriber, you have the ability to download and install Office ProPlus up to five times on a variety of devices.

For users who have relied on InfoPath 2013, you will notice that the InfoPath app is not available. In this case, you can use InfoPath 2013 but should plan on transitioning to Power Apps eventually.

Co-authoring is a powerful toolset in the Office ProPlus and Office Online ecosystems. Co-authoring is a great tool to foster collaboration with users who are geographically dispersed and may not want to send documents continually back and forth via email.

In the next chapter, I will discuss Microsoft Planner, which offers task management far superior to that of Outlook, SharePoint, or any other Microsoft task management program. Planner is aimed at project task assignment and reporting, for which Project 2019 or Project Online is overkill.

CHAPTER 8

Planner

In the previous chapter, I discussed the familiar Office applications and some of their benefits. In this chapter, I will review Microsoft Planner, which is a Microsoft 365 product that allows you and your team to create tasks and plans to manage tasks and projects. With Planner, you can assign tasks to users, monitor their statuses, and report on them. By utilizing this Microsoft 365 application, you can finally get rid of all the Post-It notes littering your desk and the countless Microsoft Excel spreadsheets and do not have to utilize Microsoft Project to manage simple or ad hoc projects, which might not be available in your workplace.

I am not discounting the need for project managers or project management software, but Planner does offer the ability to manage tasks and resources. Microsoft Project has its place, and it's a great tool to manage enterprise projects, but it does require licensing outside of the traditional Office suite licensing, and there is a bit of a learning curve to using it. Microsoft Planner is more focused on task management for projects and does not encroach on the features of Microsoft Project but does share some commonality with task management.

As I dive deeper into Microsoft Planner, I am going to touch upon some key areas that I think you will find useful. Regarding task management, you will explore not only creating tasks but also the ability to track and group them with buckets. You will also dive into reporting on tasks and their statuses. In Chapter 11, you will explore connecting Microsoft Planner with Microsoft Power Automate to create a truly remarkable integration between the two services.

But before we get too far ahead of ourselves, let's look at how to access Planner and get familiar with the interface and where you can find certain actions within Planner.

© Ralph Mercurio and Brian Merrill 2021
R. Mercurio and B. Merrill, *Beginning Microsoft 365 Collaboration Apps*,
https://doi.org/10.1007/978-1-4842-6936-7_8

Overview of the Planner Interface

Within Microsoft 365, click the app launcher in the upper-left corner and select Microsoft Planner, as shown in Figure 8-1.

 Planner

Figure 8-1. *Launching the Microsoft Planner application*

Once you click the application, you will be presented with the Planner Hub (see Figure 8-2). This Planner Hub displays all the Planner plans you create. I will discuss plans shortly.

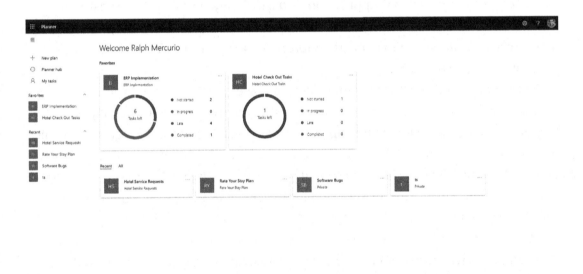

Figure 8-2. *Microsoft Planner Hub dashboard*

The Planner Hub also contains options to the left of the main section of the dashboard; see Figure 8-3. The options include creating a new plan (+ New plan), a shortcut link to the Planner Hub, My tasks, Favorites, Recent, Get the Planner app, and an icon to minimize the left menu.

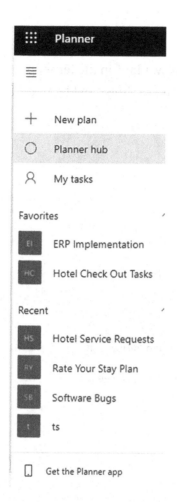

Figure 8-3. *Planner Hub left menu options*

Now that you know the layout and where actions are located within the application, let's move on to discussing plans, which provide the foundation for Planner.

Plans

Plans are a foundational element of Planner. Each plan provides the foundation for task buckets, charts, and schedules. It also provides an integration point for Microsoft 365 Groups and Teams. Microsoft 365 Groups was discussed in Chapter 4, and Teams was explored in Chapter 5.

Creating a New Plan

To create a new plan, click "+ New plan" in the left-hand menu. A modal window appears with the title "New Plan," as shown in Figure 8-4.

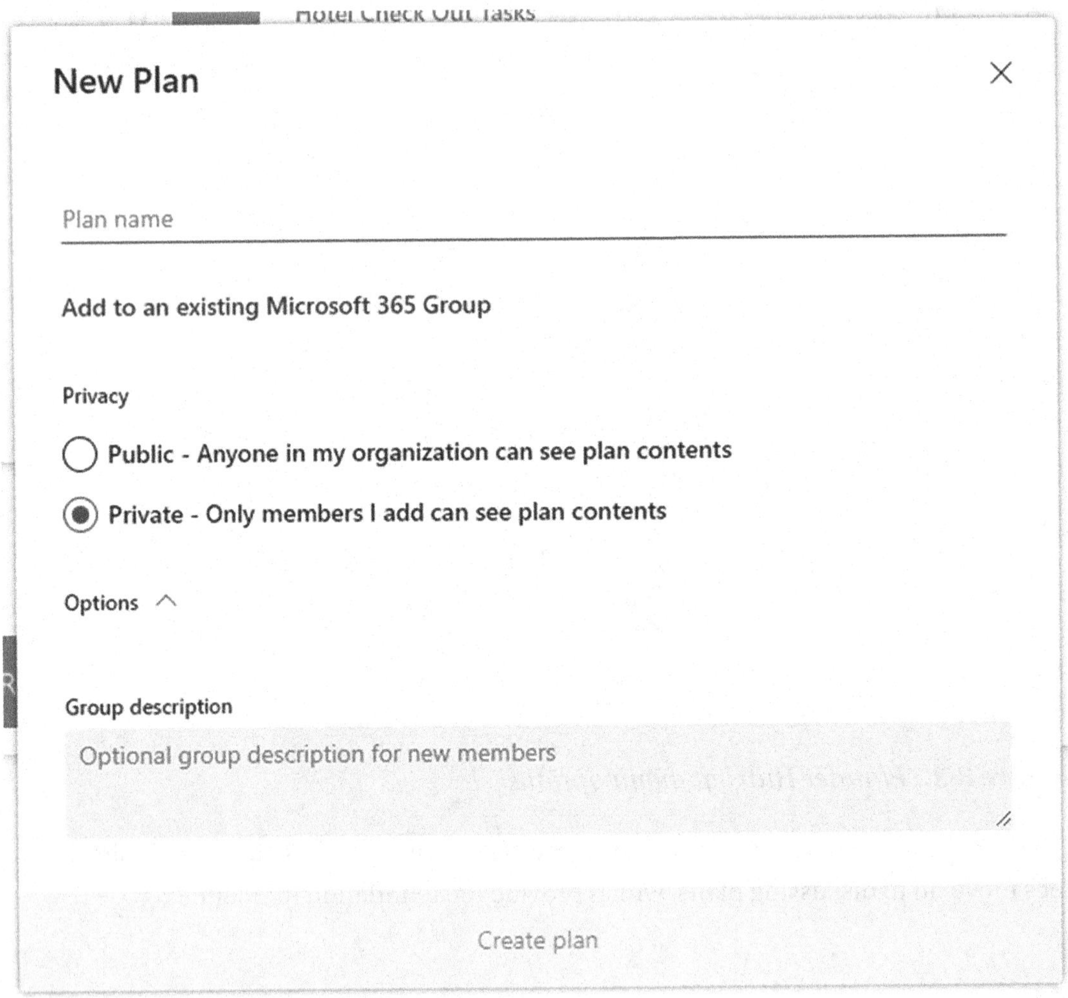

Figure 8-4. *New Plan window*

Note   Due to unmanaged proliferation of Microsoft groups and other objects, your internal IT team might have disabled the ability to create new objects including Planner plans. If you are unable to do so, please check with your service desk.

Creating a new plan is as simple as specifying a title for the plan, entering a group description if desired, and selecting the privacy settings. There are two privacy settings: public and private. If public is selected, any user within the organization can view the plan; if private is selected, the onus is on you to give access to the correct users. The easy way is to make all the plans public, but there may be reasons why this is not desired. For example, if the project deals with sensitive information about an acquisition or some other business activity, that could be sufficient reason to make it private.

Let's create a new plan with the following settings:

- **Title**: 2021 WFH Policy

- **Privacy**: Private – Only members I add can see plan contents

- **Plan description**: Plan to develop WFH Policy

Once the plan details are entered, click the Create plan button. See Figure 8-5.

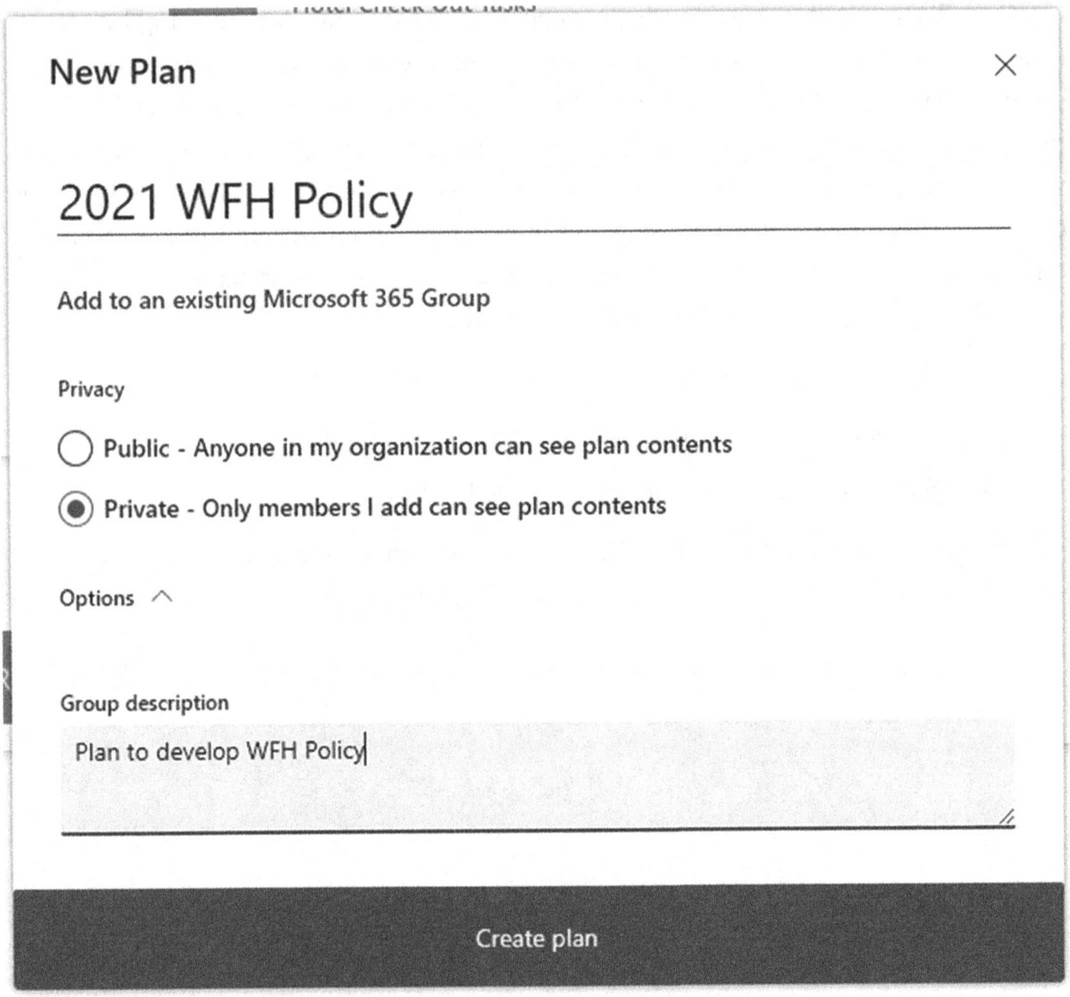

New Plan   ×

2021 WFH Policy

Add to an existing Microsoft 365 Group

Privacy

○ Public - Anyone in my organization can see plan contents

◉ Private - Only members I add can see plan contents

Options ∧

Group description

Plan to develop WFH Policy

Create plan

Figure 8-5. *New Plan settings*

Now that you have created a plan, let's get familiar with the plan's dashboard. Each plan also contains more settings available by an ellipsis (...) next to the Schedule link. This context menu contains some interesting connections as well as Planner-specific settings. Opening the menu, you will see icons for Conversation, Members, Files, Notebook, and Sites. These five options are connected to other Microsoft 365 services, and you will explore some of these options later in the chapter. The remaining six options are "Add to favorites," "Copy plan," "Export plan to Excel," "Copy link to plan," "Add plan to Outlook Calendar," and "Plan settings." The plan dashboard contains options to create tasks, add new buckets to contain tasks and group by, and invite members, six different views to view data (Boards, Assigned to, Progress, Due date, Labels, and Priority), and a settings menu. See Figure 8-6.

Figure 8-6. *Planner plan dashboard*

As you add tasks, I will explain the available options and settings. Buckets contain tasks that are assigned to resources. Buckets also contain a few settings that can be manipulated; they can be renamed, moved left or right on the plan dashboard, and deleted. The settings menu can be accessed by hovering over the bucket title and clicking the ellipsis (...). This will bring up the context menu for buckets.

There are times when you may want to group tasks by a common theme. Out of the gate, Planner creates a To-Do bucket, but you can create as many buckets as you need. Creating buckets is as simple as clicking "Add new bucket" and typing a name. For this exercise, let's create a bucket called "Internal Tasks." Now that you have a bucket to hold your tasks, let's invite users so you can assign tasks.

To invite users to a plan, click "Members" in the upper-right corner. Simply type the name of a user you want to add, and Microsoft 365 will automatically show the users that match your query. I am going to invite Brian Merrill and Sarah Merrill to the plan; the users you add will be different because these users are specific to my Microsoft 365 tenant. If you created a trial tenant, you will also need to create users; this can be accomplished by going to the admin settings, creating the users, and assigning them an appropriate license.

Note   If you made a mistake adding a user, click "Members" and hover over the name you want to remove. By hovering over the name you want to remove, an ellipsis will appear, and you can select the "Remove" option from the menu.

As Planner takes off in your organization and more and more plans are created, you may want to mark plans as favorites so they can be quickly accessed without the need to scroll through numerous plans on the Planner dashboard. By clicking the ellipsis (…) to the right of the Schedule link, you can select "Add to favorites." This will add the plan to the Favorites heading in the left-hand side of Planner.

Editing a Plan

To edit a plan, click the tile of the plan and select Plan settings. A Plan settings window will open on the right side of Planner. You will be able to change the title of the plan or background and delete the plan. You can also make a plan public or private depending on how the plan was originally created. Marking a plan as private or public does not hide the plan but limits who can access the plan. On the Plan settings screen, you can also change the email settings to send an email when a task is assigned to or completed by a group.

Deleting a Plan

Deleting a plan is as simple as choosing "Delete this plan" (Figure 8-7) in the Plan settings menu as described in the preceding.

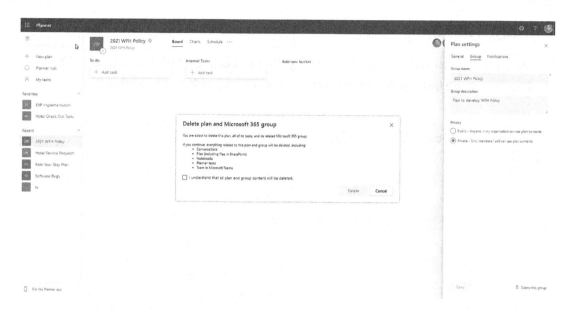

Figure 8-7. *Delete plan confirmation screen*

Deleting a plan will permanently delete the plan as well as all of the tasks. Currently, a deleted plan is nonrecoverable.

Plan Notifications and Communications

Planner offers little in the way of notifications, but as the service progresses, I can definitely see more control over the notifications received. Part of this isn't that Microsoft isn't able to accomplish it; it's more of not overloading your inbox with countless notifications about when tasks are completed or new plans are created.

To access the current notification settings available, access the cog/gear in the upper-right corner of Planner. You can tick the checkbox to alert you when someone assigns a task to you. You also can opt to be notified when a task is late, due today, or due in the next seven days. Click "Save" when you have made your choice. The default setting is that both options are selected.

Task Management

Being able to manage tasks is a cornerstone of Planner and is what makes Planner an effective application. Tasks can be added, edited, and deleted. Planner also presents dashboards to manage the number of tasks and to quickly gain an understanding of their statuses.

Adding Tasks

Create your first task in the 2021 WFH Policy plan by adding a task to the Internal Tasks bucket; see Figure 8-8. Clicking the + sign makes an Add task window appear.

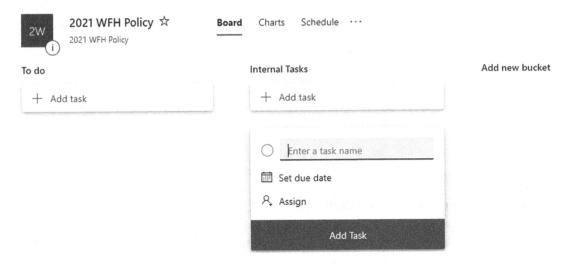

Figure 8-8. *Adding a task to a bucket*

The Add task window allows you to simply create a task name, set a due date, and assign it to a user. Once the task is added, you can further edit the task. For this scenario, I created a task with the following settings:

- **Task name**: WFH Policy Template Creation

- **Set a due date**: 2/1/2021

- **Assign**: Brian@capelesssolutions.com

Note   The values for "Assign" and "Set a due date" will be different because the users will be different in your environment. Also, the dates will be different.

Adding more tasks is as simple as following the preceding steps of adding a task to the bucket. One interesting feature about adding tasks is the ability to assign a task to more than one person. This is a great way to assign tasks to multiple users. To assign a task to multiple users, simply add those members during task creation; see Figure 8-9.

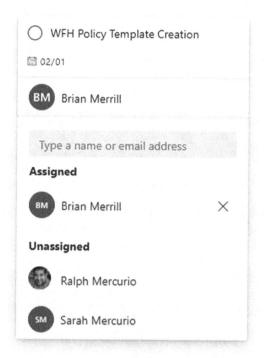

Figure 8-9. *Adding multiple members to a task*

Open the task you created before and click the "Assign" field. A list of members will be displayed; click the user to whom you want to assign the task. You can select a single user or as many users as you want by clicking their name.

Note   To remove a user from a task, open the task and hover over the "Assign" field. Once the list of users appears, select the X to the right of their name.

Because Microsoft Planner is part of the Microsoft 365 suite, there is tight integration with other Microsoft 365 applications. When a user is added to a plan or when a task gets assigned to a user, the user will receive an email in their Outlook inbox. This is great because most of us work out of our inbox and cannot be expected to check a Planner plan for tasks. Figure 8-10 shows the email that is sent to the user. Currently the email is not customizable in Microsoft Planner.

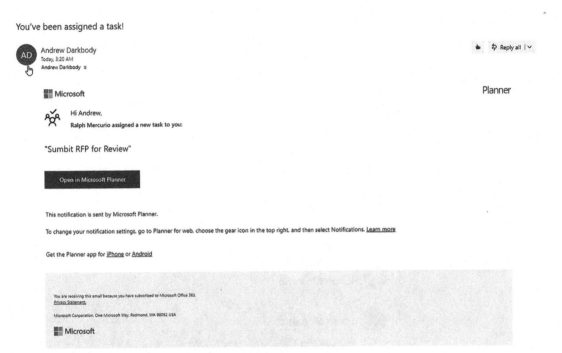

Figure 8-10. *Task assignment email from Planner*

Editing a Task

Now that you have a solid understanding of creating and assigning tasks, let's begin to edit tasks. As the creator of the task, the fields are limited to only three pertinent pieces of task information: "Task name," "Assign," and "Set a due date."

Click the task. In this case, the task is titled "WFH Policy Template Creation." Clicking the task opens a modal window with the ability to add more context to the task. See Figure 8-11 for the task detail window.

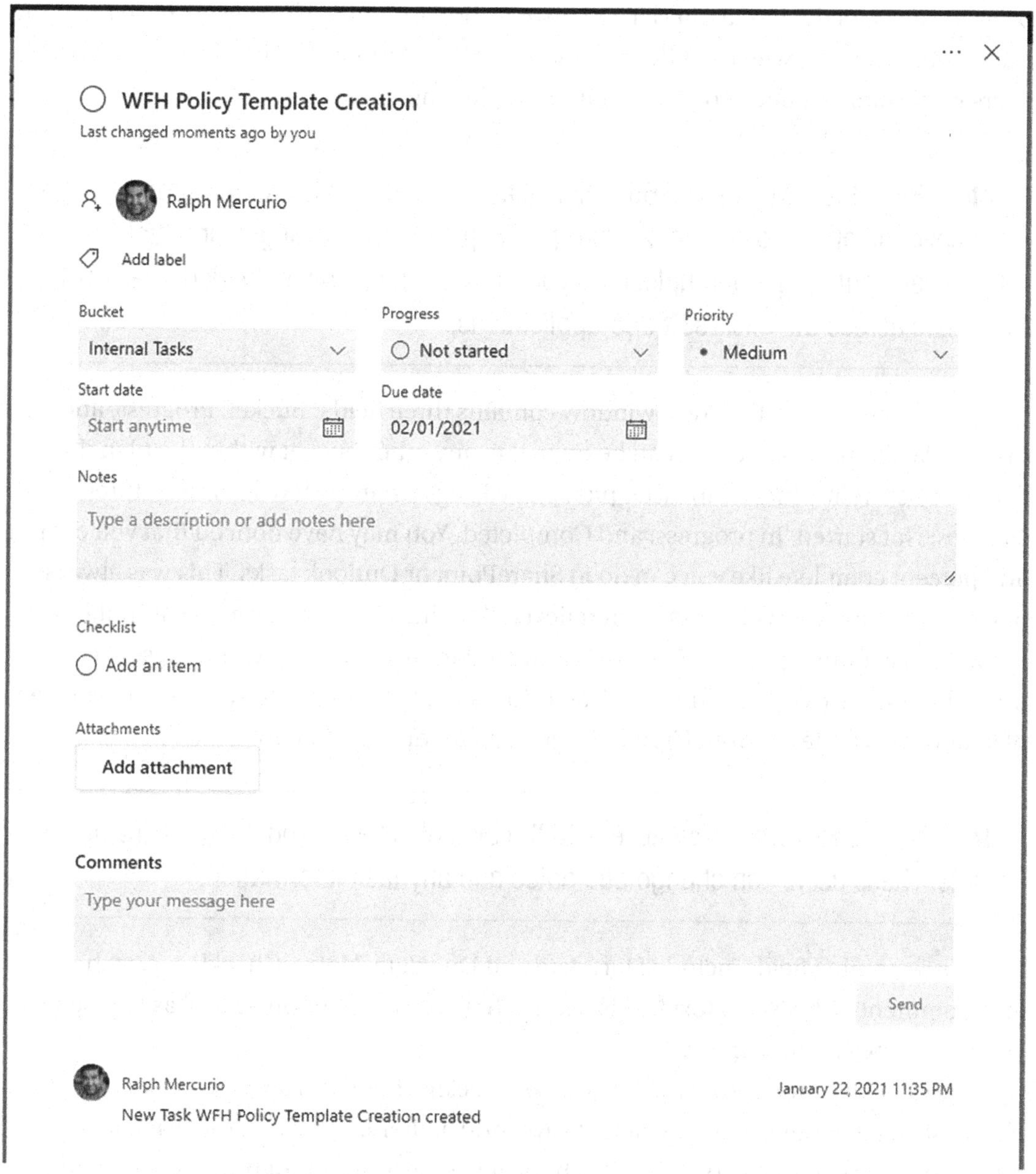

○ **WFH Policy Template Creation**
Last changed moments ago by you

    Ralph Mercurio

⬠ Add label

Bucket	Progress	Priority
Internal Tasks ⌄	○ Not started ⌄	• Medium ⌄

Start date	Due date
Start anytime 🗓	02/01/2021 🗓

Notes

Type a description or add notes here

Checklist

○ Add an item

Attachments

Add attachment

Comments

Type your message here

Send

   Ralph Mercurio   January 22, 2021 11:35 PM
New Task WFH Policy Template Creation created

Figure 8-11. *Task detail window*

This now probably looks a lot more familiar when adding a task. Now that the task detail window is open, let's explore the areas further. The first thing you will notice is the title of the task. The members assigned are located in the upper-left corner. One thing to be aware of is that Microsoft 365 displays users as initials, but you can always hover

over the image of the initials, and it will display the username. If two users have the same initial, Microsoft 365 will use different colors for the user images. You can also remove users by clicking the image of the initials and selecting the X.

Note   By default, Microsoft 365 will display a user's initials as their profile image. You have the ability to customize your profile picture by clicking your initials in the upper-right corner and uploading your image. The newly uploaded image will populate across the Microsoft 365 applications.

The first row of the Edit Task window contains three fields: Bucket, Progress, and Priority. With buckets, the task can be moved to any other bucket within the plan. It cannot be currently moved to other plans. The Progress drop-down contains three statuses: Not started, In progress, and Completed. You may have noticed that you cannot add percent complete like you can do in SharePoint or Outlook tasks. This was always one of my pet peeves with tasks; I am relieved that they decided to remove it (but it may show up in a future update). You also cannot add more statuses because these are the main three statuses that are tracked. The Priority field allows you to set the importance of it; and you can select from Urgent, Important, Medium, and Low.

Attention   Users who have access to the plan also have modify rights, including delete. These users can change due dates and any task information.

The remaining fields include Start date and Due date, Notes, Checklist, Attachments, and Comments. The Notes text box is used to hold the description as well as any details you feel are pertinent to the task.

The Checklist area allows the creation of checklist items. To add items to the checklist, begin typing an item where it says "Add an item." Be aware that each item added to the checklist can only be 100 characters long and cannot be assigned to other users. The checklist items and tasks are assigned to the same user(s). Once one item is added to the checklist, the "Show on card" and Checklist checkboxes become active. The "Show on card" (see Figure 8-13) checkbox shows all the checklist items on the main task card, while the checkbox to the left of the subtask strikes through it (completed) or not.

To further build out the exercise, I added three subtasks to the main task, "WFH Policy Template Creation." These subtasks are "Get Template," "Meet with Executive

Team," "and "Survey Workforce." I also checked "Show on card" (Figure 8-13), which displays the checklist items on the main task card.

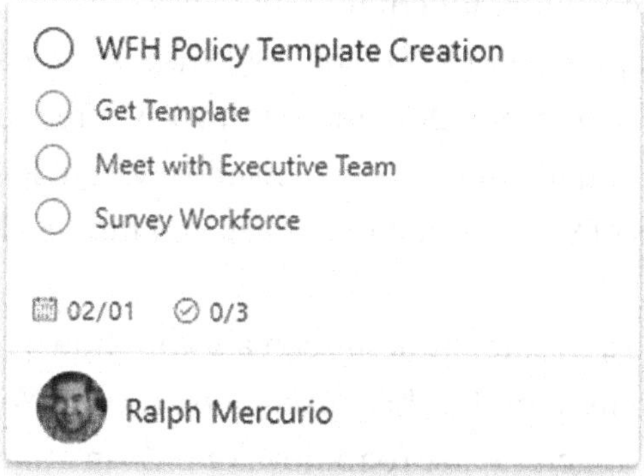

Figure 8-12.   *Task with checklist items added*

When the checklist items are shown on the card, you'll see how many checklist items are completed and the total. Checklist items can also be promoted or removed completely. When hovering the mouse pointer over a checklist item within the Edit Task window, two icons will appear to the right of the item (see Figure 8-13). These icons are the garbage can and the promoted arrow. Promotion in Planner means that the checklist item becomes an actual task and is removed from the current task. You need to fill out the task details because those properties are not carried over during the promotion.

Figure 8-13.   *Promoted arrow and trash icons*

The final two fields on the task detail window are Attachments and Comments. Attachments can be a file, a link, or a SharePoint attachment. For file attachments, an Open File dialog box appears, and you simply select the file from your local computer. A link attachment contains both an address field and text to display. For example, the link could be www.capelesssolutions.com, and the text to display would be Capeless Solutions. The next attachment I find to be very clever on Microsoft's part.

When creating a plan, Microsoft creates a SharePoint site and a Microsoft 365 group to gather and serve as a repository for content that lives outside of Planner. I discussed SharePoint Online in Chapter 2 and Microsoft 365 Groups in Chapter 4. SharePoint attachments point to the SharePoint document library where the content is stored. This ties into other Microsoft 365 services, which allow you to leverage the document management capabilities of SharePoint Online without the headache of having to create a site for each plan.

As with checklist items, the attachments can also be shown on the main task card. However, only one attachment or the checklist can be shown. You can't currently show both checklist items and attachments. To remove or edit an attachment, hover over the attachment in the task detail view and click the ellipsis (…). You can then delete the item or edit the item as desired.

The last option in the task detail window is Labels (see Figure 8-11). Planner offers six different label colors (pink, red, yellow, green, blue, and purple). You can add text to the label colors to denote severity or importance, but you can't change the actual color of a task label.

Note   These text labels will apply to all tasks in each plan.

To edit a label, open any task in detail mode and select "Label" under the members. Hover over the label you want to add text to and type the specific text. You can also quickly set the label for tasks by selecting the ellipsis in the upper-right corner.

Viewing Tasks

Planner offers a quick way to view the tasks assigned to you. On the Planner dashboard, the My tasks link (see Figure 8-3) available to the left of the main dashboard will show you tasks assigned to you either grouped by plan (Figure 8-14) or grouped by progress (Figure 8-15).

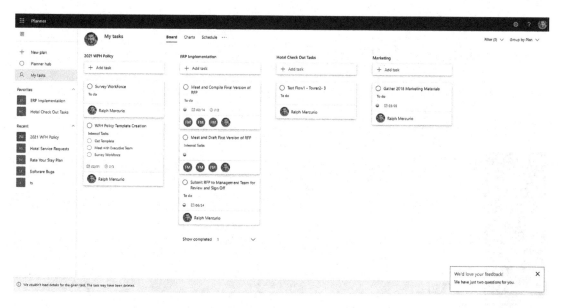

Figure 8-14. *My tasks grouped by plan*

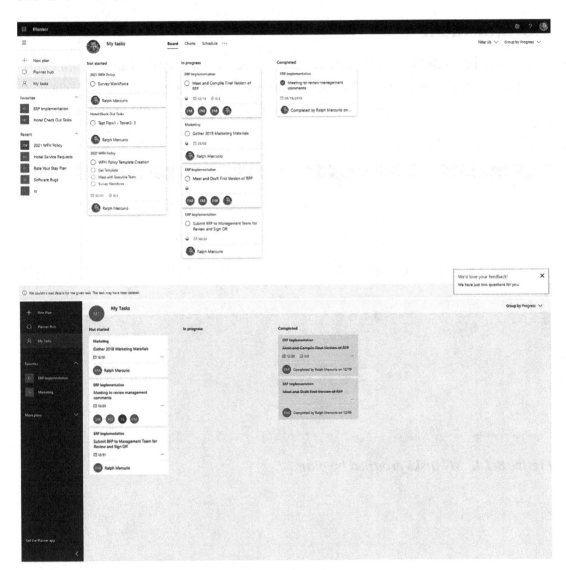

Figure 8-15. *My tasks grouped by progress*

Another way to view tasks, not just your tasks but tasks within a plan, is to click "Planner Hub" in the leftmost menu (Figure 8-3). Now that you have created a plan, added tasks, and added it as a favorite, it will show the remaining tasks within your favorite plans; see Figure 8-16.

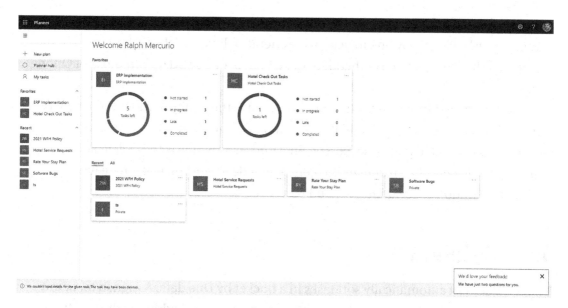

Figure 8-16. *Planner Hub with favorite plans*

As you can see, the remaining tasks inside each plan are shown in a donut chart with the appropriate status. The view does not show the tasks assigned to you but simply a count of all the tasks.

Viewing the tasks assigned to a user can be achieved in two ways. The first way is to use "Group by Assigned to" in a plan. "Group by Assigned to" will group the tasks within a plan into individual silos for each user. If a task is assigned to multiple users, the same task will be displayed in each silo.

Manage Tasks

Planner includes six options to manage tasks within a plan. Hover over the ellipsis (…) on the main task you want to manage. The options that appear are: Label, Assign, Copy task, Copy link to task, Move task, and Delete.

You can quickly apply a label to a task. In this view, you can't edit the text label, but you can do so in the task detail window, as described in the previous section.

"Assign" allows you to add assignee(s) for the task. Remember multiple people can be assigned to a task.

"Copy task" allows you to copy the task. It can duplicate the task, and it will allow you to copy over portions of the task. These portions include Assignment, Progress, Dates, Description, Checklist, Attachments, and Labels. It will also allow you to copy the task using a different task name. This is useful if you want to duplicate a task but change the title of the task. The "Copy link to task" will generate a link, which will be copied to the clipboard. This link could be embedded into an email or posted to a SharePoint Online site.

The next available option for task management is the ability to move tasks between buckets. Simply select the plan and the bucket name and click "Move." This will move the task to the selected plan/bucket. The final option available is the Delete action. Selecting the Delete option deletes the item. Upon deletion, you will have a few moments to undo it if accidently deleted.

Task Ordering

Planner does not automatically sort tasks in a bucket by Due date, Assigned to, or any other criteria. As tasks are created in a bucket, they are simply added as the first item regardless of the due date or any criteria. The tasks can be manually ordered by simply dragging the task into the correct spot.

Task Completion

You have explored creating a plan, adding buckets and tasks, and editing those tasks, but what I have not talked about is completing tasks. Tasks can be completed in a number of ways, either directly on the plan or within the task detail view. To complete a task when looking at a plan, simply hover over the task and select the circle to the left of the task title; see Figure 8-17. Clicking it marks the task complete by setting the status to "Completed." Another way to complete a task is to set the Progress drop-down to Completed within the task detail.

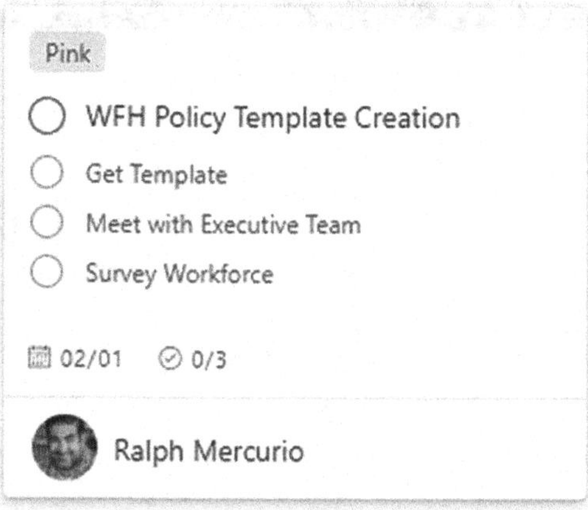

Figure 8-17. *Completing a task*

Once the task is marked Completed, it will be collapsed into a completed view. You can expand the view and see all the tasks that have been completed. Figure 8-18 shows the effect of marking a task Completed.

Show completed   1   ∨

Figure 8-18. *Completed tasks view*

If a task is marked Completed but should not have been, anyone can set the status back to "Not started" or "In progress" in the task detail view or by viewing the completed tasks and hovering over the task. Deselect the circle to the left of the task name, and the task will be marked as "Not started."

Planner Dashboards and Reporting

For the most part, you have been working in the Board view of Planner. Planner offers a Charts dashboard (Figure 8-19) to view task status and members and group tasks by Bucket, Assigned to, Progress, and Due date.

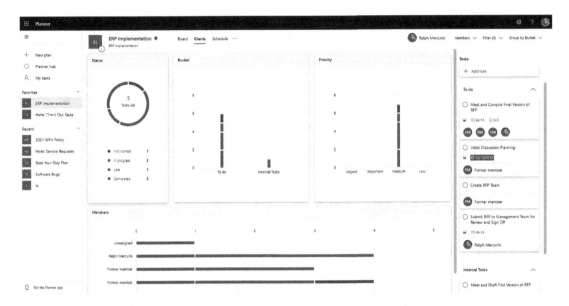

Figure 8-19. *Charts dashboard for a Planner plan*

The Charts dashboard is accessible by selecting Charts in about the center of the screen of any plan; see Figure 8-20.

Figure 8-20. *Planner Charts view*

Continuing with this example, the Charts view of the ERP plan shows a doughnut chart of task statuses and the number of tasks left in the plan. Each status is color-coded: gray for not started, blue for in progress, red for late, and green for completed. The Members line chart shows the number of tasks assigned to a member and the status of those assigned tasks. The rightmost column of the Charts dashboard for the ERP plan allows for grouping by Bucket, Assigned to, Progress, Due date, and Labels.

Note   For the other tasks, I promoted the checklist items I added earlier to tasks and assigned them to members of the ERP plan.

Planner also has a calendar view called Schedule (Figure 8-21). This displays the tasks in a calendar view based on the task details.

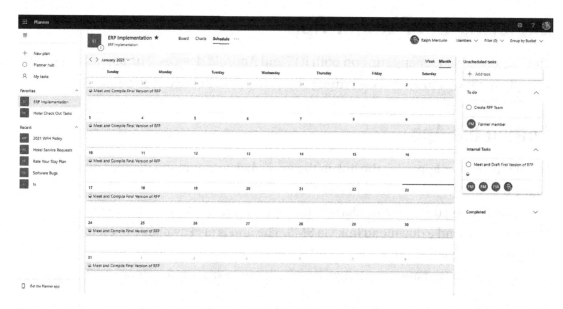

Figure 8-21. *Monthly schedule view of Planner*

This view uses the start date and due date to calculate the duration. For example, if only the start date is populated, the Schedule view will use that value and place the task on the corresponding date. If the due date is the only populated value, the task will be placed on the due date of the task. If both the start date and due date are populated, the task will appear as a duration (days in between) in the Schedule view.

Planner Integrations

As you may have noticed while reading this book, Microsoft has done a great job of building separate applications that can entirely function on their own but also can be utilized within other applications to form a cohesive collaboration toolset.

Planner is no different. As you saw at the beginning of the chapter, Planner integrates with Microsoft 365 Groups as well as SharePoint Online. You explored both Microsoft 365 Groups in Chapter 4 and SharePoint Online in Chapter 2; and in a later chapter, you will see the integration with Automate (formerly Flow) (Chapter 11).

There is a one-to-one relationship between Microsoft 365 Groups and Planner. Each group has a Planner plan; each time a plan is created, a corresponding Microsoft 365 group is created.

Exploring the Planner App

The Microsoft Planner app runs on both iOS and Android devices. The app allows you to view plans, tasks, and almost everything else you can do in the web version.

Getting the App

To get the Planner app, click the link in the lower-left corner in the Planner menu; see Figure 8-3.

Upon clicking the link, a modal window opens, asking for your mobile number. Microsoft will send a download link via SMS. The app is also available in either the Google or Apple app store.

Once the Planner app is installed, it will ask you to sign in; see Figure 8-22.

Figure 8-22. *The Sign in screen*

Signing into the Planner App

Sign in with your credentials. Once the app loads, you will be directed to the Planner Hub. Keep in mind that the experience doesn't translate fully from the web version to a mobile device. There just is not enough room to show everything on the smaller screen sizes of mobile devices.

Creating a Plan

The Planner Hub on a mobile device shows the current plans. You also have the ability to create a new plan by clicking the + located in the upper-right corner. The experience of creating a plan in the app is very similar to the web version; the only option not available is to "Subscribe new members to notification emails." Once you input the plan title, privacy settings, and a description if needed, you will be directed to add members to the plan. Choose the members as you did earlier in this chapter. Once that is completed, the plan will sync with Microsoft 365 and in moments will show up in the Planner Hub in the web version.

To explore a little deeper, go ahead and click a plan. The experience is similar, and the Planner app will render the plan that you clicked almost the same way as the web version. If you swipe left in the app, you will see the buckets and any tasks in them. By clicking and holding on the task, you can move it to another bucket.

Task Management

As with the web version, the app also allows for adding, editing, and deleting tasks. The experience is similar to the web version without any lack of capabilities.

Adding Tasks

In the Planner app, open the 2021 WFH Policy plan you created earlier in this chapter. To open the plan, click 2021 WFH Policy in the Planner Hub. When the plan opens, you will see the task buckets: To-Do and Internal Tasks. You can view the buckets by swiping left or right.

In the Internal Tasks bucket, click "Add a task..." as seen in Figure 8-23.

Figure 8-23. *Adding a task through the Planner app*

Clicking "Add a task…" allows you to type the task name, set a due date, and assign to a team member of the plan; see Figure 8-24. Go ahead and add a task.

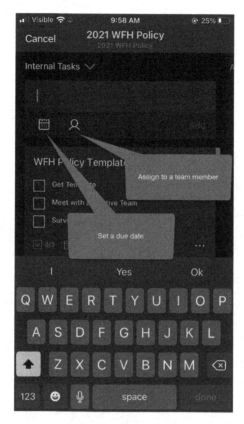

Figure 8-24. *Adding a task and its associated properties*

The task is added to the plan and in near real time is available in the web version as well.

Editing Tasks

Editing tasks is like editing tasks in the web version with near one-to-one functionality. Clicking the task in the Planner app brings up the Edit task view; see Figure 8-25.

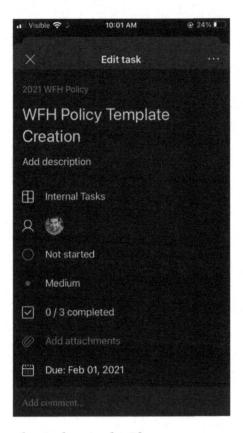

Figure 8-25. *The Edit task window in the Planner app*

As you can see, you can do almost everything in the web version. The big difference is the experience on the mobile device vs. the desktop/laptop.

Deleting Tasks

Deleting a task can be done when the task is in edit mode. It's available via the horizontal ellipsis in the upper-right corner of the window.

Summary

Microsoft Planner is like the big brother to the way we have been managing tasks currently in the Microsoft ecosystem; Excel spreadsheets, Microsoft Project, Microsoft SharePoint, and Microsoft Outlook. The ability to easily create plans and group tasks together allows users everywhere to have a formidable task management system. In my opinion, what sets this apart from the other ways we have managed tasks is the Charts dashboard. The ability to report graphically without heavy customization or manipulating the data in Excel is well worth the use of Planner.

The integration with Microsoft 365 Groups and SharePoint Online provides a cohesive set of services that can be used to support collaboration in any business environment. Instead of trying to force an application into unorthodox situations, Microsoft is utilizing all the apps to do what they do best and integrate them. Gone are the days of having super-rich feature sets with product overlap and the ensuing confusion over how to use an application.

Not only is the integration into existing services great but so is the cross-platform functionality. Whether you are using the web versions of the products in a variety of browsers (IE, Chrome, Firefox, etc.) or an array of devices utilizing the Planner app, the experience is strikingly similar. This new Microsoft is getting back to its core: building apps that accomplish a goal, not overextending apps to be overly complex.

In the next chapter, I will discuss Microsoft Stream, which allows companies to create video libraries in Microsoft 365. This new application is built to be an enterprise video platform and improve video capabilities and delivery.

CHAPTER 9

Stream

In Chapter 8, I reviewed Planner, a new application to manage tasks within Microsoft 365. In this chapter, I will discuss Microsoft Stream, an application to upload and consume video. Over the past few years, video content has exploded and arguably has invaded both our personal and business lives.

Video can now be produced with a smartphone, uploaded to the Web, and consumed quickly by anyone. No longer is expensive camera equipment, well-lit studio, or top-of-the-line editing equipment needed to produce video content and distribute it. Video content can be created and edited to quickly disseminate information in a new, accepted format that is consumable by almost everyone.

If you happen to be an existing subscriber to Office 365 Video, Stream is the replacement application as designated by Microsoft. Stream does have some limits, and it is essential to be aware of them prior to using Stream in a production scenario. Video files in Stream can be no larger than 50 GB as of the publication of this book. I doubt that most video files you create will ever be that large, but if they are, Microsoft Stream can't support them.

Microsoft Stream attempts to bridge the divide for video content in a business environment by creating an innovative platform for video content. With Stream, you can search for the title of a video file, and you can search within a video because every video is transcribed. As I progress through the chapter, I will highlight all that Stream has to offer and how it can provide a new communication platform for any organization.

Using Microsoft Stream

In the Office 365 tenant, click the app launcher in the upper-left corner and select Stream; see Figure 9-1. If you do not see Microsoft Stream, click the "All apps" link and select it from there.

© Ralph Mercurio and Brian Merrill 2021
R. Mercurio and B. Merrill, *Beginning Microsoft 365 Collaboration Apps*,
https://doi.org/10.1007/978-1-4842-6936-7_9

Stream

Figure 9-1. *Launching Microsoft Stream from the app launcher*

After clicking the application link, Microsoft Stream will launch as depicted in Figure 9-2.

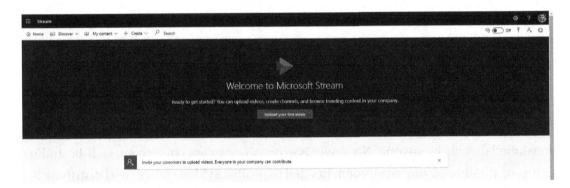

Figure 9-2. *The Microsoft Stream application*

Looking at the interface of Stream, let's review the navigational and essential elements. At first glance, there is not much happening with the application, but that is part of the simplicity of the Stream platform. Figure 9-3 depicts the primary navigational elements.

Figure 9-3. *Microsoft Stream navigational elements*

- **Discover**: Allows you to search Stream by specifying keywords, and then you can sort by a variety of attributes, such as "Name," "Relevance," "Trending," "Publish date," "Views," and "Likes."

- **My content**

  - **Videos**

This portal allows you to see the videos you have uploaded to Microsoft Stream, as shown in Figure 9-4.

Figure 9-4. *Videos page of Microsoft Stream*

You can also view the videos in a variety of ways: "Name," "Upload date," "Relevance," "Views," and "Likes." The "State" drop-down refers to if a video file is still in draft or published. If a video is marked as published, it is fully viewable and searchable by the users who have permission. Draft is the opposite state, and videos marked as draft will not be viewable by anyone except the uploader.

The final available drop-down choice is Privacy. It filters the videos based on if they are viewable by everyone (company), limited people, or both.

- **Channels**

Channels are another foundational element of Microsoft 365, which I discussed in Microsoft Teams. Channels in Microsoft Stream are similar and so have similar properties. In Stream, channels can be created and scoped to either the entire company, meaning that everyone has access, or to a Microsoft 365 group.

- **Meetings**

A list where recorded meetings from Teams will be stored that are initiated by you.

- **Watchlist**

A watchlist is a list where video content that you want to see has been tagged for further viewing. This watchlist is also searchable and sortable via "Relevance," "Trending," Added date," "Views," and "Likes."

- **Groups**

  Groups in Microsoft Stream are the same as Microsoft 365
  groups. Making a group via Microsoft Stream is similar to making
  a Microsoft 365 group via Outlook. You will notice that every
  Microsoft 365 group also has a Microsoft Stream component.
  Unfortunately, at the time of writing this book, the integration
  between Outlook and Stream appears to be quite limited.

Note   Be aware that deleting a group via Microsoft Stream will also delete the
corresponding Microsoft 365 group. This includes deletion of conversations, files,
sites, and so on.

- **Followed channels**

  Followed channels are channels that you have selected to follow
  and get notifications from. The followed channel list can be
  searched and sorted by "Number of followers," "Number of
  videos," and "Relevance."

- **Create**

  - **Upload video**

    Allows you to upload a video to Microsoft Stream. This will be
    discussed later in this chapter.

  - **Live event**

  - **Group**

    This link allows you to create a Microsoft 365 group via Microsoft
    Stream. This group retains all the properties of a Microsoft 365
    group but can also leverage Stream to upload and play video
    content.

  - **Channel**

    Creating a channel allows similar content to be classified together.
    This makes it easy to find content on a specific topic. Creating
    channels is also discussed later in the chapter.

- **Record screen or video**

  This will allow you to record both the screen and your voice and upload the video to Stream. This is useful when recording training sessions or anything else that needs to be saved. There is a 15-minute time limit per video.

- **Search**

  Allows you to search Stream by specifying keywords, and then you can also sort by a variety of attributes. You can sort the result set by "Name," "Relevance," "Trending," "Publish date," "Views," and "Likes."

Walking Through Stream

Even though Stream is centered around video content through a simple, clean interface, let's go through the process of uploading a video, creating a channel, and navigating around Stream.

Uploading Your First Video

To upload a video to Stream, either select the "Upload video" link located within the "Create" navigational element, as discussed, or drag the file onto the Videos page accessible from the "My content" link. Instead of the traditional upload form with a variety of fields, Microsoft presents just a page (Figure 9-5) where a file can be dragged onto, or you can choose to upload files through a Windows Explorer–like interface.

Figure 9-5. *Uploading a video file to Microsoft Stream through My content ➤ Videos*

Once a file is uploaded by either dragging the file or uploading a selected file, you must populate the details of the video file, as shown in Figure 9-6.

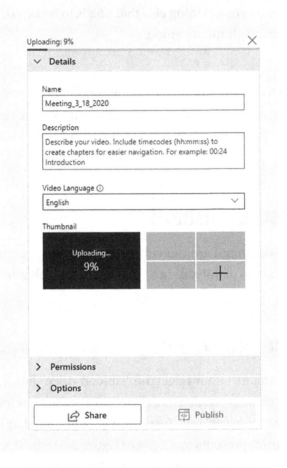

Figure 9-6. *Populating the details of an uploaded video*

Provide the name, description, video language, and thumbnail. The thumbnails auto-generate, but you can also specify your own. You also need to set the appropriate permissions. By default, videos are viewable by the entire organization, but you can share the video with a specific group, channel, or set of people.

Note   You can share with a combination of channels, groups, and people so that you can upload and post to specific areas of Microsoft Stream instead of the traditional method of sharing with users.

There are three options available under the Options heading. By default, Comments and Captions are enabled. These settings allow others to post comments, thus creating another way users can collaborate and post feedback throughout Stream.

Creating a Channel

As discussed, channels are a way to group videos that have a similar context, department, or theme. To create a new channel, click the "Channel" link under the Create navigational element. Once you click the link, you will be presented with the Create a Channel interface depicted in Figure 9-7.

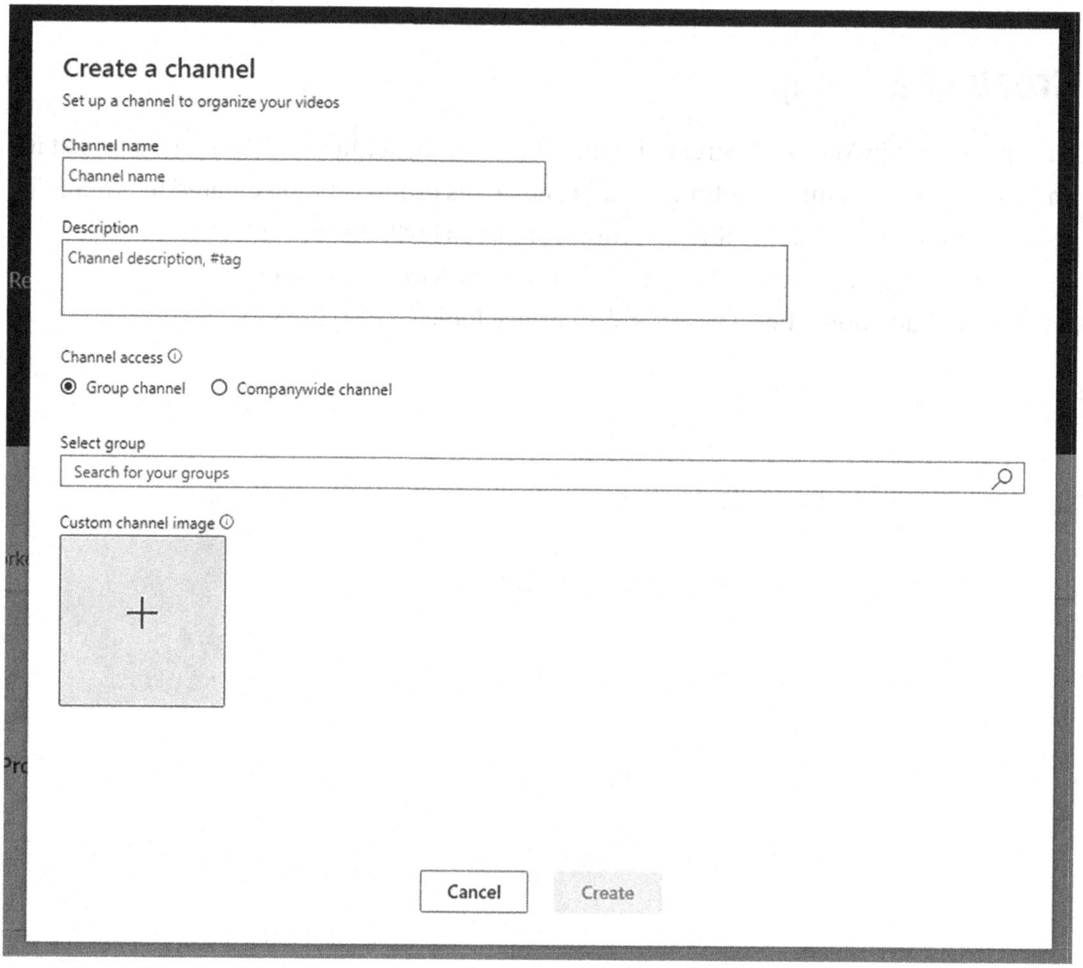

Figure 9-7. *Creating a new channel in Microsoft Stream*

When creating the channel, you need to specify a channel name and, if desired, a description. Select either "Companywide channel" or "Group channel" under Channel access. A companywide channel allows anyone in the organization who has access to Stream to upload and watch videos. This option might be preferable in some circumstances, but I would venture to say that corporate communications would like to check for content and message. With that, you can also select Group channel, which allows a group to manage videos; this option limits who can view or post, and only users who have access to the group also have access to the channel.

You also have the option to choose a channel image. Once you are satisfied with your settings, click the Create button. You can also access your channels by selecting the "Channels" link under the My content heading.

Creating a Group

Group creation in Microsoft Stream is similar to creating a Microsoft 365 group in that it shares some of the familiar settings, but because this group is being created in Stream, it also presents you with some Stream-only options, as I will discuss shortly.

To create a group within Microsoft Stream, click "Group" from the Create navigational heading. The "New group" interface looks like Figure 9-8.

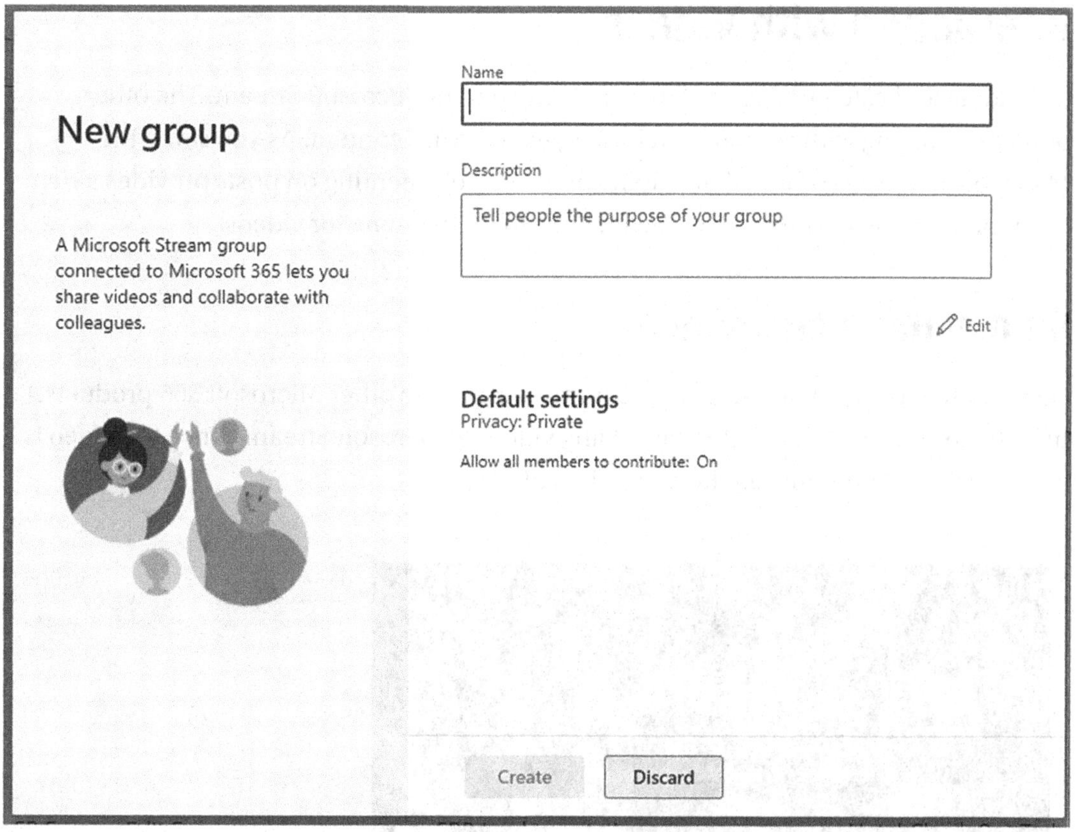

Figure 9-8. *Creating a group in Microsoft Stream*

To create the group, you need to specify a name and a description if needed. As with creating a Microsoft 365 group, you need to choose either a private or public group, which is available from the Edit link. To recap, a public group is a group that is searchable, and anyone can join. In a private group, the members must be invited to participate.

The "Allow all members to contribute" toggle button is only available when creating a group within Microsoft Stream. This group setting by default (On) gives all members of the group the ability to upload videos, delete videos, create and delete channels, and edit the membership of the group; if that is not a desired scenario, set the toggle to Off.

Interacting with Videos

Uploading and categorizing content is just one part of Microsoft Stream. The other part is interacting with content and finding the relevant content. As you saw with Microsoft Teams and chats, liking, following, and commenting on posts provides a rich collaboration environment, and Stream aims to do the same for videos.

Commenting on a Video

Commenting on a video is similar to commenting in the other Microsoft 365 products. In order to comment on a video, select any video in Microsoft Stream. Once the video is loaded, click "Comment," as shown in Figure 9-9.

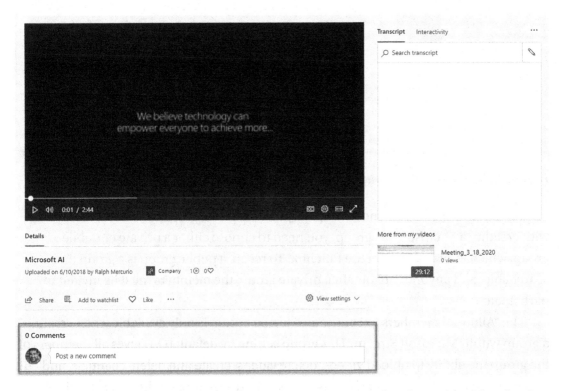

Figure 9-9. *Commenting on a video, as seen in a screenshot from the video "AI for Accessibility" recorded by Microsoft for Build 2019*

At the time of writing this book, Microsoft Stream only supports comments in plain text. Plain text refers strictly to text without the ability to embellish, such as using bold or italics, changing the font, or embedding documents or links to other content. Once you have typed your comment, select "Post" in the lower-right corner.

Your comment will be posted, and if needed you will be able to edit or delete the comment.

Liking a Video

Liking a video in Stream increases its relevancy and also gives a user the ability to refine when searching because Likes is one of the search refiners. By liking videos, it shows that the content is relevant and that it might be useful to others. In order to like a video, browse for the video you want to like, and choose "Like," as shown in Figure 9-10.

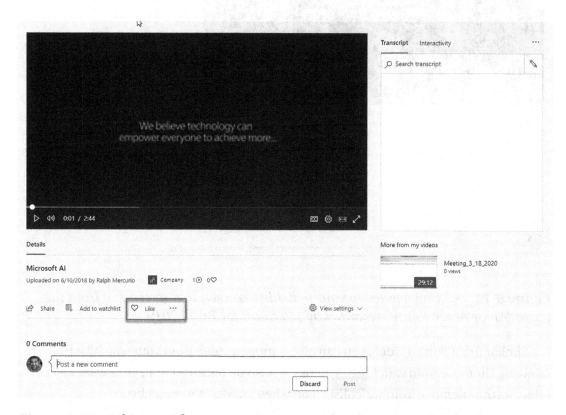

Figure 9-10. *Liking a video, as seen in a screenshot from the video "AI for Accessibility" recorded by Microsoft for Build 2019*

Choosing "Like" will switch the Like button to "Liked." If needed, you can also unlike a previously liked video.

Adding a Video to Your Watchlist

Watchlists are a great feature because they allow you to save videos to watch at a later date. As discussed, the watchlist can be sorted by a variety of refiners as well as full index searching. In order to save a video to your watchlist, select "Add to watchlist," as shown in Figure 9-11.

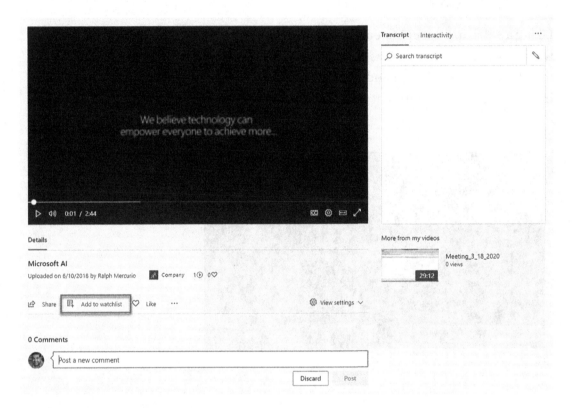

Figure 9-11. *Adding a video to your watchlist, as seen in a screenshot from the video "AI for Accessibility" recorded by Microsoft for Build 2019*

Similar to unliking a video, you can also remove a video from your watchlist by selecting "Remove from watchlist." Videos can also be removed from your watchlist by selecting the "Remove from watchlist" icon when viewing the watchlist.

Transcript

Microsoft Stream introduces the ability for videos to be transcribed. A transcript is generated automatically without any user interaction. The transcript is also searchable, so any search terms in the transcript will be found and shown in the specific time location. In order to view the transcript if it is not being shown, enable it via the cog in the lower-right corner, as shown in Figure 9-12.

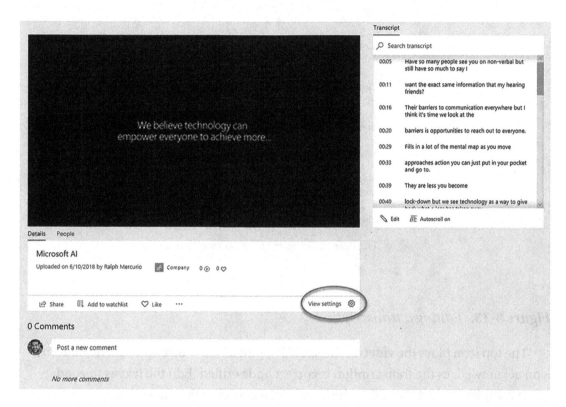

Figure 9-12. *Showing the transcription for a video, as seen in a screenshot from the video "AI for Accessibility" recorded by Microsoft for Build 2019*

The transcript autoscrolls as the video is playing so it can be consumed. Microsoft Stream gives you the option to disable the autoscroll so you can scroll to any point of the transcription whether the video is currently playing or not.

As with any transcription service, the success rate varies, and a number of factors play a role in how well it is transcribed. At this point, technology still can't replace a person, but as innovations occur, the service will ultimately get better. Because of this, Microsoft Stream allows you to edit the transcription of any video by selecting the text in the transcription and choosing "Edit."

When the transcription is in edit mode and a specific section is highlighted, two icons will appear to the right of the selected text, as shown in Figure 9-13.

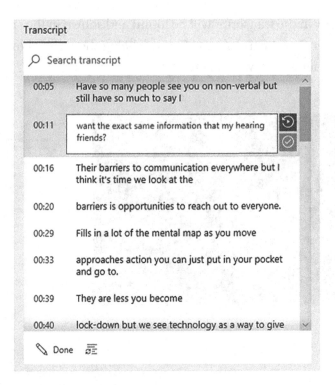

Figure 9-13. *Editing a transcription*

The top icon plays the video at the specific point of the transcription. The bottom icon acknowledges the transcription is correct and verified. Edit the text as needed; when complete, select "Done" in the bottom-left corner of the transcript.

Note   This feature is not perfect. I have noticed that it struggles a little bit to transcribe each word correctly when there is background music or accents.

Accessibility in Stream

Ensuring that all users can create and consume content is the main priority for not only organizations but also Microsoft 365. Microsoft introduced features that make accessibility a priority and allow all users to be part of the experience.

Closed Captioning

Closed captioning, which has been around since the 1970s, aims to transcribe the speech portion of a broadcast or video and display it on the screen for people who have hearing limitations. With Microsoft Stream, closed captioning is available for any video uploaded.

To enable closed captioning for a video, click the closed captioning icon displayed in Figure 9-14. Likewise, to disable closed captioning for the video, click the same icon.

Figure 9-14. *Enable/disable closed captioning for a video*

Note   By default, closed captioning is not enabled for a video, but the user can select it to show.

By accessing the cog next to the closed captioning button, you can also change the look and feel of the captions. You have control over the size of text, color, and background transparency setting.

Screen Readers

Many users around the world use screen readers to aid them in their day-to-day tasks. Screen readers allow the text displayed in Windows, on a web page, and so on to be read aloud to the user. Microsoft Stream supports many screen readers to aid the user in both consuming video content and navigating around the application.

High Contrast

Microsoft Stream supports high-contrast scenarios set at the operating system level. For example, in Windows 10, you can access the High contrast settings shown in Figure 9-15 by searching for "high contrast" in the Windows 10 search bar located next to the Windows Start menu.

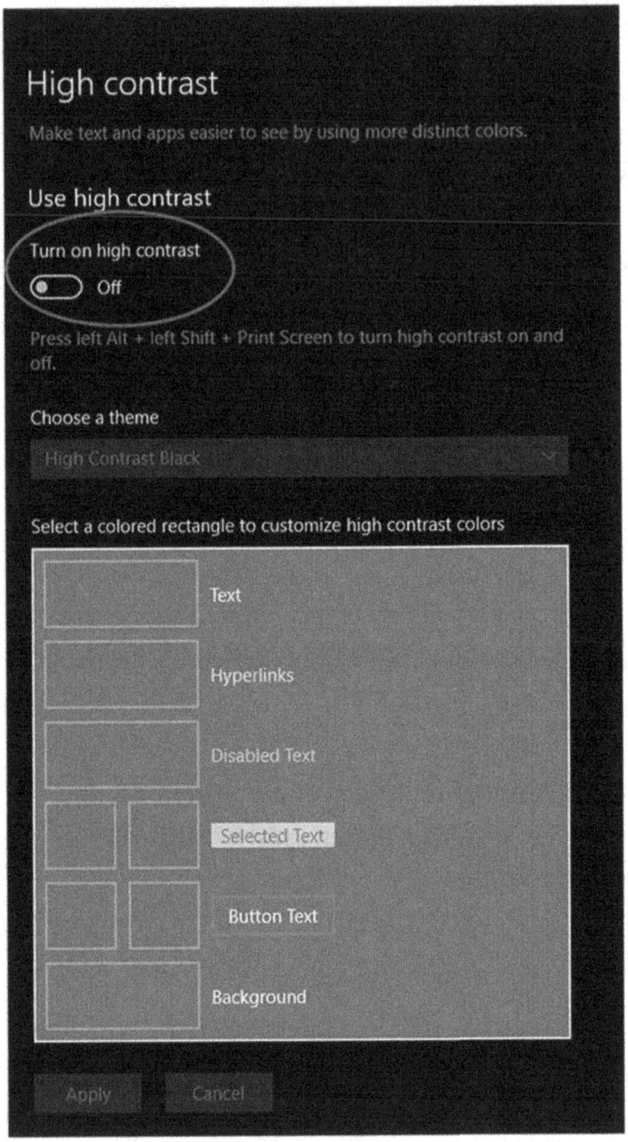

Figure 9-15. *High contrast settings in Windows 10*

After enabling high contrast, Stream will adjust and display in high-contrast mode, as shown in Figure 9-16.

Figure 9-16. *Viewing Stream in high-contrast mode*

Keyboard Navigations

Microsoft Stream supports keyboard navigations and hotkeys to control the video or choose a specific element of Microsoft Stream. For instance, while a video is playing, the hotkeys in Table 9-1 become active.

Table 9-1. *Microsoft Stream Hotkeys*

Hotkey	Hotkey Action
F	Exits full-screen mode
M	Mutes the video
Up arrow/down arrow	Increases/decreases volume
Left arrow/right arrow	Rewind/fast-forward
Numbers (0, 1, 2, 3, 4, 5, 6, 7, 8, 9)	Quick jump to the percentage of the video. For example, pressing 4 jumps the video to the 40% played mark and begins to play from there.
Space bar	Pauses/plays the current video

With keyboard navigation, pressing Tab advances the cursor to the next element on the page; pressing Shift+Tab moves the cursor to the previous element. This is like pressing Tab in other applications. Clicking the space bar resembles a left-mouse click.

Integrations with Other Microsoft 365 Apps

Other Microsoft 365 applications are making guest appearances in other apps. You saw that Planner is a supporting app in Microsoft 365 Groups and that Planner is also available within Microsoft Teams. Stream is no different; it is a stand-alone enterprise video platform, but it can be integrated into other applications to provide a video platform and capabilities.

The first integration is with SharePoint. As you saw in Chapter 2, SharePoint has many web parts that can be added to a site to provide some context. SharePoint Online has a Stream web part that can be configured to show a single video or videos from a specific channel. To add the Stream web part, put the SharePoint page in edit mode and add a web part. Select the Stream web part; upon adding it to the page, the web part properties will appear as shown in Figure 9-17.

Select "Single video" or "Channel" from the Source drop-down. You must also specify the video or channel URL in the Video address text box. Hopefully, in a future update, you will not have to specify the URL and will be able to select it directly.

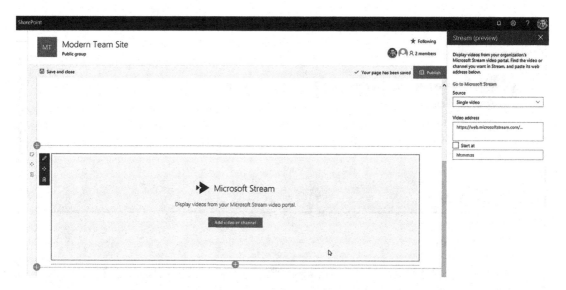

Figure 9-17. *Adding Stream to a SharePoint site*

With Microsoft Teams, Stream is available to add as a tab within a team; I discussed teams in Chapter 5. Navigate to any of your teams and select the + sign next to Wiki. Select Stream from the available options. After selecting Stream, you will be presented with a modal window titled Stream; you need to provide the tab name and the URL, as shown in Figure 9-18.

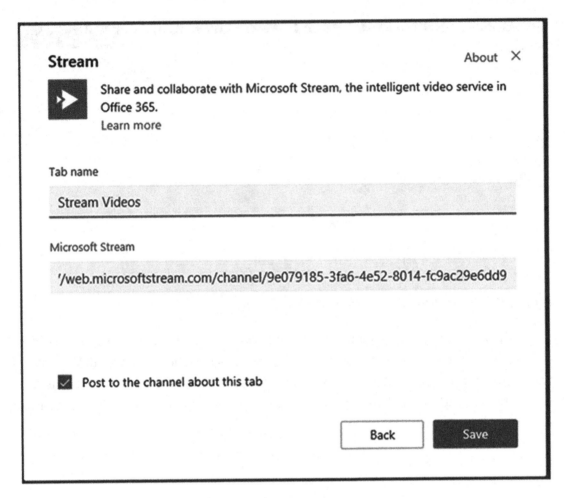

Figure 9-18. *Adding Stream to a Microsoft team*

Once you specify the appropriate values and click the Save button in the lower-right corner, a new tab is added and displayed as shown in Figure 9-19.

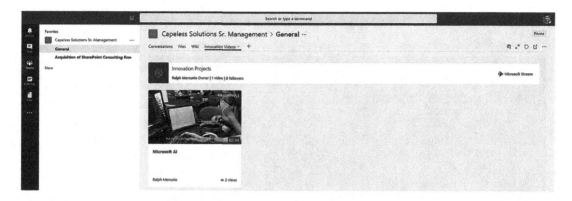

Figure 9-19. *Stream integrated with Microsoft Teams*

As videos are uploaded to Stream and tagged with the appropriate channel, the team will be able to update itself with the current videos. Part of the allure of this integration is that video files are stored on the appropriate enterprise product and not stored and uploaded to Microsoft Teams or stored in a document library.

Summary

Microsoft Stream is the next-level video platform that enterprises need. Gone are the days of storing videos on YouTube or buying expensive video platforms. Stream provides needed capabilities such as transcription, facial recognition, and ways to group videos together through channels.

Even though Stream is still relatively new, it is based on the current Microsoft 365 video product titled Video. Microsoft learned its lessons with Video, responded to customer feedback, and crafted a powerful application that is more than suited to handle the video needs of an enterprise moving forward.

In the next chapter, I will discuss Microsoft Forms, which is also relatively new to Microsoft 365 and is designed to provide an interface (forms) to collect information from users.

CHAPTER 10

Forms

In Chapter 9, I discussed Stream, which provides video capabilities and a platform for enterprises. Microsoft Forms is an application from Microsoft that is used to create forms and surveys to collect information and quizzes that can be shared and graded. Forms is built with a mobile-first approach, ensuring that it works not only on the mobile platform but also on many other devices.

A distinction needs to be made before we start, and that is that Microsoft Forms is not an InfoPath replacement. There are similarities between the two, but the intended purpose of Microsoft Forms is for quizzes, surveys, and polls. Microsoft is moving in the direction of using Power Apps to be the replacement for InfoPath, the last released version of which was included in Office 2013.

In this chapter, you will create a form to collect responses from employees about the annual company picnic, exploring the available data types you can use to create the questions. You will also create a quiz to demonstrate how quizzes can be created and graded. Finally, you will look at the reporting features so you can view metrics about the forms.

Using Microsoft Forms

In the Microsoft 365 tenant, click the app launcher in the upper-left corner and select Microsoft Forms; see Figure 10-1.

 Forms

Figure 10-1. *Microsoft Forms application*

© Ralph Mercurio and Brian Merrill 2021
R. Mercurio and B. Merrill, *Beginning Microsoft 365 Collaboration Apps*,
https://doi.org/10.1007/978-1-4842-6936-7_10

Once you click the application, you will be presented with the Forms dashboard (see Figure 10-2). This dashboard allows you to create a new form, search for existing forms, create a new quiz, or create a group form.

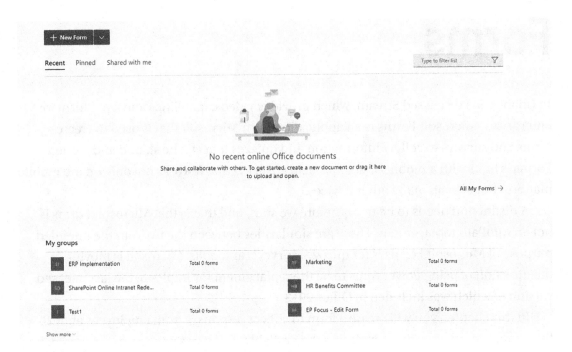

Figure 10-2. *Microsoft Forms application dashboard*

Editing/Creating Workspace

When editing or creating a form or quiz, the Preview, Theme, Share, and ellipsis (...) options (Figure 10-3) become available.

Figure 10-3. *Microsoft Forms dashboard menu*

The Preview button allows you to preview the form or quiz to see how your form or quiz renders. The preview mode offers an interesting function: it allows you to preview the form on both a typical mobile device and a computer.

The Theme button allows you to change the look and feel of the form. You can select from an available theme or upload your own image to use as a background image. If you choose to add an image, you can connect to the Bing search engine for pictures, OneDrive, or your local computer. Currently, you can only upload one picture to create a custom theme.

The Share button allows you to share your completed form or quiz in various ways (Figure 10-4) with any user. The form or quiz can be shared internally or externally because the object is hosted within Microsoft 365, so the object can be filled out from anywhere. The form can also be sent via email with a link, embedded in a web page, or accessed via QR code (barcode), or the link can be shared.

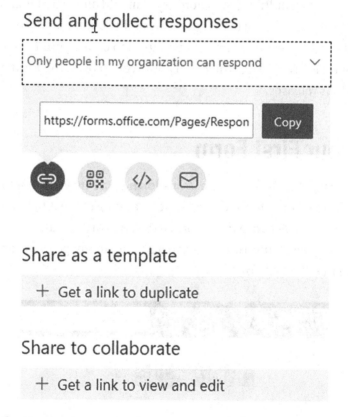

Figure 10-4. *Sharing menu*

Part of collaboration is the ability to share your data with others. By selecting the "Share as a template" link, other users can duplicate your form and use it as a base for their own form. By selecting the "Share to collaborate" link, you can send the form to others to edit the questions and/or add values to the questions.

The ellipsis (…) (Figure 10-3) offers some additional functionality when the form in edit mode.

The first advanced feature is the settings menu. These options let you allow anyone to fill out the form (anonymous) or restrict it to just internal company users. This setting isn't permanent; when you go to share the form, you can change the option. This simply sets the default for the form.

The options for responses are whether you can accept responses, the Start date and End date of when the form can be filled out, whether to shuffle or lock the questions, and if you want to receive a notification of each response. These advanced settings are useful if you need the form filled out prior to a deadline.

The second option is Multilingual where you can add alternate languages so the submitter of the form can change to one of the available choices. This is useful; however, it does not translate the questions/answers you used to create your form or quiz.

The third option is Print form, which will allow you to print the form; this was not available in previous releases.

Creating Your First Form

Click + New Form (Figure 10-5) from the drop-down to create your first form. Give your form a title by clicking "Untitled form" and changing the text to "Annual Company Picnic." It's also a wise choice to give the form a description, so edit the description to "Basic Survey Form." See Figure 10-6. You can also add an image to the area by clicking the image icon in the title text box.

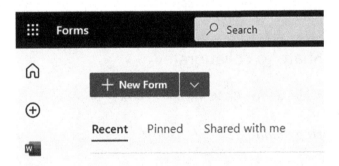

Figure 10-5. *Creating a new form*

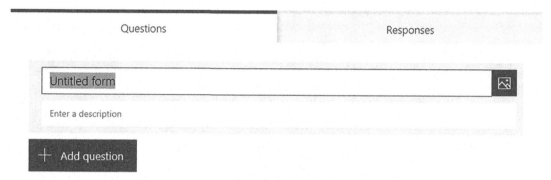

Figure 10-6. *Editing the title and description*

Clicking + New Form creates an empty form that you will add your questions to. Note that there are two tabs: Questions and Responses. Within the Questions tabs, you add your questions to create the form. The Responses tab, discussed later in this chapter, shows the responses to the form in a graphical format.

In the next section, I will discuss the available data types and how they can be used to craft forms and quizzes.

Data Types

On the form, select "+ Add question." In the resulting menu (Figure 10-7), each button represents a different data type that can be used in your form. These data types control the way a user can respond.

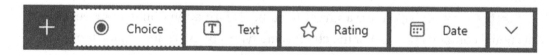

Figure 10-7. *Microsoft Forms data types*

Choice

Choice is the basic multiple-choice data type we all know. A predetermined set of choices is presented, and a user selects one of them (or multiple selections, if allowed). These details are controlled in the interface (Figure 10-8).

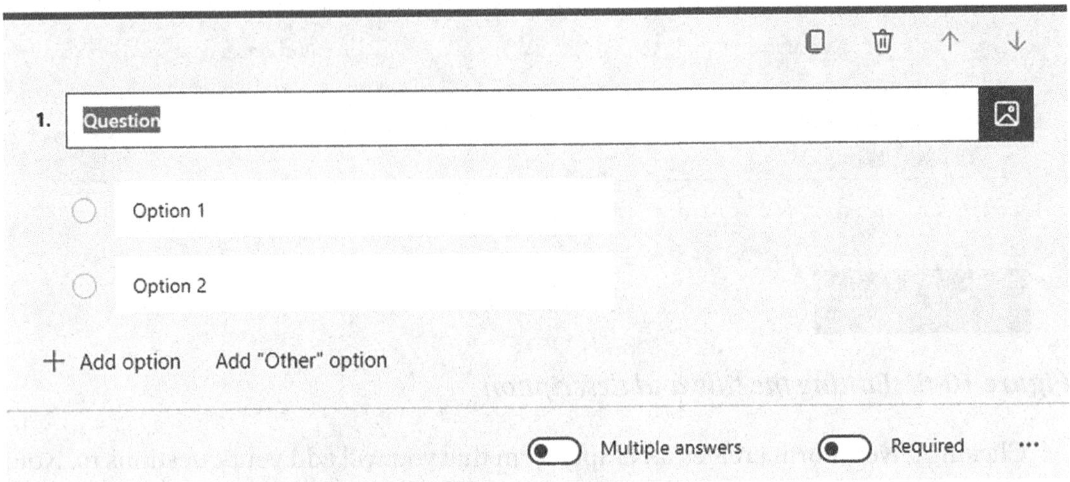

Figure 10-8. The choice data type

With this data type, Microsoft Forms allows two options: "Multiple answers" and "Required." Selecting "Multiple answers" allows the submitter to select more than one choice. You will notice that the radio buttons turn into checkboxes when "Multiple answers" is selected.

Multiple answers are useful when there is more than one choice that could be selected or a submitter can select multiple correct answers to a question. Selecting the "Required" toggle forces the user to answer the question; the form can't be submitted if the question is not answered. Selecting the ellipsis (…) shows the options to add a subtitle and set the questions to shuffle, which presents the questions in a different order to individuals.

For this exercise, let's create a survey to gather information from employees about the annual company picnic. For the choice data type, add two choice questions:

Question 1: Are you likely to attend this year's company picnic?

- **Choice options:** Yes, No

- **Allow multiple choices:** No

- **Required:** No

Question 2: Please select an activity that you will like to participate in.

- **Choice options**: Basketball, Bocce, Horseshoes

  - **Select "Add "Other" Option" to add a freeform field**

- **Allow multiple choices:** No

- **Required:** Yes

Once you are satisfied with the questions and choices, select "+ Add question" and add another question using the date data type.

Questions also contain three other functions: copying a question, deleting a question via the trash can icon, and moving the question up or down in the form. See Figure 10-9.

Figure 10-9. *Question options*

Note   When creating questions, you can also insert a video or image into the question. This is done by selecting the image icon to the right of the text box.

Date

The date data type allows a user to answer the question with a date (Figure 10-10). Unlike the other data types, the configuration is quite limited to a question field and a date field. This data type also has the Required switch.

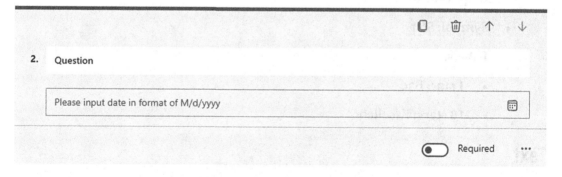

Figure 10-10. *The date data type*

Question 3: Select the date that would be best for the company picnic.

- **Required:** Yes.

- **Subtitle**: Please select a date in June 2021 or August 2021.

Rating

The rating data type (Figure 10-11) asks users to rate using either the familiar stars or numbers. The form creator has the option to display five or ten stars or numbers. Utilizing ten stars is effectively a scale of 1–10.

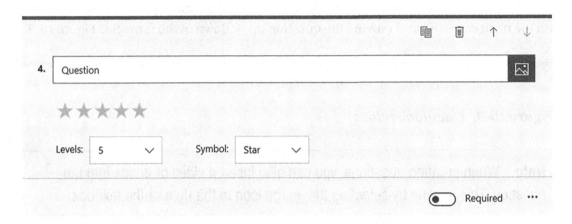

Figure 10-11. *The rating data type*

Selecting the ellipsis (…) presents the opportunity to add labels to your rating. Labels help define what a single star/number is in terms of the lowest and highest.

Question 4: How would you rate last year's company picnic activities?

- **Required:** Yes

- **Symbol:** Star

- **Labels:**

    - **1 star:** Bad

    - **10 stars:** Excellent

Text

The text data type allows free entry of data and doesn't have preset options like the choice data type. This data type has similar options to the choice data type (Figure 10-12).

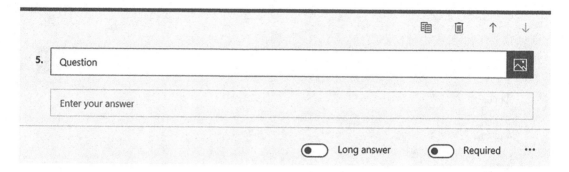

Figure 10-12. *The text data type*

The text data type does contain a "Long answer" toggle. Selecting this toggle increases the number of lines available for the user to fill out. This is preferred because you do not want to abruptly cut off an answer unless there is absolute certainty that the answer will be short.

Selecting the ellipsis (...) presents the option to restrict the data entered to a restriction value. The restrictions are limited to numbers only and cannot be used to restrict text.

Question 5: Please describe the best part of last year's annual outing.

Long answer: Yes

Required: Yes

Ranking

The ranking data type (Figure 10-13) allows the options to be sorted or ranked in an order. This is useful if you are trying to schedule a team meeting. Submitters can sort the available times from best to worst time slots.

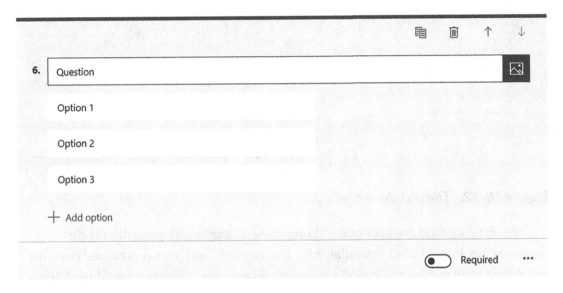

Figure 10-13. *The ranking data type*

The ranking data type does not contain any other configurable properties besides Required and Subtitle.

Note   One issue with the ranking data type is that if the field is set to Required, the order must be changed and set back to the default if the submitter agrees to that ranking.

To complete the form, use the following values for Question 6:

Question 6: Please rank the following food options from most desirable to least.

- **Required:** Yes

- **Options:** Seafood, Barbeque, Vegan, Italian, Sandwiches

Likert

Microsoft Forms also includes the Likert (Figure 10-14) data type. This data type is available by clicking the down arrow when adding a question. This data type strives to gauge a statement by having the user select one of the corresponding options.

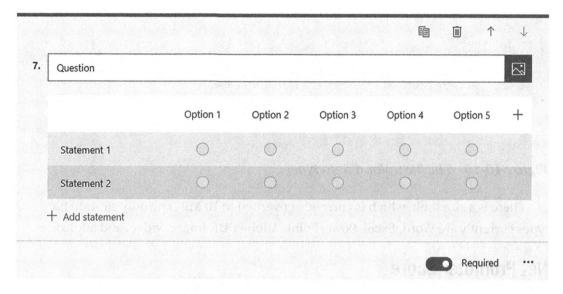

Figure 10-14. *The Likert data type*

You aren't going to use the Likert data type in your survey, but let's review the configuration of it. The keys to this data type are both the options and statements. The options are the gauge and are most commonly "Strongly Disagree," "Disagree," "Neutral," "Agree," and "Strongly Agree." You can have more, but I think five is the perfect level of granularity and offers clear definitive lines between the options. The statements of the Likert data type are the statements that are gauged by the user.

We will discuss three new data types; they won't be part of the form, but it's good to be aware of these data types as they have specific uses and cases.

File Upload

Microsoft Forms also includes the file upload (Figure 10-15) data type. This data type is available by clicking the down arrow when adding a question. This data type strives to give the user the ability to upload a file. The file is then stored in SharePoint Online.

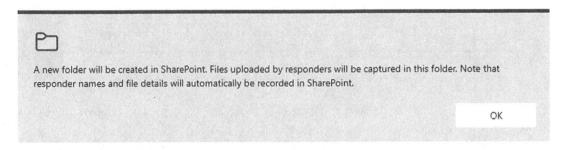

Figure 10-15. *The file upload data type*

There is a size limit, which is currently governed to 10 MB. The only allowed file types currently are Word, Excel, PowerPoint, Adobe PDF, image, video, and audio files.

Net Promoter Score

Microsoft Forms also includes the Net Promoter Score (Figure 10-16) data type. This data type is available by clicking the down arrow when adding a question. This is similar to a Likert data type.

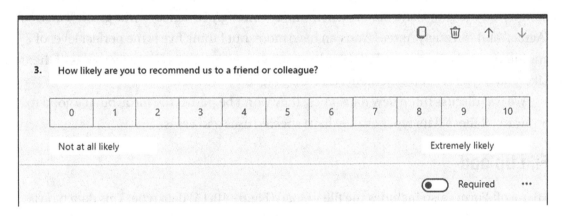

Figure 10-16. *The Net Promoter Score data type*

Section

Microsoft Forms also includes the ability to create a section (Figure 10-17) data type. This data type is available by clicking the down arrow when adding a question. This data type when configured will allow the form to be broken up by sections, providing the user with a "Next" button to progress through the form.

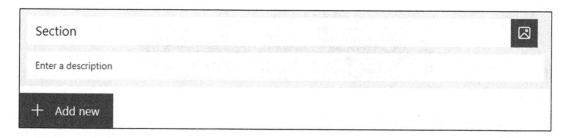

Figure 10-17. *The section data type*

Once all the questions have been entered, your form should look like Figure 10-18.

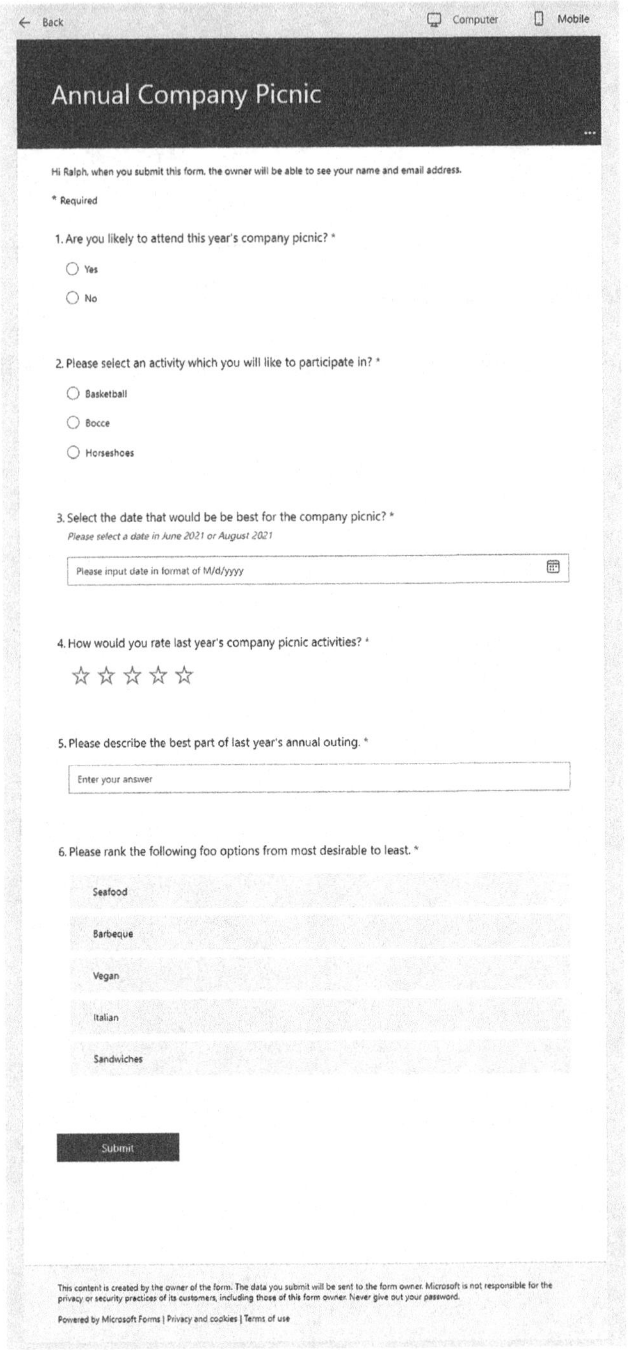

Figure 10-18. *The completed Annual Company Picnic form*

Branching

Microsoft Forms contains a feature called branching. This feature allows you to tailor the questions asked or to end the form based on an answer to a question. This feature can be used in forms, surveys, or quizzes.

In this example, let's create a new form titled "Company Picnic Survey." Create the following questions with the following details:

Question 1: Did you attend the company picnic last year?

- **Data type:** Choice

- **Choice options:** Yes, No

- **Allow multiple choices**: No

- **Required**: No

Question 2: Why did you not attend the company picnic last year?

- **Data type**: Text

- **Long answer**: Yes

Your finished form should look like Figure 10-19.

Figure 10-19. Company Picnic Survey with branching

Now that the form is created, let's add branching logic to the form to end the survey for users who answer "Yes" to the first question. By doing so, users will not have to worry about answering the second question, which in this context means nothing to them.

To add branching to the form, click the settings (...) located in the lower-right corner in the question when the form is in edit mode. Clicking the Add branching option reveals the interface in Figure 10-20.

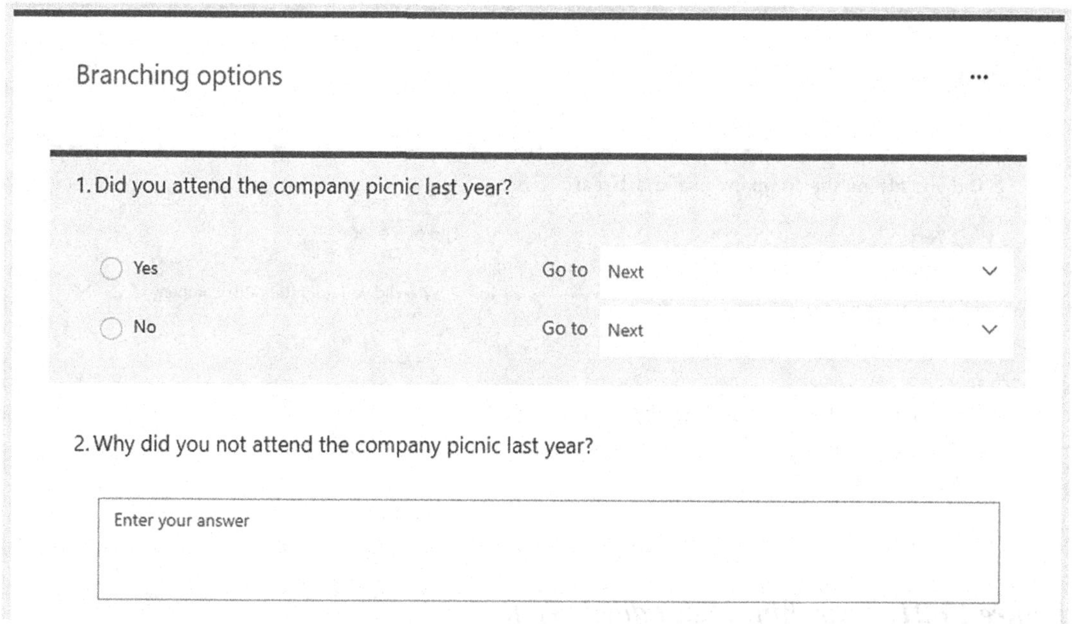

Branching options   ...

1. Did you attend the company picnic last year?

　　○ Yes   Go to   Next   ⌄

　　○ No   Go to   Next   ⌄

2. Why did you not attend the company picnic last year?

　　Enter your answer

Figure 10-20. *The branching interface*

Based on your example, when a user answers Yes to Question 1, you want to skip the next question and end the form for the user. In Question 1 of the form, select "End of the form" from the "Go to" drop-down on the Yes row. The branching logic should now look like Figure 10-21.

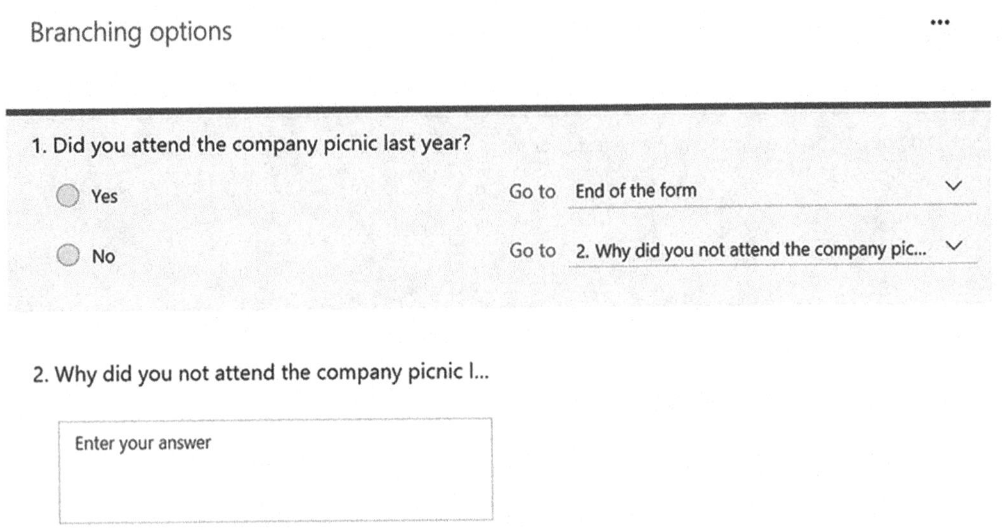

Branching options   •••

1. Did you attend the company picnic last year?

   ○ Yes   Go to   End of the form   ∨

   ○ No   Go to   2. Why did you not attend the company pic... ∨

2. Why did you not attend the company picnic I...

   ┌───┐
   │ Enter your answer   │
   │   │
   │   │
   └───┘

Figure 10-21. *Branching logic added to a form*

Once the logic is added, click the Back button in the interface, and it will reload the form in edit mode. Go ahead and preview the form; if done correctly, Question 2 will be hidden unless you select "No" for the first question.

Note   If you make a mistake in the branching logic, you can reset all the branching logic by selecting the ellipsis (…) in the Branching options interface and selecting "Reset" in the upper corner.

Quizzes

Quizzes and forms are quite similar and share the corresponding Microsoft Forms platform. A big difference between a quiz and form is that the quiz can be auto-graded (provided you specify the answers) and the results can be shown automatically at the end of the quiz or after the author has marked them. The settings for the quiz can be selected from the ellipsis (…) when the quiz is being created. The default setting is that responders will see their results upon completion. See Figure 10-22.

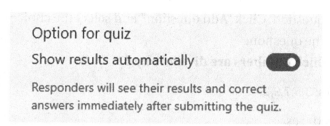

Figure 10-22. *Grading options for a quiz*

Quizzes are extremely useful in the workplace or classroom. One excellent use of them is to test the knowledge of an employee after human resources or safety training. Obtaining a certain percentage shows understanding of a concept. The quiz can even be restricted so it can be filled out only once by a person once their quiz is graded. You will explore more of quizzes when you build a sample quiz shortly. See Figure 10-23.

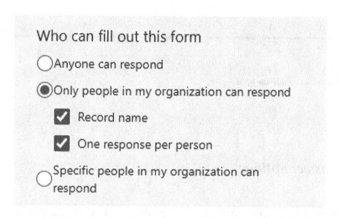

Figure 10-23. *Who can take the quiz*

The data types are the same as when creating a form: choice, text, rating, date, ranking, Likert, file upload, Net Promoter Score, and section. However, quizzes contain some special elements that you will explore further. To explore the full feature set of quizzes, you will construct a quiz that will be used in an educational setting.

Creating Your First Quiz

On the Microsoft Forms dashboard, select "New Quiz" from the drop-down menu in the upper-left corner. This creates an empty quiz where you can enter the questions and answers. Start by changing the title of "Untitled Quiz" to "Weekly Quiz" by clicking "Untitled Quiz" and entering the new title.

Add your first question. Click "Add question" and select the choice data type. Use the following data for the question:

Question 1: Which numbers are divisible by 3?

- **Answers:** 3,5,7,9,23

- **Required:** Yes

- **Multiple answers:** Yes

If you hover over the answers 3 and 9, three options appear to the right of the answer. See Figure 10-24.

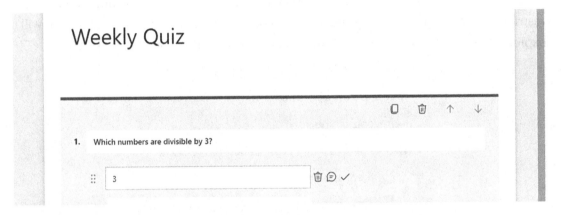

Figure 10-24. *Answer options*

The trash can, message box, and correct answer icons appear. If you click the trash can icon, the answer will be deleted. The next two options separate forms from quizzes. The message box allows the quiz author to display a message when the answer is selected, and the correct answer icon marks the answer correct if chosen. At the end of the quiz, the correct answers are tallied, and a score is displayed.

Mark answers 3 and 9 correct using the correct answer icon when hovering over each value. On answer values 5, 7, and 23, add a message box to each one informing the user that "The answer selected is incorrect." Add a point value of 10 points in the Points box in the lower-left corner. The question should now look like Figure 10-25.

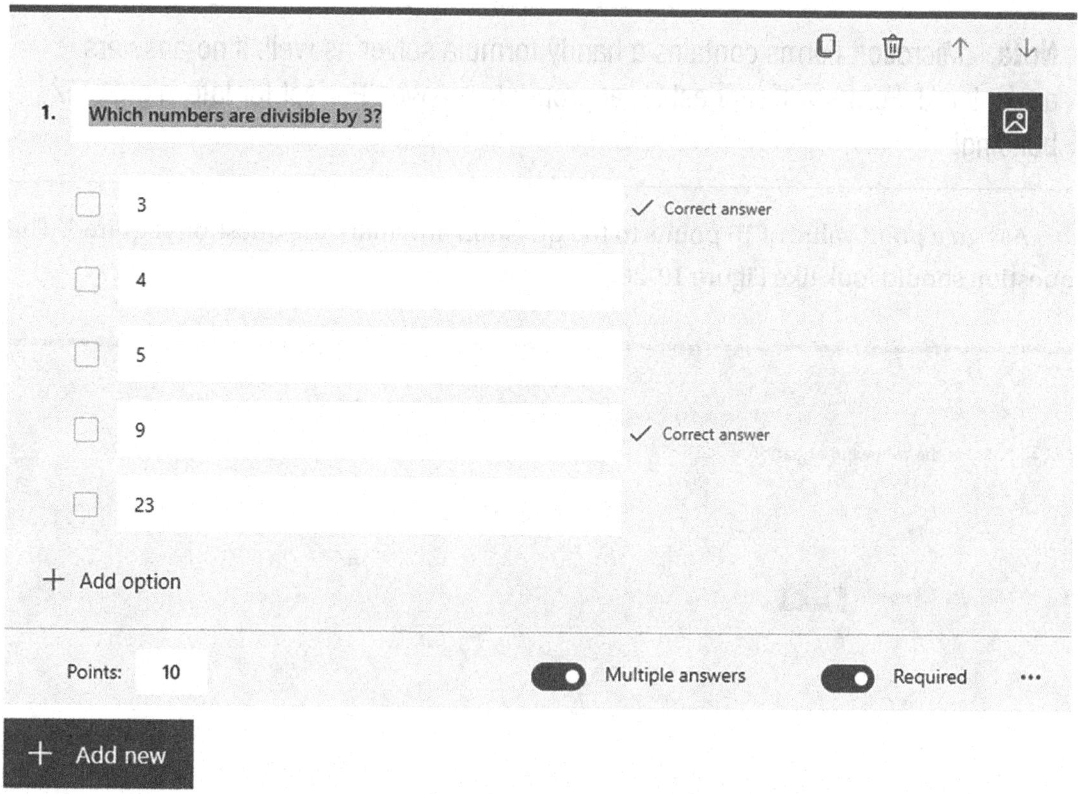

Figure 10-25. *The finished first question*

Add a second choice question by selecting the "Add new" box and choosing the choice data type. Use the following info to build the question:

Question 2: Solve the following equation:

- **Answers:** 7, 14, 18
  - **Correct answer:** 7
- **Required:** Yes
- **Multiple answers:** Yes

Click the ellipsis (…) in the lower-right of Question 2. Select the "Math" and "Subtitle" options, and an equation editor will appear where you can enter a math equation in the subtitle box. This formula editor offers a wide range of complex mathematical formulas. Currently you are only able to add mathematical formulas that are visible, but I could see where this could be extended to include chemistry, computer science, or physics formulas. For now, add the square root symbol with a value of 49.

Note   Microsoft Forms contains a handy formula solver as well. If no answers are entered, Forms will suggest an appropriate answer. Perfect for late-night quiz building!

Assign a point value of 10 points to the question and mark the question required. The question should look like Figure 10-26.

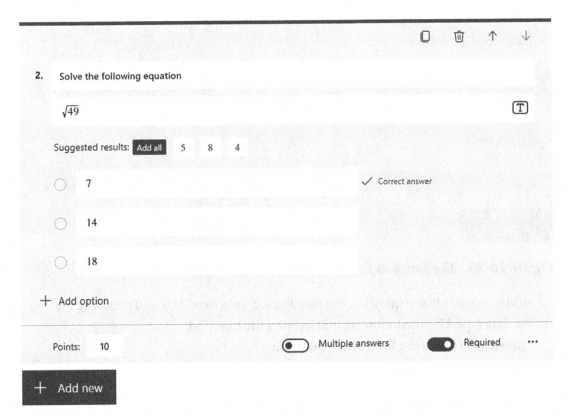

Figure 10-26.   Question 2 with the correct answer marked and a point total assessed

The completed quiz should now look like Figure 10-27. Feel free to add more questions.

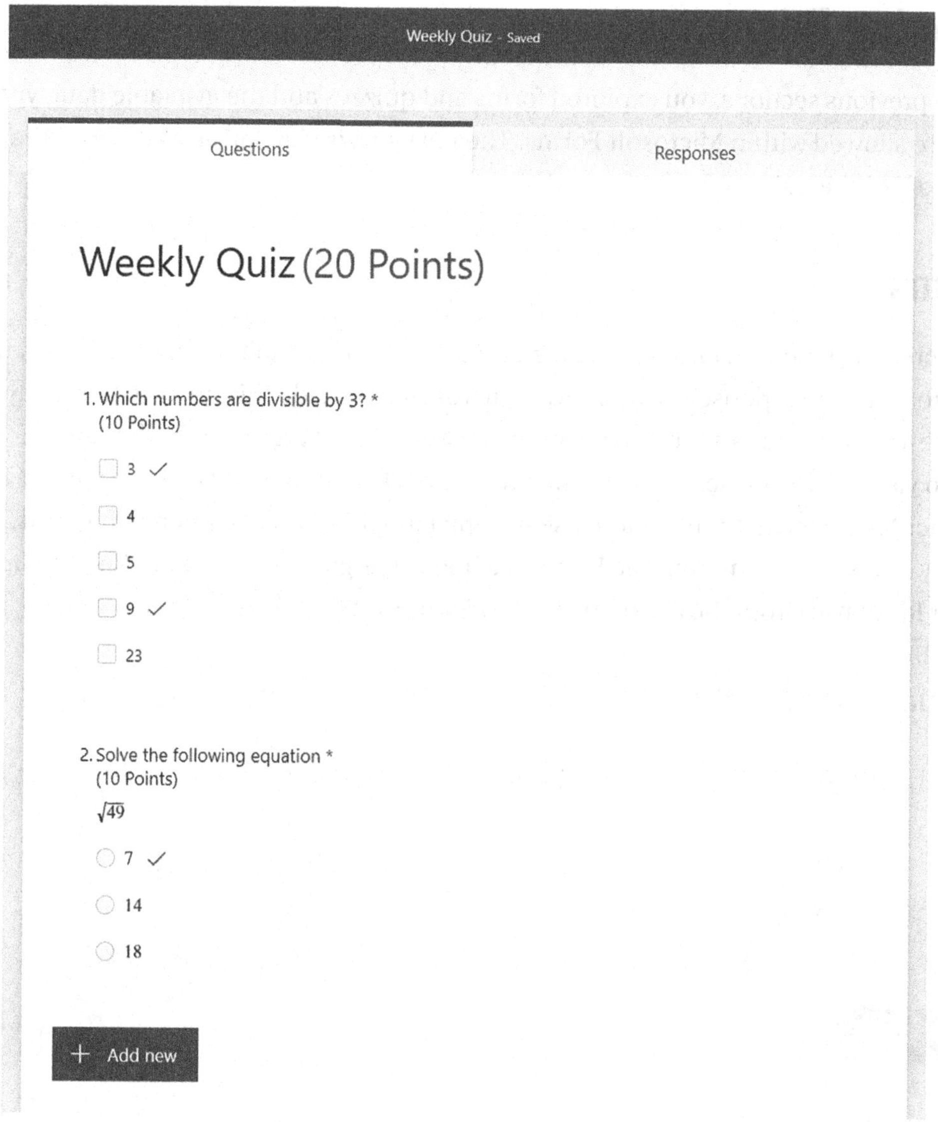

Figure 10-27. The completed quiz

Select the Preview button and go ahead and complete your first quiz. Once completed, you will see your score, and you can view the responses.

Note   Only choice data types can be auto-graded. All other data types need to be graded by reviewing the answers, which is discussed in the next section.

Viewing Responses

In the previous sections, you explored forms and quizzes and the available data types that are allowed within Microsoft Forms. The next part is viewing and acting on the data collected or the quiz graded.

Forms

After creating your first form and distributing it through one of the share methods, it's time to view the responses to your form. Microsoft has made this process extremely simple and consolidates the responses in an easy-to-read graphical dashboard.

To view the responses to the form, navigate back to Microsoft Forms; if you are in another Microsoft 365 application, use the app launcher. Once in Microsoft Forms, simply select your form from the Forms dashboard (Figure 10-2). When the form opens, select Responses from the top of the form (Figure 10-28).

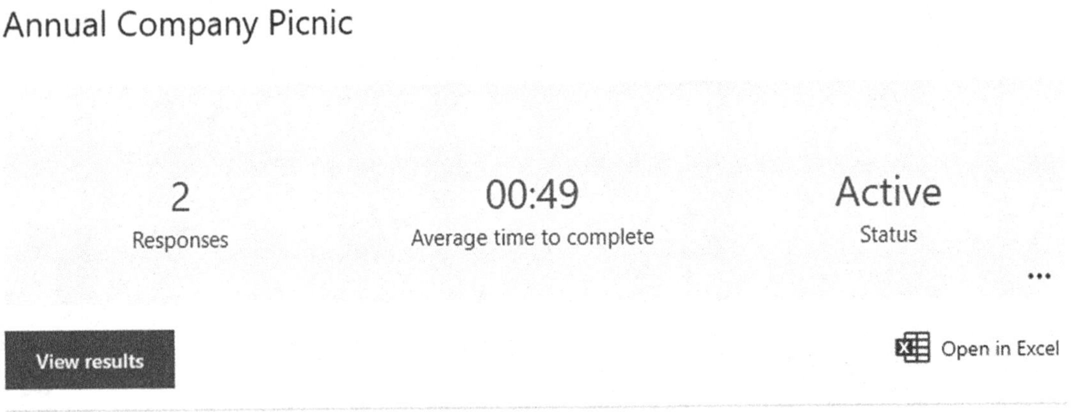

Annual Company Picnic

2	00:49	Active
Responses	Average time to complete	Status

•••

View results   Open in Excel

Figure 10-28. *Questions and Reponses tabs*

Note   In this example, you will view the responses for the Annual Company Picnic form. You need to fill out the form or share the link with your colleagues.

Click the Responses tab (Figure 10-28) to see the responses displayed in a graphical format; see Figure 10-29. The summary includes the number of responders, the average time to complete the form, and whether the form is active or not. Clicking "View results" shows the individual responses for each submitter. If the form is set for anonymous or you chose not to record the name in the settings of the form, you will not know who filled out the form.

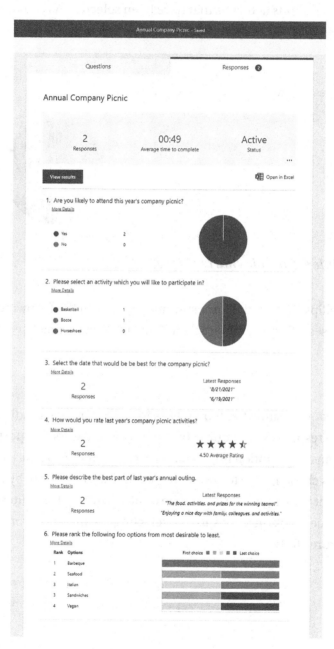

Figure 10-29. *Form responses*

You can also export the results to Excel for further data analysis or if you want to create different charts from the dataset. In most cases, the displayed results are sufficient. Take, for example, Question 2 (Figure 10-30); the data is displayed in an interactive pie chart totaling the sports activities that have been selected. As you hover over each segment of the pie chart, the chart renders the total responses for the answer chosen.

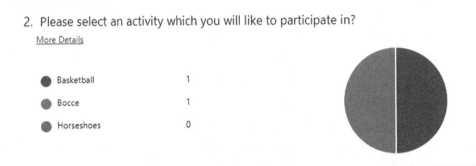

2. Please select an activity which you will like to participate in?
   More Details

   ● Basketball   1
   ● Bocce   1
   ● Horseshoes   0

Figure 10-30. *Interactive pie chart for Question 2*

Clicking the ellipsis (…) in the form summary gives you the following options: "Delete all responses," "Print summary," and "Get a summary link."

Quizzes

Quizzes share a lot of the same functionality as forms but offer a few different options. When viewing the responses for a quiz, you can review answers and post scores.

The "Review answers" option is located underneath the responses for the quiz and shows the answers chosen, time to complete the quiz, and the score by quiz taker. You can adjust the point values given. This can be done by editing the "Auto-graded" total. You can also give feedback on a question by selecting the message icon and adding feedback. See Figure 10-31.

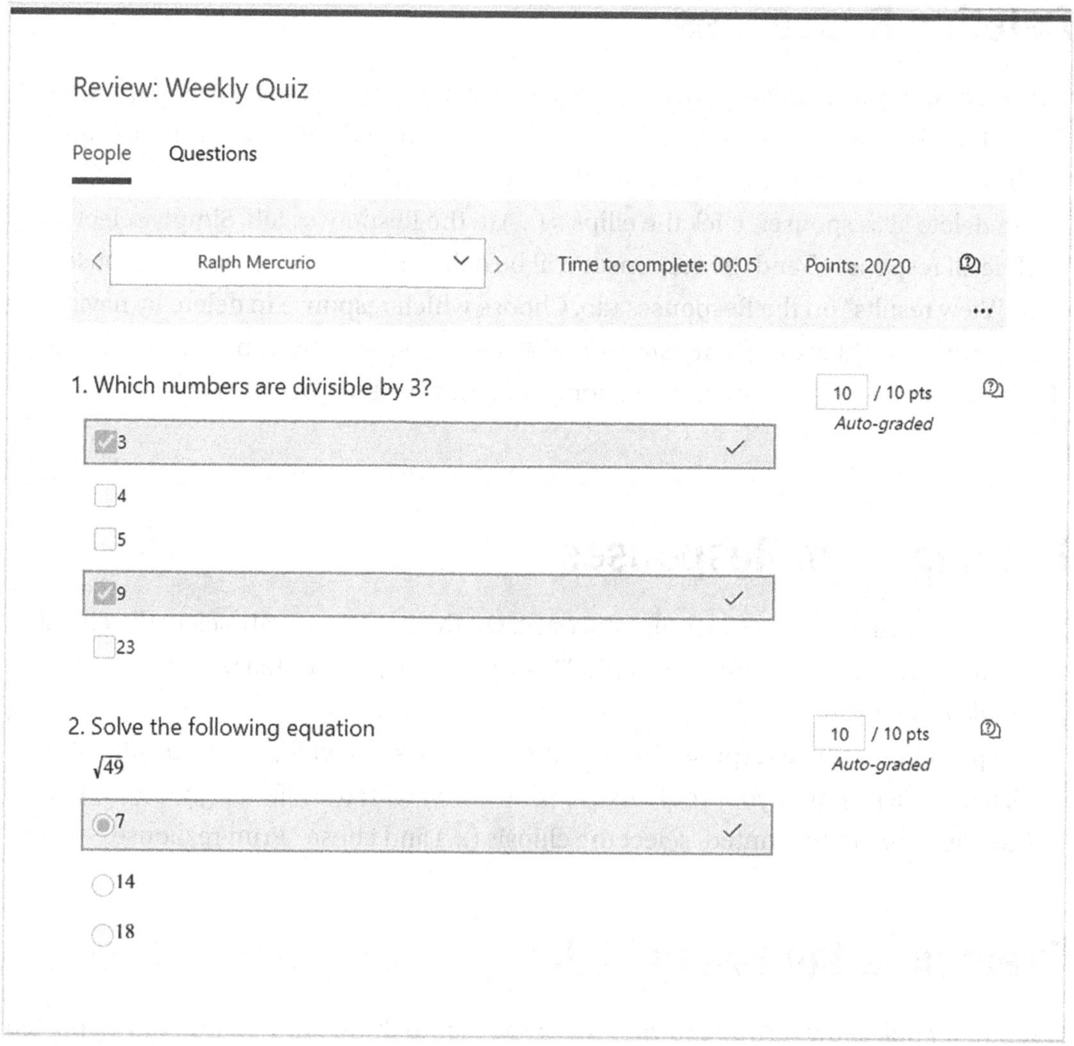

Review: Weekly Quiz

People   Questions

<	Ralph Mercurio ∨	>	Time to complete: 00:05 Points: 20/20

...

1. Which numbers are divisible by 3?   `10` / 10 pts
                                          Auto-graded

☑ 3   ✓

☐ 4

☐ 5

☑ 9   ✓

☐ 23

2. Solve the following equation   `10` / 10 pts
$\sqrt{49}$ *Auto-graded*

◉ 7   ✓

○ 14

○ 18

Figure 10-31. *Review options by quiz taker*

Under the Questions tab, the form author can review the questions or print all the answers for each question.

Back on the Responses tab of the quiz, select "Post scores." Posting scores allows you to view the feedback, if any, and the correct questions. There currently is no portal, so you need to use the same link to view the completed graded quiz. To provide immediate feedback, set the "Option for quiz" to show results automatically. This option is located in the settings menu of the quiz.

Deleting Responses

There may come a time when you want to delete all the responses or a singular response from a form or a quiz. Perhaps you want to remove incorrectly filled-out forms so they don't skew the dataset or delete quizzes that are not filled out.

To delete all responses, click the ellipsis (...) in the Responses tab. Simply select "Delete all responses," and the responses will be deleted. To delete a single response, click "View results" on the Responses tab. Choose which response to delete by navigating with the left or right arrow. To delete a single response, select the ellipsis (...) and click "Delete response." Agree with the deletion, and Forms will remove the response from the form.

Printing Form Responses

Printing the form responses is straightforward. On the Responses tab, select the ellipsis (...) and select the "Print summary" link. This will render the summary of the results in a printable format.

To print just a single response from all the responses, select the "View results" link. Navigate to the response you would like to print either with the left or right arrow. On the desired response to be printed, select the ellipsis (...) and chose "Print response."

Creating a Summary Link

A summary link allows anyone to view the responses to the form. This link can be posted on an internal intranet (SharePoint), sent through email, or shared in Microsoft Teams. The summary link is created by Microsoft Forms and can be created by selecting the ellipsis (...) and choosing "Get a summary link."

Summary

Microsoft Forms has the potential to be an innovative product in the Microsoft 365 application suite. In this chapter, you reviewed the Forms interfaces and available options, created your first form, shared the form with others, and viewed the responses.

This application can also be used to create online quizzes and have them graded automatically. This type of application can be used to streamline quiz taking in education environments, moving away from Scantron tests and moving to an interactive online experience for students.

This is a powerful application; and future updates should add more functionality, provide more data types, and add more equations. I am excited to see what Microsoft does with this product and how it can streamline surveys and quizzes and provide the analytical data we crave without using other Microsoft applications such as Excel.

In the next chapter, you will explore Microsoft Power Automate, which is designed to automate reparative actions in not only Microsoft 365 but also third-party services.

CHAPTER 11

Power Automate

In Chapter 10, I discussed Microsoft Forms, which allows for the creation of web-based forms for data collection, surveys, or quizzes. In this chapter, I will focus on Power Automate, which is an application from Microsoft centered on automation and integration between many services. Power Automate is an important part of Microsoft's Power Platform.

Power Automate aims to automate tasks or repetitive actions and create a "flow" that will run automatically. These flows are similar to IFTTT, which is an open source protocol to link multiple third-party services together. For example, using IFTTT and the appropriate hardware/software, you can create an IFTTT that will turn on your house lights as you approach the front door carrying your mobile phone.

Microsoft aims to deliver a similar service in Microsoft 365 that links not only the Microsoft 365 collaborative applications I have discussed but also connects with third-party services such as Twitter, Instagram, and Adobe.

Before you dive into Power Automate, I do want to discuss the currently available plans for Power Automate; there are three different tiers included in the platform. Users can create and execute unlimited flows or unlimited flows with RPA (Robotic Process Automation) and have the ability to subscribe the enterprise to Power Automate.

Overview of the Power Automate Interface

To launch Microsoft Power Automate, click the app launcher in the upper-left corner of Microsoft 365 and select Power Automate, as shown in Figure 11-1. If it is not visible, select the "All apps" link under Yammer in the app launcher. Power Automate is available from OneDrive and SharePoint as well.

© Ralph Mercurio and Brian Merrill 2021
R. Mercurio and B. Merrill, *Beginning Microsoft 365 Collaboration Apps*,
https://doi.org/10.1007/978-1-4842-6936-7_11

Power Automate

Figure 11-1. *Launching Power Automate from the app launcher of Microsoft 365*

Upon clicking the icon, you will be presented with the Microsoft Power Automate initial screen, as shown in Figure 11-2.

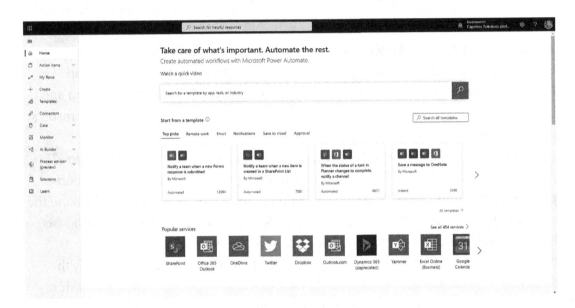

Figure 11-2. *Power Automate introductory screen*

Before you create your first flow, let's review the interface and where to find the right resources with Power Automate. As shown in Figure 11-2, the global navigation contains the following headings:

- **Action items:** Contains two submenus: Approvals and Business process flows. Approvals relate to approvals sent and received and their history. Business process flows defines a set of steps you want a user to follow.

- **My flows:** All the flows you create, both personal and team.

- **Create:** Allows you to create a template from a variety of templates or start with a blank template.

- **Templates:** Preconfigured flow templates to use. Some of the flows do require subscription outside of Microsoft 365 and may contain premium connectors. In order to use premium connectors, you must subscribe to a plan that includes them.

- **Connectors:** The building blocks to connect not only to Microsoft 365 but also a variety of third-party services. Some connectors are marked "Premium," meaning you must subscribe to the correct Power Automate plan. There may be a cost associated with subscribing to a third-party connector/service.

- **Data:** The Data menu contains Tables, Connections, Custom Connectors, and Gateways. Tables are a way to structure and store data. Power Automate and Power Apps share tables. Connections will allow you to see all the connections that are used for your account, while Custom Connectors will list any custom connectors used. Gateways, which refer to data gateways, allow the cloud services to reach on-premises data.

- **Monitor:** Contains links to view the status and history of all flows that have been executed.

- **AI Builder:** Allows you to add artificial intelligence to your flows. This functionality can be used to extract information, detect objects, or utilize predication.

- **Process advisor:** Aims to identify issues within the process, which then can be resolved to improve efficiencies within flows.

- **Solutions:** Allows you to import prebuilt solutions from the marketplace or from software providers. These solutions can then be used within the Power Automate platform.

- **Learn:** Resources such as training, support, and documentation.

In the upper-right corner of Power Automate, you will also find specific Power Automate settings as designated by the cog next to your initials or profile image.

Connectors

Before you create your first flow, let's look at the available connectors by clicking "Connectors" in the left-hand menu. The page will refresh, and all the available connectors will load. You will notice that some connectors are tagged with a green "Premium" label, meaning you need to subscribe to at least Power Automate Plan 1 to access them; see Figure 11-3.

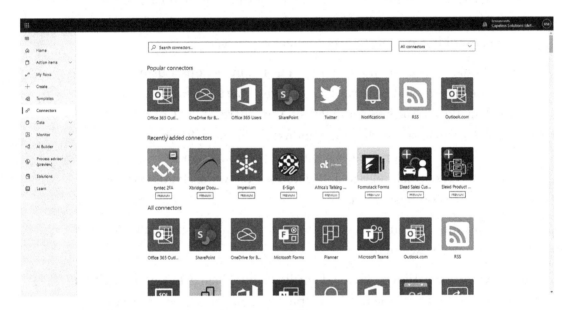

Figure 11-3. *Power Automate connector library*

Let's explore a connector a little further by clicking one of the available connectors. For this example, click the SharePoint connector. It will show the available configurations for that connector; see Figure 11-4.

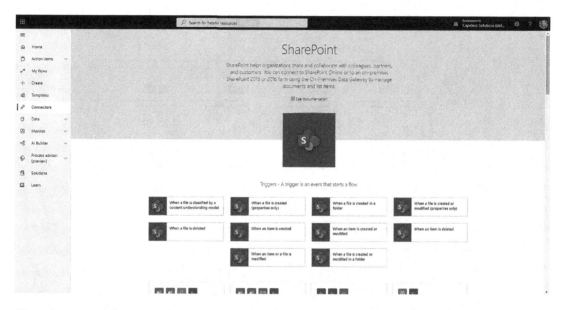

Figure 11-4. *SharePoint connector configuration settings*

On the SharePoint connector page, below the SharePoint logo, you will notice that ten triggers are available. A trigger is defined as a starting event that begins a flow. Currently the ten triggers for SharePoint center around document and item management. When a user creates/modifies/deletes a document or item, a flow can then be created to perform some action.

Note   Connectors are configured and use the credentials of the creator of the flow. The Microsoft Power Automate team will be releasing updates to the application to overcome this limitation in the future.

Templates

On the same page, there are also preconfigured flow templates where the SharePoint connector is used. Many of the templates are created and published by Microsoft, but some are published by the community.

Connectors power a flow by connecting it with services, and when combined with logic operators, they create a flow. To view the available templates, click "Templates" in the left-hand menu. The Templates page (Figure 11-5) contains all the available templates, categorized into specific categories such as Approval, Data collection, Email, Productivity, and Social media.

291

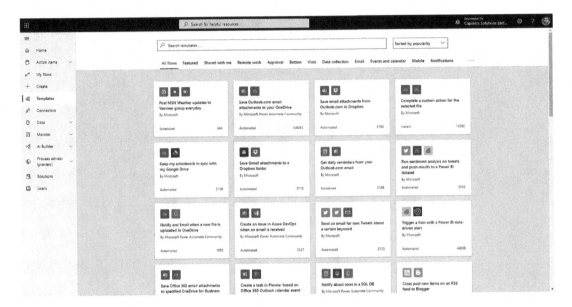

Figure 11-5. *Available templates*

You can also search for a specific template by specifying a connector or a service. The search result set can also be refined further by popularity, name, and published time.

As you can see, flows are not complicated and rely on the foundational building block of connectors and logic actions. Microsoft has also done a great job of creating templates that you might find useful and can use to automate a basic task or repetitive action.

Creating Flows

For the remainder of this chapter, you will focus on creating flows to approve an item, report software bugs, and apply an electronic signature to a document. These flows will be based on preconfigured templates so you can easily become familiar with flows and the related interfaces.

Approval Flow

The first flow you are going to create is a flow to start an approval on an item in a SharePoint library. To create your first flow, click "Create" in the left-hand navigation and search for the "Start approval when a new item is added" template as shown in Figure 11-6.

Figure 11-6. *Adding the "Start approval when a new item is added" template*

Go ahead and click "Continue." The page will refresh, and you will be presented with the template configuration screen depicted in Figure 11-7.

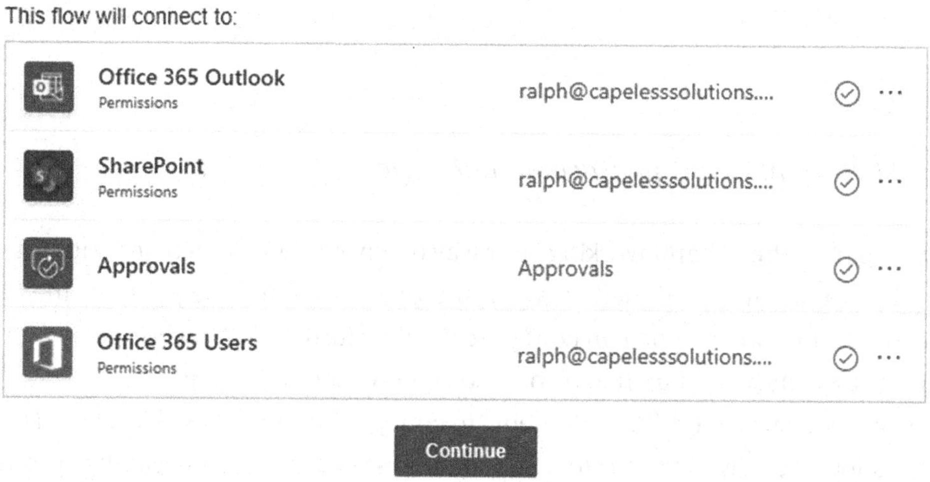

This flow will connect to:

Office 365 Outlook Permissions	ralph@capelesssolutions....	⊘	···
SharePoint Permissions	ralph@capelesssolutions....	⊘	···
Approvals	Approvals	⊘	···
Office 365 Users Permissions	ralph@capelesssolutions....	⊘	···

Continue

Figure 11-7. *Template configuration settings*

On this page, you will notice a few items. The first item is that this flow will use SharePoint, Outlook, the Power Automate Approvals engine, and Microsoft 365 users. It also provides a definition of the flow, so you can be sure that this is the correct flow you want to use. Click "Continue" to configure the flow.

The flow design page shows the associated actions and needed logic for the flow; see Figure 11-8.

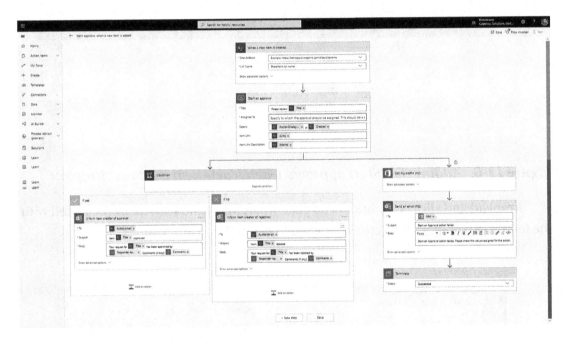

Figure 11-8. *Configuring flow actions and logic*

Starting from the top and working your way down, configure each box with the appropriate values. As mentioned, this flow uses a SharePoint library to store the item and begin the flow. Before you can configure the flow further, let's switch gears and open SharePoint from the app launcher. If you need a refresher, see Chapter 2.

Create a new site called "Procurement" to configure for this flow. The goal of this flow is to allow users to add items to a SharePoint list so the purchase can be approved in as little time as possible and to ensure the appropriate information is provided before the request approval flow is started.

Note   When a Microsoft 365 group is created, a corresponding SharePoint site is also created.

On the newly created Procurement site, create a new library to store the items needing approvals. To create a list, select "List" from the "+ New" drop-down located directly below the title of the site and title the list "Procurement Items." As discussed in Chapter 2, you need to add appropriate metadata to the list so that you can capture the information that is relevant. Create the columns shown in Table 11-1.

Table 11-1. *Procurement Items Columns*

Column Name	Type	Values
Description	Multiple lines of text	
Vendor	Choice	Amazon, OfficeMax, Staples, Target
Cost	Currency	
Notes	Multiple lines of text	
Approval	Single line of text	

Upon completion, the SharePoint list should look exactly like Figure 11-9.

Figure 11-9. *Configured Procurement Items list with added columns*

Now that the SharePoint list is configured correctly, switch back to Power Automate. In the first action, "When a new item is created," specify the SharePoint site and associated list. If it does not appear in the drop-down list, choose "Enter custom value" and add the Procurement site URL. Select the "Procurement Items" list from the List Name drop-down. The completed action should look like Figure 11-10.

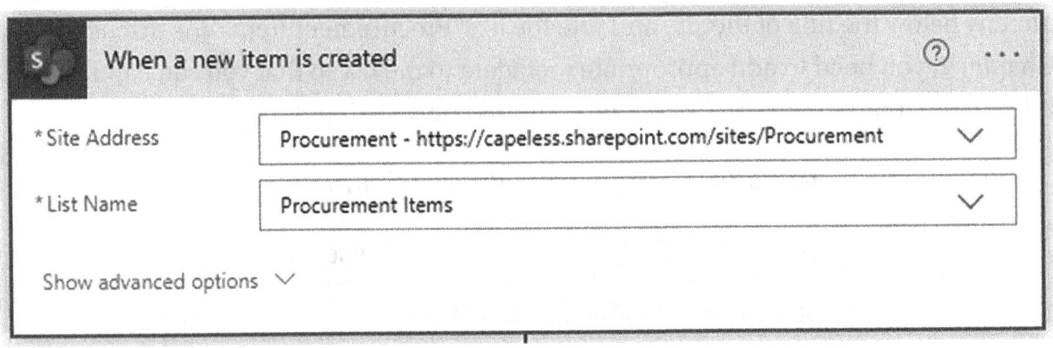

Figure 11-10. *Configured action with Procurement site URL and associated list*

Moving on to the next action, "Start an approval," specify the "Assigned To" value. In this case, you'll send all approvals to a single user; in a true production scenario, it would be ideal to send to multiple approvers because a single approver could be out of the office or not available and the requests could queue waiting for approval. In my case, I added Sarah Merrill as the approver; see Figure 11-11.

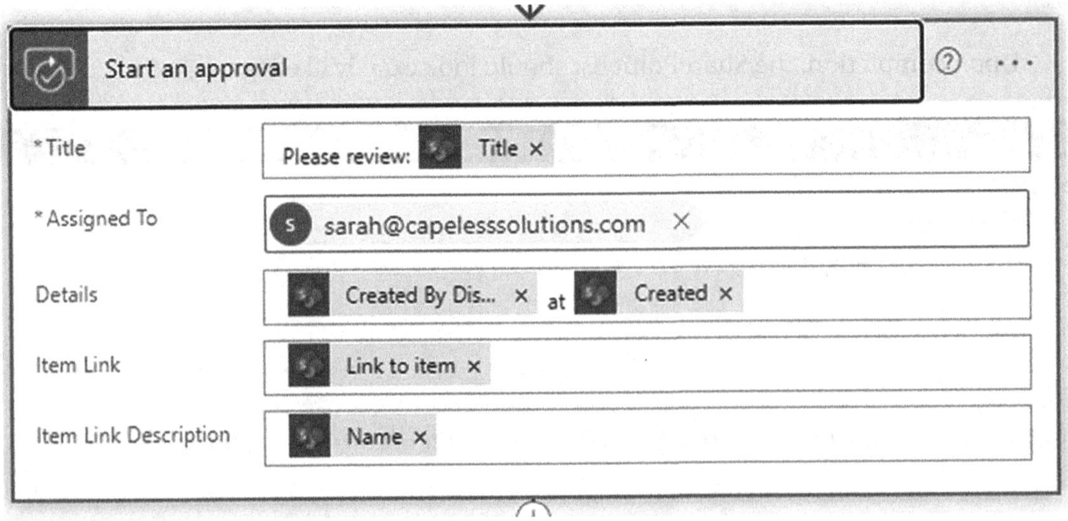

Figure 11-11. *Adding an approver to the flow*

Note   Remember that the approver and other variables will be specific to your own instance of Microsoft 365.

The final change you will make to the flow is to set the "Approval" field in the Procurement Items list with an appropriate status of Approved or Rejected. In the "If yes" action box shown in Figure 11-12, click "Add an action."

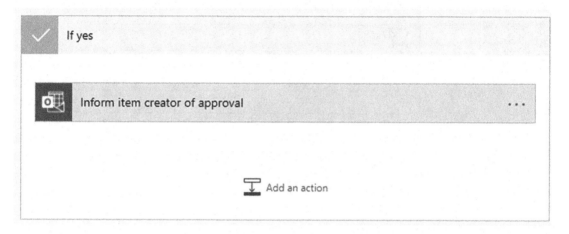

Figure 11-12. *Adding an action in Microsoft Power Automate*

In the "Choose an action" box, search for SharePoint and then select the Update item action. Once the action is added, it needs to be configured to update the item. Specify the site address, list name, ID, title, and approval, as shown in Figure 11-13.

Figure 11-13. *Configuring the Update item action to update a SharePoint list item*

To set both the ID and Title fields, place the cursor inside the corresponding text box. For instance, to set the ID to the current item you are approving, select ID, as shown in Figure 11-14.

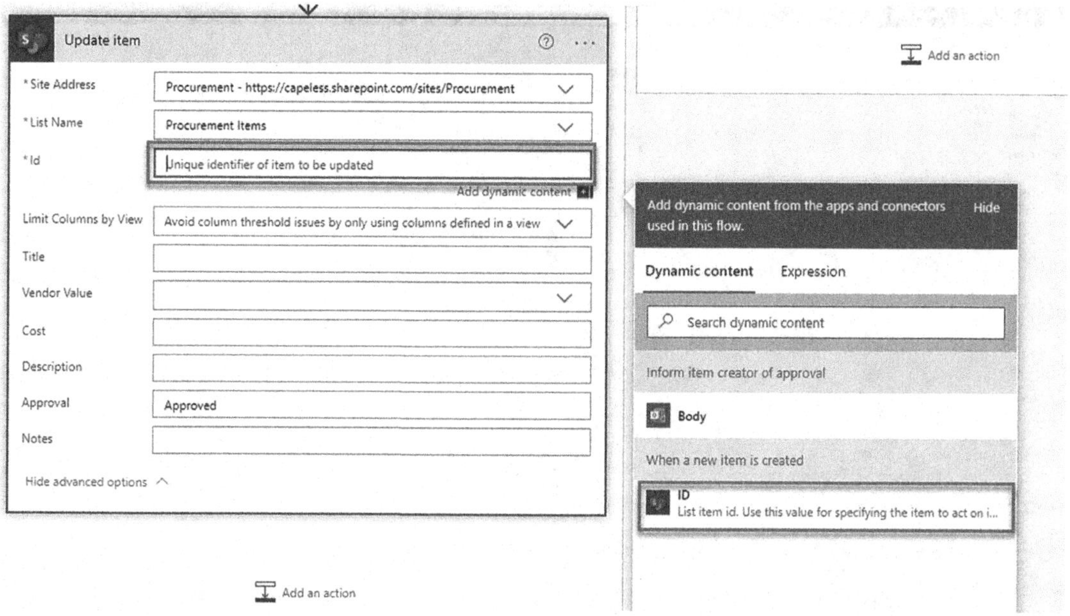

Figure 11-14. Set the ID of an item within a flow

Perform the same action for the Title field, selecting Title from the available choices. Repeat the same steps to set the Approval field to Rejected when the approver rejects the procurement request. The completed flow should be similar to Figure 11-15.

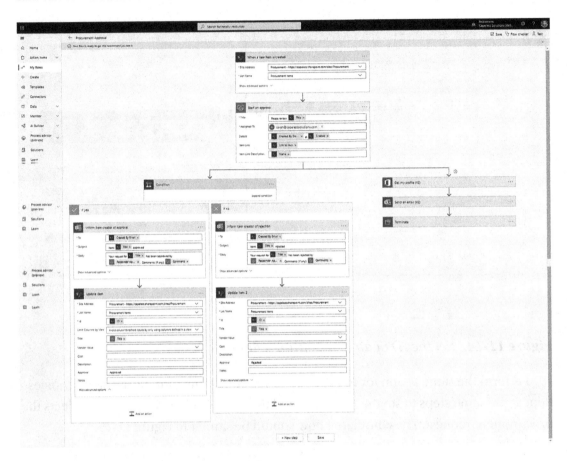

Figure 11-15. *Completed approval flow*

Each action also has a set of options that are available to configure the action further. Clicking the ellipsis in the upper-right corner of each action reveals a context menu. For the purposes of this book, I will discuss the "Add a comment" and "Rename" menu options. Clicking "Add a comment" allows a comment to be made to describe what the action is doing or a specific configuration setting. This is a good practice in the event that someone else needs to debug your flow or make changes or if you need to make changes down the road but don't entirely remember why you created specific actions. The other context menu of importance is the Rename link. It allows you to rename an action to a friendlier name and give some context to the flow.

Saving and Testing

Once the actions are appropriately named and you added comments as you saw fit, the next step is to save the flow and test it. In the upper-right corner underneath your profile picture or initials, click Save. After the save is performed, click Test to execute a test of the flow and see if there are any errors or issues. Clicking Test opens a modal dialog with two options: "Manually" or "Automatically." The first option requires you to add an item to the list in SharePoint, while the second option uses data already on the list from a previous flow to execute the flow. For the purposes of this book, let's use the first radio button: "Manually." Select the radio button and click "Save & Test." In the SharePoint list you created earlier, add a list item, updating the fields as needed. This includes title, vendor, cost, and description. Once an item is added, return back to the flow to see the progress; see Figure 11-16.

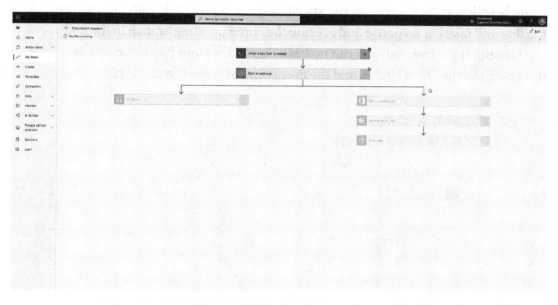

Figure 11-16. *Viewing the status of the approval flow*

By looking at the flow, you can tell that the first step was successful, as designated by a green circle with a white checkmark. You can also infer that you are on the "Start an approval" action as designated by the orange processing icon. The actions following "Start an approval" have not executed yet because they are grayed out. In this flow, Sarah Mercurio is the approver, and in her inbox, she did receive an email from Power Automate concerning the approval request, as shown in Figure 11-17.

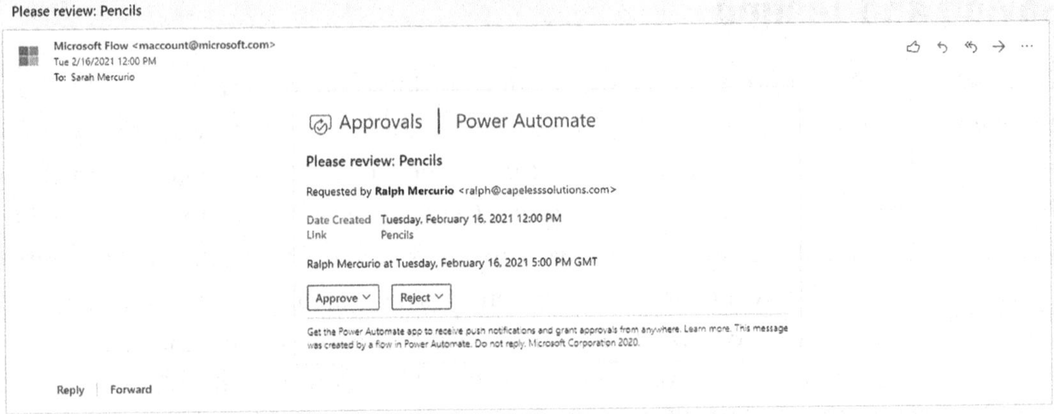

Please review: Pencils

Microsoft Flow <maccount@microsoft.com>
Tue 2/16/2021 12:00 PM
To: Sarah Mercurio

Approvals | Power Automate

Please review: Pencils

Requested by **Ralph Mercurio** <ralph@capelesssolutions.com>

Date Created   Tuesday, February 16, 2021 12:00 PM
Link   Pencils

Ralph Mercurio at Tuesday, February 16, 2021 5:00 PM GMT

Approve ⌄   Reject ⌄

Get the Power Automate app to receive push notifications and grant approvals from anywhere. Learn more. This message was created by a flow in Power Automate. Do not reply. Microsoft Corporation 2020.

Reply | Forward

Figure 11-17. *Approval email sent to the approver in a flow*

As the approver, Sarah has two choices. She can either approve or reject the item. Upon her clicking "Approve," she can specify any notes and click "Submit" in the email; the flow will take her response and execute the corresponding branch in the flow.

Looking at the flow test, you can now see that all the steps have executed, as designated by the green circles, and the flow is finished; see Figure 11-18.

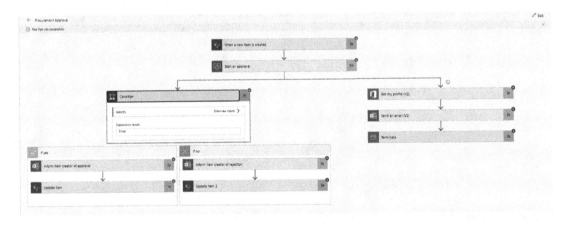

Figure 11-18. *Completed flow diagram*

As specified in the flow, you also set the Approval column to either Approved or Rejected. Examining the SharePoint list, you can see the Approval column is set to the correct value; see Figure 11-19.

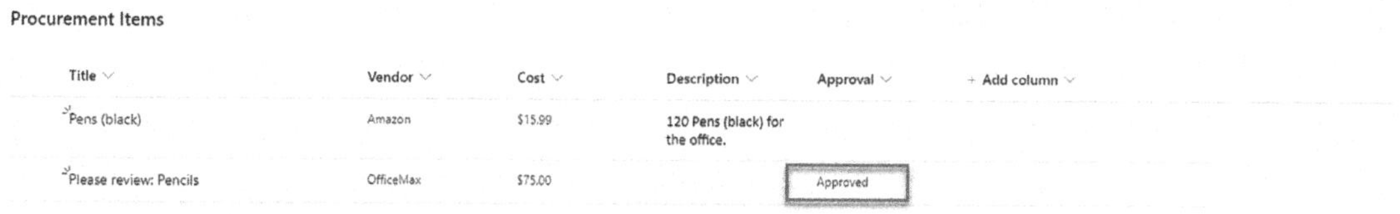

Procurement Items

Title ∨	Vendor ∨	Cost ∨	Description ∨	Approval ∨	+ Add column ∨
Pens (black)	Amazon	$15.99	120 Pens (black) for the office.		
Please review: Pencils	OfficeMax	$75.00		Approved	

Figure 11-19. *SharePoint column value set from Power Automate*

The submitter will also receive a notification in their respective inbox when the flow is complete about whether the item was approved or rejected.

Creating a Flow Between Microsoft 365 Applications

In this example, you will link Microsoft Forms, Planner, and Power Automate together to create a software bug submission flow. When a user finds a software bug, they can fill out the form located within a SharePoint site, and upon submission, a Planner task will be created for the software debug lead to perform. The lead can also reassign the task to one of the available developers. Before you create the flow, you need to configure the form, SharePoint site, and Planner.

In Microsoft Forms, which was discussed in Chapter 10, create a simple form like the one in Figure 11-20.

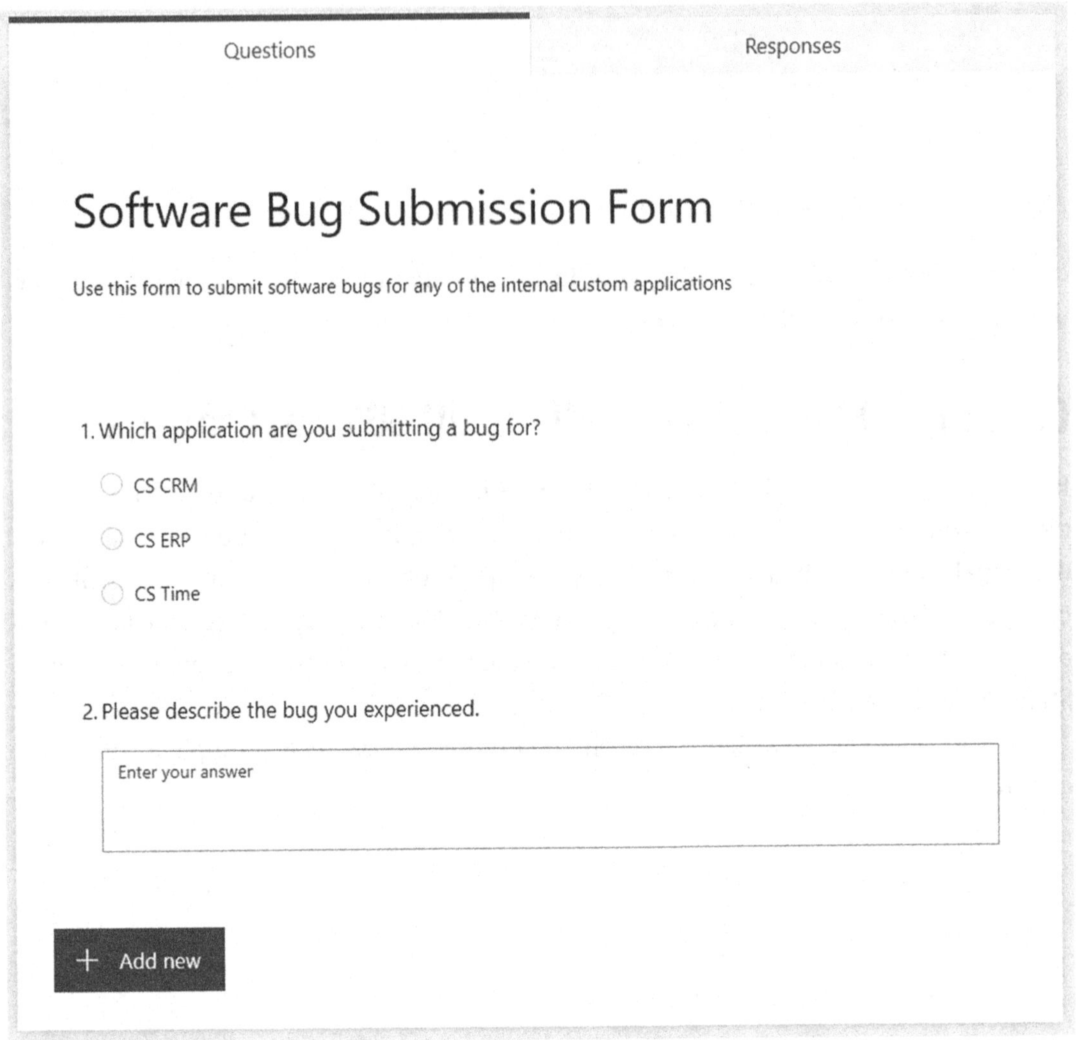

Figure 11-20. Form for submission of software bugs

Now that you have the form, let's configure Planner to support this solution. Planner was discussed previously in Chapter 8.

In Planner, create a new plan by selecting "+ New plan" in the left-hand navigation of Planner. In the New Plan modal window, title your plan and set the privacy to private, as shown in Figure 11-21. Be sure to click "Create plan."

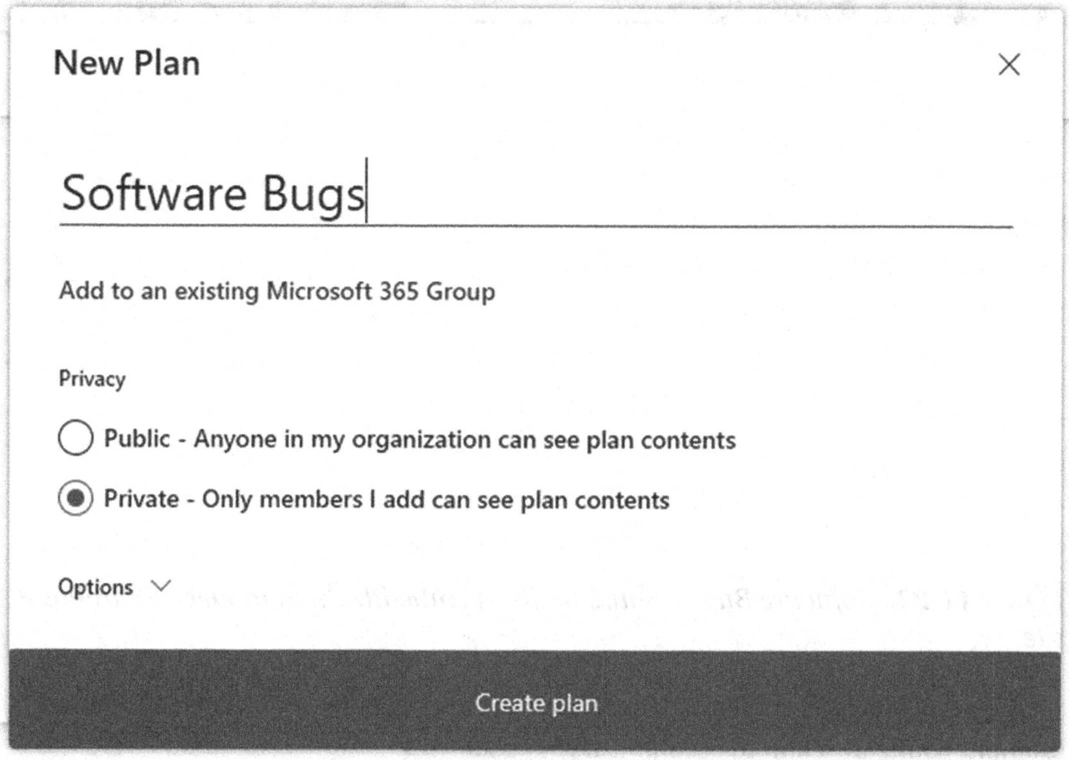

New Plan   ×

Software Bugs

Add to an existing Microsoft 365 Group

Privacy

○ Public - Anyone in my organization can see plan contents

◉ Private - Only members I add can see plan contents

Options ∨

Create plan

Figure 11-21. Planner plan to support software bug tasks

For the final setup step, let's embed the Microsoft form you created into a SharePoint site so that it is easily accessible to the users.

In a SharePoint site (which was discussed in Chapter 2; any site will do), put the page into edit mode. Select a section of the page and add the Forms web part. Once the web part is added, paste the link of the form into the configuration settings and click "Ok" and then "Republish." To get the form link, click "Share" in Microsoft Forms and copy the available link. If done correctly, it will look like Figure 11-22.

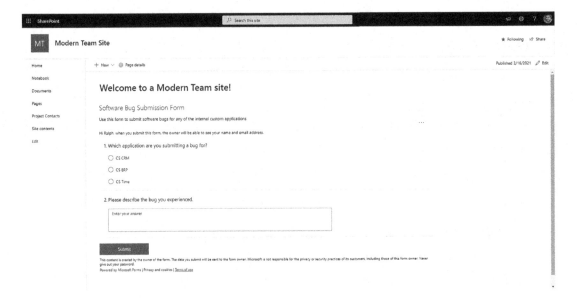

Figure 11-22. *Software Bug Submission form embedded in a modern SharePoint site*

Now that you have configured the supporting applications in this Power Automate example, configure a flow to accomplish your goal.

In Power Automate, click "+ Create" in the left-hand navigation and then click "Automated cloud flow." The first step is to find the form triggers so the flow can execute an action. In the search box, type "Forms" and choose "When a new response is submitted." Click "Create" when done. Once the trigger is added, choose the form we previously created, and click "New step" and then "Choose an action." In the search box, search for Planner and add the "Planner – Create a task" action to the flow. If done correctly, your flow should resemble Figure 11-23.

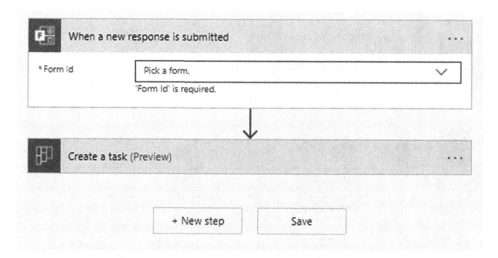

Figure 11-23. *A flow with Forms and Planner*

Configure the trigger by choosing the name of the form from the drop-down box for Form Id. In the "Create a task" action, configure the Group Id and Plan Id and add a title to the Title text box. Leave all other fields blank for now. The trigger and the action should resemble Figure 11-24.

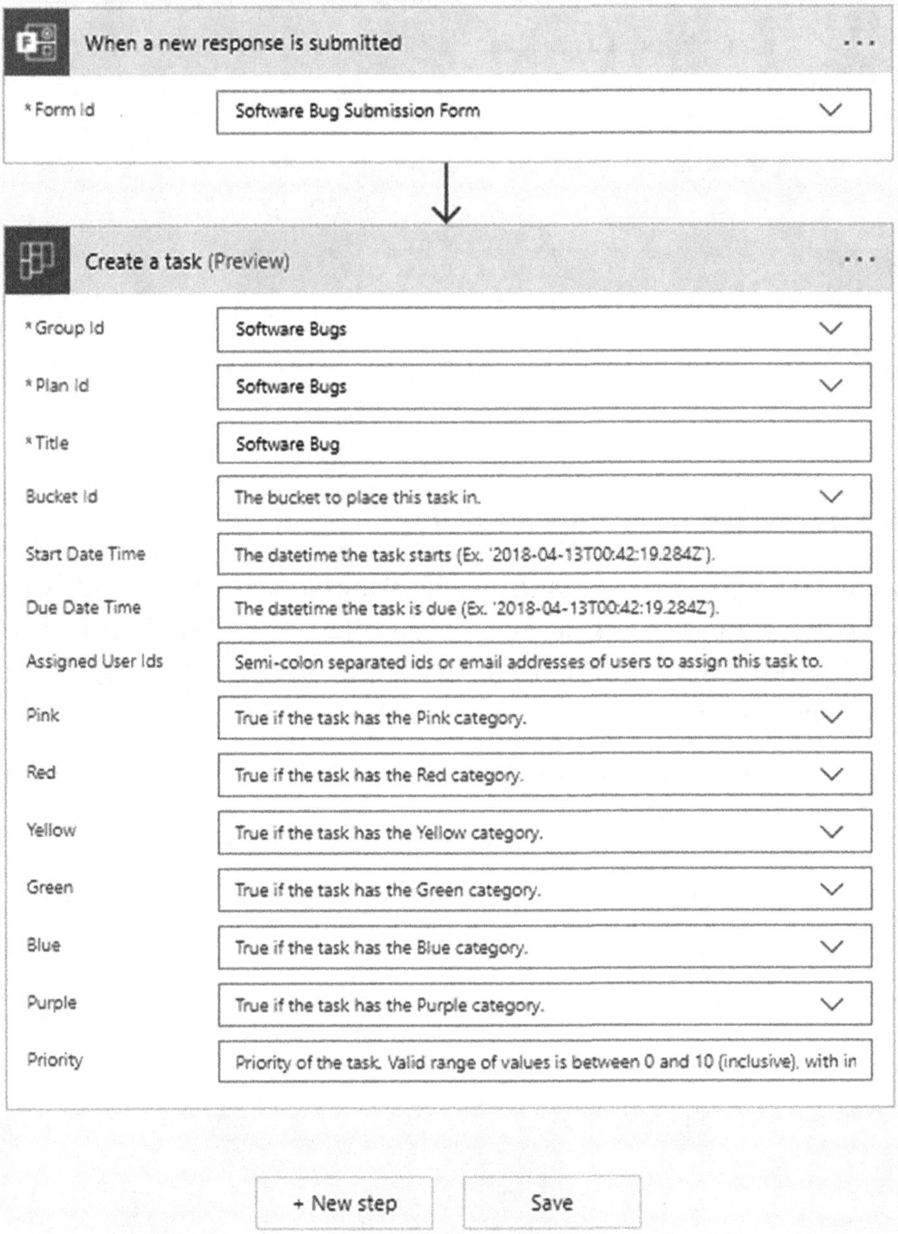

Figure 11-24. *Configuring the trigger and action to create a Planner task via a form*

At this point, you added a trigger and an action to create a flow. If you were to run the flow, a user would fill out the form, and a task would be created in Planner with very little detail. Let's add a little bit of logic so that you can use the form responses to update the task details.

Between the two current actions, click the + sign and choose to add an action. Within the search box, search for Microsoft Forms and select "Microsoft Forms – Get response details" under the Actions tab. This action requires two pieces of information: the Form Id and Response Id. For the Form Id, choose the "Software Bug Submission Form" from the drop-down. For the Response Id, click the "Response Id" field and click "See more" within the Dynamic content window. The window will refresh, and a single value will be displayed: Response Id. Click "Response Id," as shown in Figure 11-25.

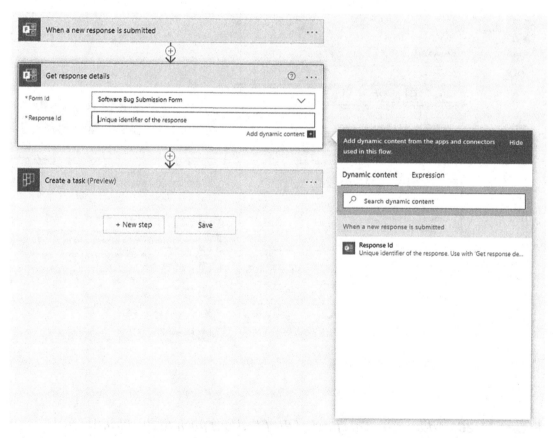

Figure 11-25. *Choosing Response Id for the "Get response details" action*

Once the field is added, the "Get response details" action is enveloped within an "Apply to each" for loop. This loop will iterate through the responses and expose the form data. In this case, the response set is a single item.

The next step is to move the "Create a task" action into the "Apply to each" action. This is done by clicking the header of the "Create a task" action and dragging it onto the "Apply to each" action. If done correctly, the "Create a task" action should be below the "Get response details" action.

Open the "Create a task" action and click the Title field. Delete the existing text and type "New Bug for: ." Clicking the Title field allows you to insert dynamic content after your text; click the "Which application are you submitting a bug for?" detail shown in Figure 11-26.

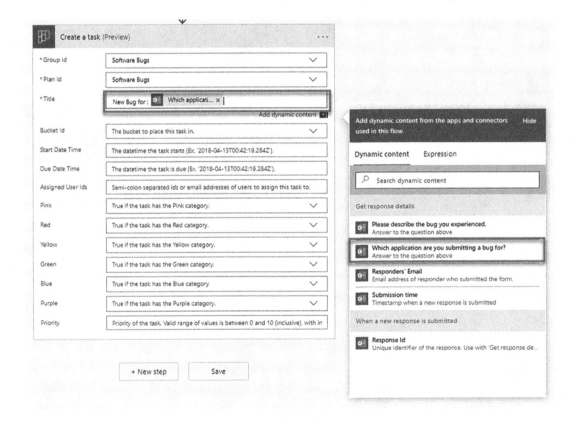

Figure 11-26. *Adding the Title field of the filled-out form to the Planner task*

Leave the other fields empty for now because you will update the details via a different action because you can't update the details of the task in the current action.

At this point, you can take data entered into Microsoft Forms and use it to create a task in Planner. You have only set the Title field and the Plan Id for tasks to be created; now let's set the other fields to add context.

To accomplish this, you need to add two actions: Delay and "Planner – Update task details." To add the Delay action, click "Add an action" below the "Create a task" action. Using the search box, search for "Delay" and select it. Set the count to 20 and the unit to second. This delay is needed to allow Planner to create the task before you attempt to update it.

Repeat the adding action sequence and search for "Planner – Update task details" and add it to the flow you are working on below the Delay action. In this action, you provide two values: a Task Id to tell Planner what to update and a Description to add context to the newly created task. Clicking the Task Id text box and then "Enter custom value," it will open the Dynamic content window. Select "ID" located in the "Create a task" section. The next update is to the Description field. Click the field and select the "Please describe the bug you experienced" tag located in the "Get response details" section. The entire flow will look like Figure 11-27.

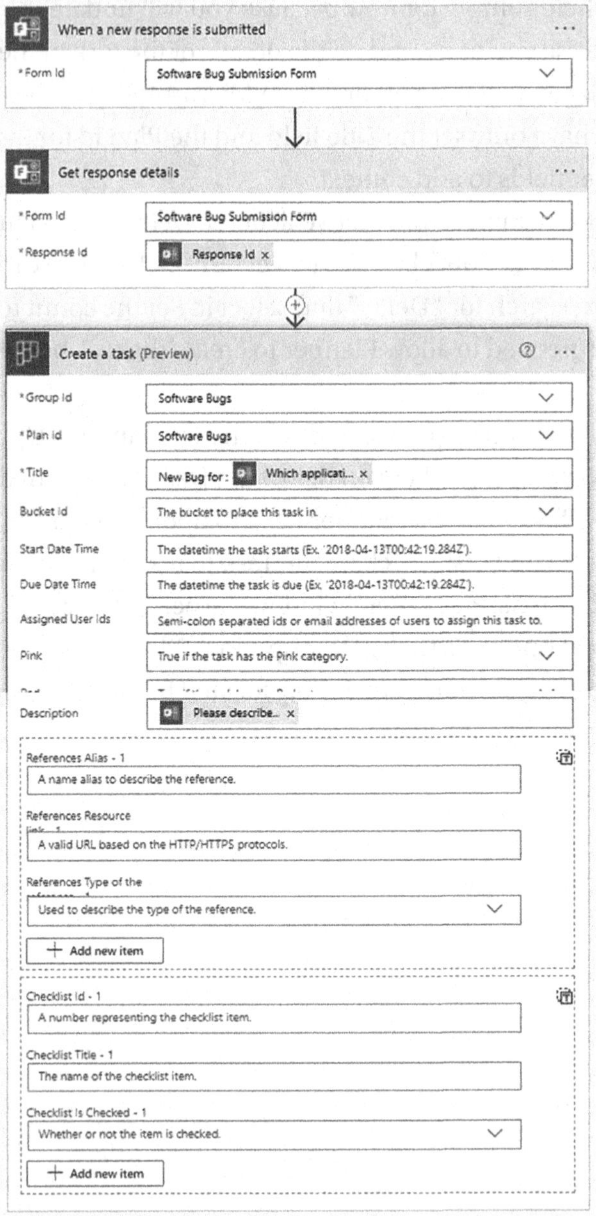

Figure 11-27. *Completed flow for software bug collection*

In this example, you connected three separate applications (Forms, SharePoint, and Planner) using Power Automate to create a cohesive work scenario without any heavy coding or custom work. This example can be further refined in numerous ways, such as adding a notification action, emailing a user, posting in a team, or even potentially integrating with a third-party software bug tracking system.

The final step is to test the flow, as you did earlier in this chapter, and ensure the task gets created with the correct metadata and bucket. In Figure 11-28, you can see that based on the form data submitted, the appropriate task is created in Planner.

Figure 11-28. *Newly created task from data entered in Microsoft Forms*

At this point, you have seen Power Automate cross Microsoft 365 application boundaries, but Power Automate also has the ability via actions to connect to third-party services.

Creating an Advanced Flow to Interact with a Third-Party Service

In this section, you will configure a flow to step outside the bounds of Microsoft 365 and integrate with an entirely separate third-party service.

In this example, when a document is saved to a particular SharePoint site, the document will be routed for electronic signature using GetAccept. GetAccept is an electronic signature platform similar to DocuSign or Adobe Sign. This app does require separate licensing since it is a service offered strictly from GetAccept. Electronic signatures are becoming more common in enterprises because they are legal time stamp signatures that can be integrated into workflows to automate requests, similar to this example.

In order to create the flow, navigate to "Templates" in the left-hand navigation. In this example, you are interested in having a document electronically signed in GetAccept whenever a file is added to a specific folder in SharePoint. Search for "Get signatures for a selected SharePoint file." Clicking the item opens the template and as seen in Figure 11-29.

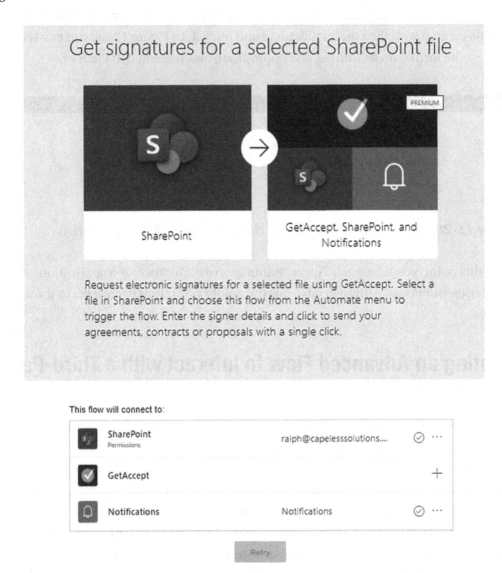

Figure 11-29. *The SharePoint/GetAccept template*

Selecting this flow requires an account to connect to GetAccept. Since this is not a Microsoft product, you will need to create an account with GetAccept to proceed.

Once you have authenticated to GetAccept with valid credentials, you can begin customizing the actions to meet your intended goal. The flow is quite simple and is comprised of three actions, shown in Figure 11-30.

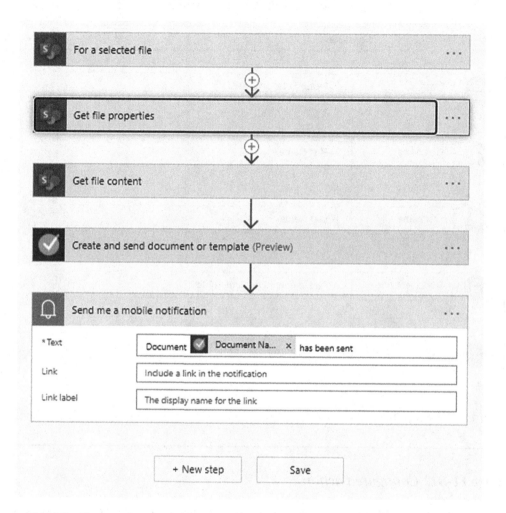

Figure 11-30. Power Automate – Get signatures for a selected SharePoint file

The first action, "For a selected file," requires the site address and library of the file on which the flow will be executed. Like in the previous sections, remove and choose the correct site address and library name as required for this action, as seen in Figure 11-31. My values will be slightly different than the values you choose.

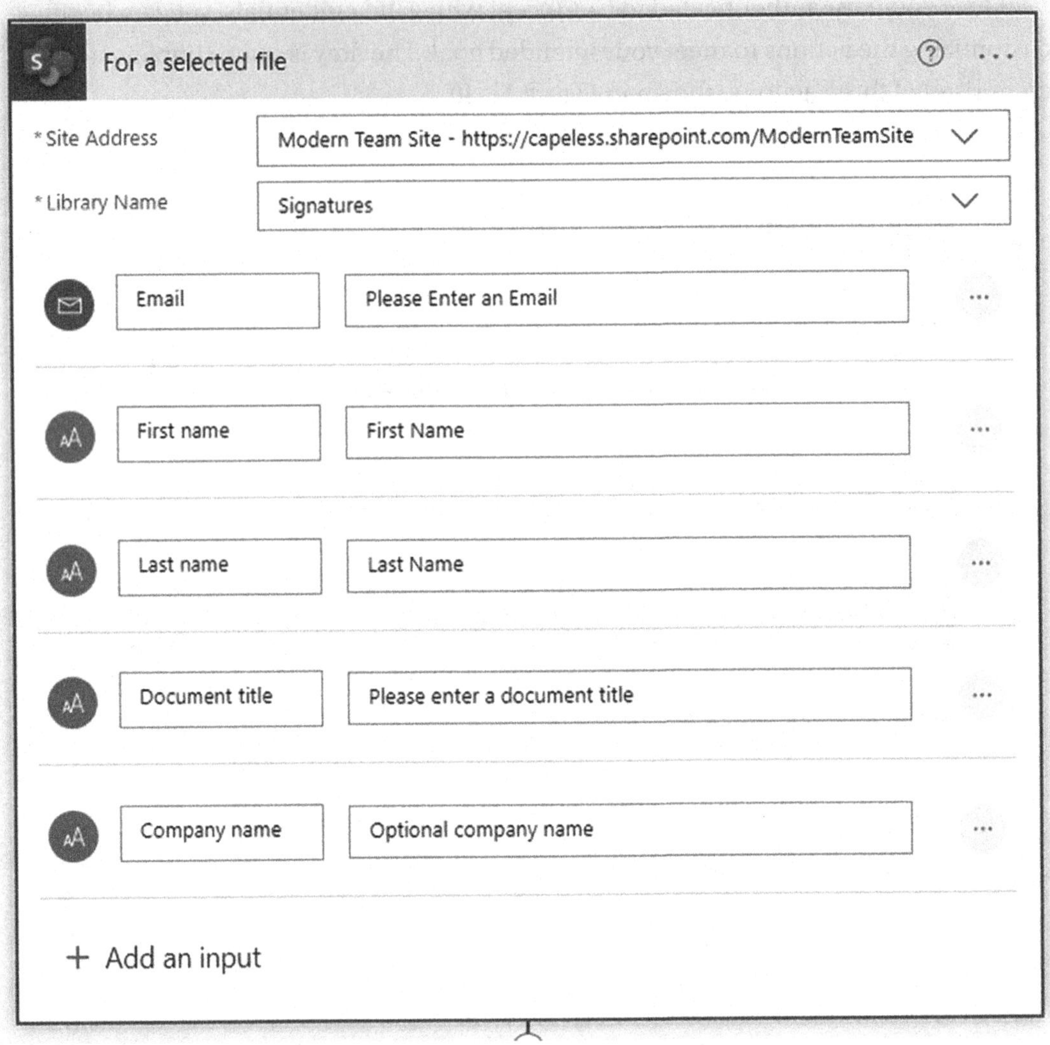

Figure 11-31. *Configured action*

The second and third actions are very easy to configure. For the "Get file properties" action, configure the site address and library name, and choose the ID of the item. It might be prepopulated already. The third action, "Get file content," requires the site address as well as the file identifier. Choose the site address that was selected in the previous actions; see Figure 11-32.

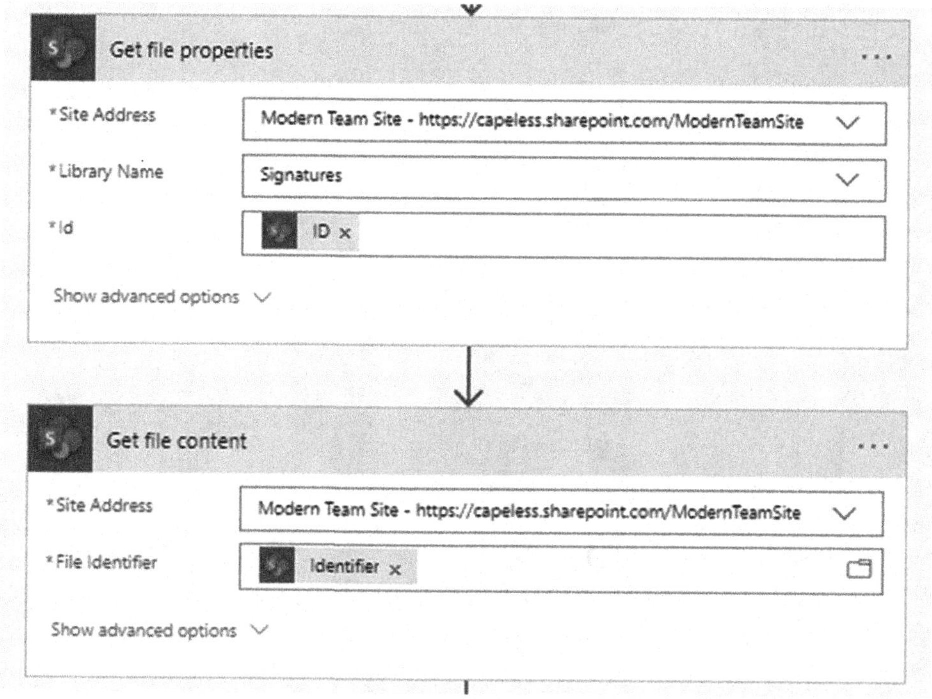

Figure 11-32. *Configured File Properties action*

The fourth action, "Create and send document or template (Preview)," is the action that will leverage the GetAccept action to send the document for electronic signature as seen in Figure 11-33.

Figure 11-33. *Configured GetAccept action*

The variables for this action are taken from the previous actions and used to configure this action. As you look through this action, there are numerous different settings, which you can configure. The final action, "Send me a mobile notification," will send an alert to the Power Automate mobile app.

As the flow progresses through the actions, it will send emails to the parties involved: Sarah will receive an email asking her to sign, as shown in Figure 11-34.

Figure 11-34. *Email sent to Sarah from GetAccept*

Once Sarah clicks the link within the email and signs the document, we all will receive a PDF in our inboxes with her signature applied. As a future exercise, the signed document can be deposited into another folder or even a SharePoint library.

Summary

Microsoft Power Automate is an innovative application that has the ability to connect the services we use, whether they are Microsoft 365 applications or external third-party services. Power Automate takes workflow to another level by providing an easy and intuitive way to create flows. I was not able to cover the advanced logic and conditions available, but this chapter should have provided you with the foundation and understanding of Power Automate.

With Power Automate, triggers are the key to starting a flow, while actions are the building blocks to perform a simple approval process or even a complicated process involving third-party services.

Flows are aimed at the user executing the flow and are not technically the same as workflows. As Power Automate evolves, the possibility if not the opportunity is available for Power Automate to become the de facto workflow engine for Microsoft 365.

You created a basic approval flow that sent a document for electronic signature and a flow to ease the tedious process of software bug tracking. I am excited for what Microsoft has in store for Power Automate in the upcoming update cycles.

CHAPTER 12

Power BI

In the first chapter, you created the Microsoft 365 environment to begin your journey through the collaboration apps. An important piece of Microsoft's "Power Platform" is Power BI. Power BI is Microsoft's data visualization software. Power BI is a lot more than the graphs and charts that you can make in Excel. The charts and graphs are not static, but reactive. When you click an element, the rest of the report will change to reveal information specific to where you clicked. Your data can also be drilled down into more specific information or related information to what is currently being displayed. It is more than just that a single graph or dataset, but how multiple sets of data are related to one another. In this way, you are able to explore your data in a way you never could with static charts.

Microsoft offers three flavors of Power BI: Power BI Desktop, Power BI Service, and the Power BI mobile app for iOS and Android. Power BI has two different licensing models: Power BI Free and Power BI Pro. The license type granted to you will determine what features of Power BI you are able to utilize. In this book, we will focus on the free licensing of Power BI, which is included with a Microsoft 365 subscription. Power BI free licensing will severely limit the collaboration and publishing abilities of the license holder; however, one will still be able to consume data published by a Power BI Pro license holder. We will explore both the capabilities of Power BI Service and Power BI Desktop under the free licensing.

The Starting Line of Power BI Service

Power BI Service is accessible via the app launcher located in the upper left of the Microsoft 365 site, as shown in Figure 12-1.

© Ralph Mercurio and Brian Merrill 2021
R. Mercurio and B. Merrill, *Beginning Microsoft 365 Collaboration Apps*,
https://doi.org/10.1007/978-1-4842-6936-7_12

Figure 12-1. *Accessing the Power BI icon from the Microsoft 365 app launcher*

Clicking the Power BI icon opens your Power BI Service environment, which presents a single pane to access published Power BI reports as well as build simple visualizations (Figure 12-2).

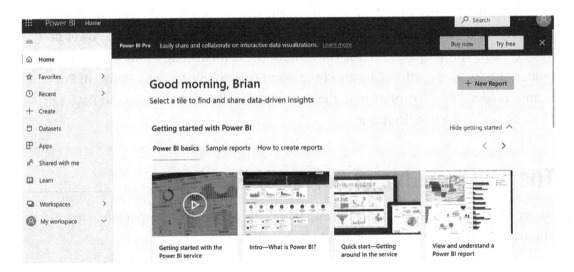

Figure 12-2. *Power BI Service Home*

Power BI Service Navigation

Navigational elements, shown in Figure 12-4, are consistent in Power BI with other pieces of the Microsoft 365 environment.

Under the **Favorites** tab, you will find visuals and workspaces that you have designated as favorites, just as in other areas of the Microsoft 365 environment. Additionally, you will find your recent actions right at your fingertips under the **Recent** tab. As in other Office areas, this section will show you what has been worked on recently, either by you or in a workspace you have access to. This access can be granted by the user sharing with you or the workspace being part of a team you are a member of.

Click **Create** to start to create a report in the Power BI Service environment. This is currently in preview and restricted to manually entered or published data. The majority of creation still exists in the desktop tool. The **Datasets** tab will show you what data you have to work with for creation in the Service environment.

Apps is another new element currently in preview. This space allows an institution to publish frequently used dashboards to their entire institution to use as needed. It is the equivalent to the "Anyone with the link" share option in OneDrive. It would be cumbersome to provision a dashboard or report to everyone in your institution. **Apps** allows you to easily deploy a collection of dashboards or reports to a large number of users. Users in your environment would be able to click **Apps** and choose from previously published dashboards and reports to use in their rolls.

The **Shared with me** tab, as in other areas of Microsoft 365, will show you dashboards and reports that people have shared specifically with you. You will be able to view any of these items until access has been taken away by the report or dashboard owner.

The **Learn** tab, pictured in Figure 12-3, is a wonderful addition to the Power BI Service. By clicking this tab, you will be taken to free, on-demand training, documentation, and testimonials.

Figure 12-3. *Power BI Service Learn tab*

Figure 12-4. *Power BI Service navigation menu*

Published Reports

Under "My workspaces," you will be able to access all published reports that you have created and published. This includes Dashboards, Reports, Workbooks, as well as Datasets. **The My workspace** area, shown in Figure 12-5, is private to you and is comprised of items that are your work only. You are able to share these published items with others; however, they are not worked on collaboratively.

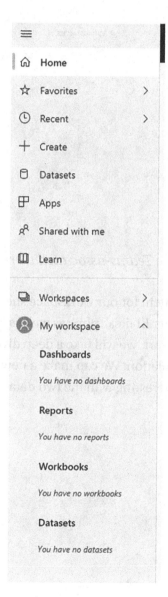

Figure 12-5. *Power BI Service My workspace*

Work published inside a team that you are a member of can be found by clicking the "Workspaces" button and navigating to the workspace associated with that team as shown in Figure 12-6. This will give you access to reports published by anyone in that team with a Power BI Pro license.

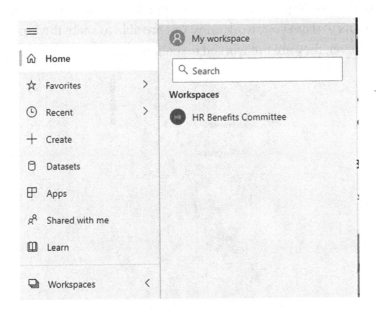

Figure 12-6. *Power BI Service Teams-associated workspace*

We can also create new content for our workspace shown in Figure 12-7. Here we can upload files, including Power BI files, .pbix, as well as Excel files and CSV files. The Report option creates a new report; we will take a deep dive into this shortly. Paginated Report requires a desktop installation. We can make a new dashboard, which is a single-paged data story. Things get interesting with the two dataset options: Dataset and Streaming dataset.

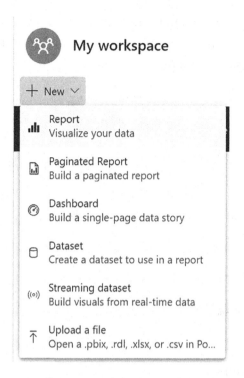

Figure 12-7. *Adding to a workspace*

The Streaming dataset option, shown in Figure 12-8, will allow you to stream data using Azure Stream, Power BI Pro required, PUBNUB, or other APIs.

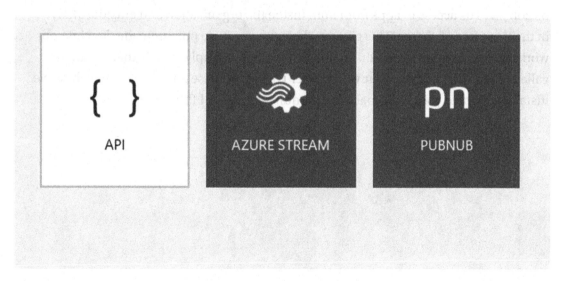

Figure 12-8. *Power BI Service streaming datasets*

The Dataset option, shown in Figure 12-9, gives us many ways to pull in new data. Many of these options work much better in Power BI Desktop, and Power BI Service is quick to remind us of this on this screen.

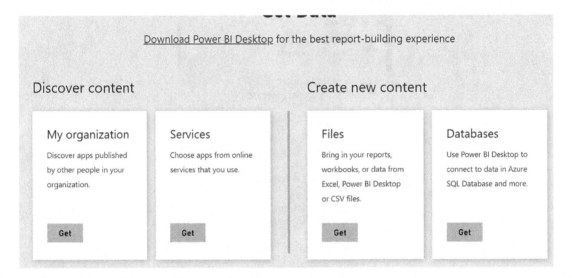

Figure 12-9. Dataset options

This menu is divided into two sections: Discover content and Create new content. Most of their options either require that you have the data already or use the desktop tool. An area worth exploring, however, is the Services area shown in Figure 12-10. This option gives us access to apps from both inside the organization and outside. Many of them are free of charge. This gives us the opportunity to pull premade data into our workspace and use as we see fit. To utilize these apps, simply choose them from the gallery and install them to your workspace. The use of these apps may be free; however, installing them to your workspace does require a Power BI Pro license.

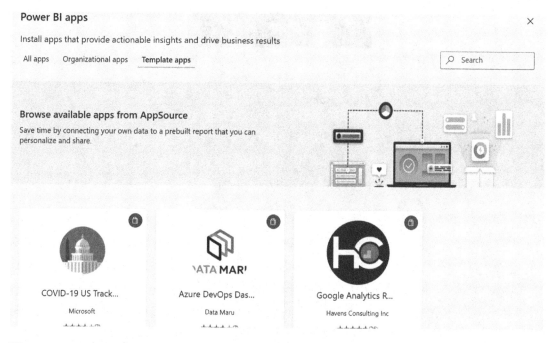

Figure 12-10. *Power BI Service Services tab*

First Visual in Power BI Service

Creation in Power BI Service is new and limited. One of the first things you will notice is the entire creation mechanism in Power BI Service is labeled as "Preview." This indicates that it is not ready and may produce less than desirable outcomes and be slow to respond. To get started, you will click the "**Create**" item from the navigation as shown in Figure 12-11.

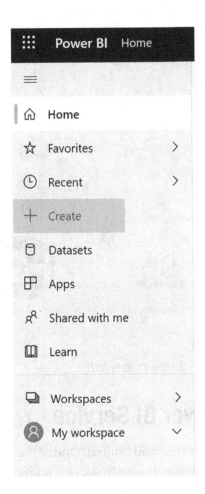

Figure 12-11. *Power BI Service Create button*

Once in the creation menu, you have two options: posting or manually entering data or using published datasets. At the time of this writing, using Excel datasheets in Power BI Service is not supported; however, it is on Microsoft's road map for inclusion. To utilize other data sources, you would need to use Power BI Desktop, which we will be covering later in the chapter.

Using published datasets, as shown in Figure 12-12, is the easiest way to create functional items in Power BI Service. These items can be published by you or by others in your institution and shared with you. To create a published dataset, the user will need to possess the Power BI Pro licensing.

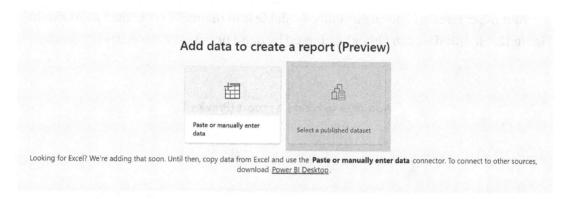

Figure 12-12. Power BI Service published datasets

Once you select the "Select a published dataset" option, you will be taken to a menu of all the published datasets to which you have access. This list will be sorted by what has recently been worked with. You would then select the dataset you would like to use, and click "**Create**" as shown in Figure 12-13.

Select a dataset to create a report

Name		Endorsement	Owner	Workspace	Refreshed
Table					2 days ago

Create   Cance

Figure 12-13. Power BI Service Create post data insert

Once clicking Create, you will be brought into your workspace to create this new report. We will explore the workspace shortly.

Your other creation option currently available is to manually enter data as shown in Figure 12-14. This data can either be entered by hand or pasted from your clipboard.

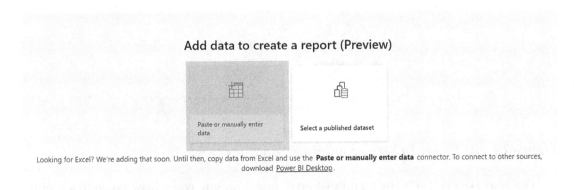

Add data to create a report (Preview)

Paste or manually enter data

Select a published dataset

Looking for Excel? We're adding that soon. Until then, copy data from Excel and use the **Paste or manually enter data** connector. To connect to other sources, download Power BI Desktop.

Figure 12-14. *Create a report with manually entered data*

Once the manual option is selected, you will be brought to Power Query, Power BI's manual table building product. Once in, you will need to select how you are labeling your table. You can either use the first row as headers or use headers as the first row as shown in Figure 12-15. These options do sound similar but are importantly different.

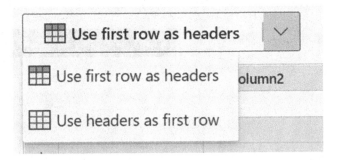

Use first row as headers

Use first row as headers

Use headers as first row

Figure 12-15. *Header row options*

The first option will give you a heading row, that is, unlabeled with a row number. This is beneficial if you are entering the data by hand or if the data you are about to paste has unlabeled table headers. The second option takes your header row and moves it down into row 1. This is helpful if your data is again unlabeled and you need to make room for headers.

Once you have selected how your headers will be determined, it is time to name your table. This name will be visible going forward to create workspace from published data, so something should be picked that you will remember later.

Now that all the labeling is complete, you can create the actual dataset. Again, this can be either pasted from your clipboard or entered manually. To enter data, simply click the cell and enter the data field required. New columns and rows will be created as you click new cells. Once all your data is entered, you can click **Create**, as shown in Figure 12-16.

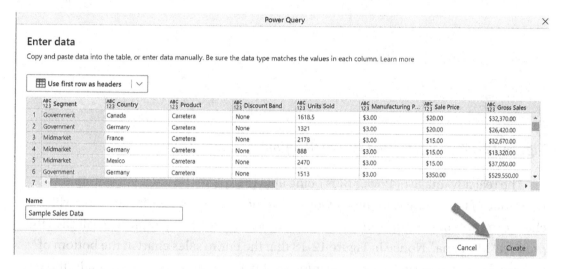

Figure 12-16. *Create post manually entering data*

Once **Create** is clicked, Power BI will create a visualization for you, as shown in Figure 12-17, if it is able to make sense of your data automatically. If there are ways to relate your tables, it will make a report for you. For example, here is the report visualization that Power BI Service made for us with the sample data that was pasted in the previous step.

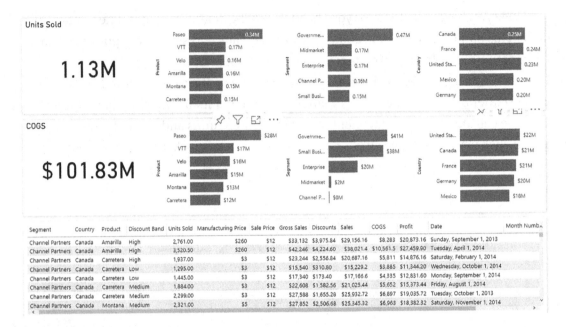

Figure 12-17. *Auto-created Power BI report*

The real advantage of Power BI is being able to explore the data. For example, if I click one of the products in the previous example, the rest of the visualization will change to show me just information on that product. For this example, we will click the product "Montana." Notice in Figure 12-18 that the entire sales chart at the bottom of the visualization now only shows me information about Montana. Additionally, the next visualization also only shows me sales figures for Montana. The same would happen had we clicked any of the elements in the visualization. Change the information given to reflect what we are trying to investigate.

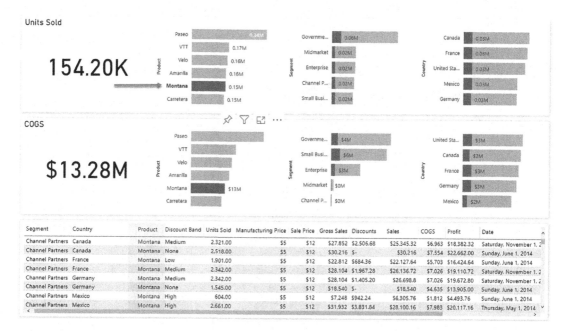

Figure 12-18. *Report data change*

We can add additional items to this report by selecting additional items under **Summarize**. The section will list all of the headings from the table we imported earlier. Currently the only headings selected can be seen in Figure 12-19.

Summarize

Figure 12-19. *Report data selection*

Let us select some additional items from the Summarize section and see how the report changes. We would like to see Sales in addition to the items we already had, as well as a breakdown of each Month, by checking the Sales and Month headers under Summarize. My workspace now looks like Figure 12-20.

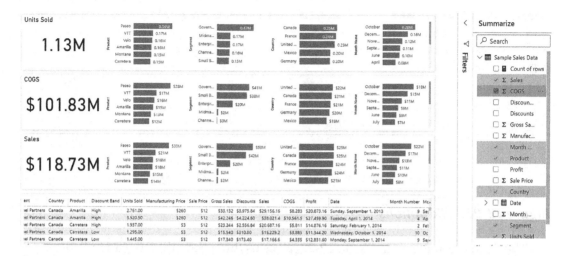

Figure 12-20. *Adding additional elements*

Notice there is a brand-new visualization showing Sales, and a breakdown by Month has been added to all three visualizations. We can continue to fine-tune which elements we would like to see added to this workspace into the visualizations that have been created for us.

This is the workspace that Power BI made for us by relating the data we presented in our table. We can now save a copy of this workspace should we want to keep it. Once we have the workspace saved, we now have an expanded report ribbon.

Under the **File** option, shown in Figure 12-21, we can "Save a copy." This is helpful should we want to create a few different workspaces that select different elements from our table. We can also download the .pbix file. This is the file we would want to give to others to share this workspace. Remember we are unable to publish this workspace under our current licensing, so this is a helpful tool to be able to share our work. We can also print our current workspace as an image. The final option, Settings, gives us a wide array of options of how others are allowed to interact with our workspace.

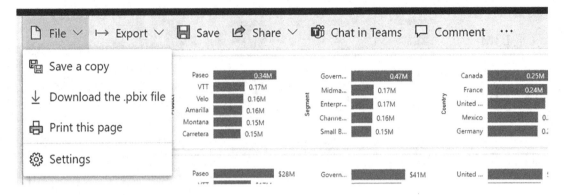

Figure 12-21. *File options*

The Export tab, shown in Figure 12-22, gives us three ways that we can pull our workspace out of Power BI and into other applications. With any export, we have options to use current or default values, exclude hidden report tabs, and either export the entire workspace or only the current page.

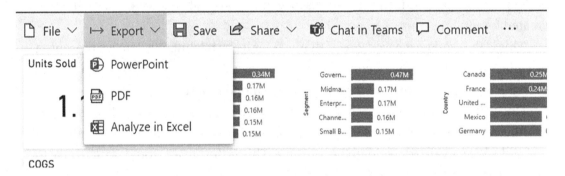

Figure 12-22. *Export options*

Exporting to PowerPoint will take our workspace and turn those visualizations into a PowerPoint slide. At this point, the visualizations are fixed and can no longer be manipulated to investigate the data. Exporting to a PDF will create a PDF document of our workspace. The final option, Analyze in Excel, is limited to Power BI Pro subscriptions.

The next four items are fairly simple, so we will quickly discuss them. The Save option allows us to save our changes to our current workspace. The items under Share are limited to Power BI Pro subscriptions, so we will skip them here. Chat in Teams allows you to add a link to the workspace to a particular Teams channel, allowing the workspace to become part of the conversation as needed. The Comment option works the same as it does in other areas of Microsoft 365, allowing you to have a conversation with collaborators right on the workspace as you are working on it.

There are many interesting options under the ellipsis as seen in Figure 12-23. We can subscribe to the workspace. This will alert us should anyone else working on the space make changes. The Edit option will allow us make changes to the workspace. Remember that up to this point this is the workspace the Power BI made for us automatically. We will discuss the many changes we can make if we edit in a moment. The See related content option will show us if this workspace is related to any other content. This can happen by design or by using the same dataset in multiple workspaces. Open lineage view will show from what dataset is the workspace derived. Pin to dashboard functions like pinning does in the rest of our environment, putting the workspace at our fingertips for easy access.

Figure 12-23. Ellipsis options

Report Editor in Power BI Service

Once we start editing a report, we are given a much more expansive ribbon as seen in Figure 12-24. We can now change any of the visualizations in our report or add new ones, by making choices from the Visualizations menu. For example, if we would like to see our Month charts vertically instead of horizontally, as we previously had, we could simply select our month visualizations and choose the stacked column chart from the Visualizations menu. You can see in the following image that the visualizations for the months are now vertical.

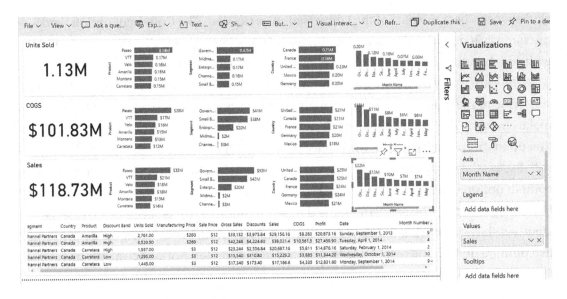

Figure 12-24. *Report editing ribbon*

By clicking the ellipsis in the Visualizations menu, we are able to add additional options not available by default. In addition to visualizations, we are now also able to add text, shapes, and buttons as seen in Figure 12-25. This is extremely helpful to build context into our reports. We can also determine if we would like our report to filter out other visuals when we filter data. This is a prime example of why Power BI is useful and should be turned on whenever possible.

Figure 12-25. *Additional visual options*

The Starting Line of Power BI Desktop

Power BI Desktop is the main tool for creation in Power BI. To get started, the desktop tool can be downloaded from Microsoft at this website: `http://powerbi.microsoft.com/en-us/desktop/`. The Power BI Desktop app is also available from the Windows 10 store. Much of what we can do in the desktop tool is limited by our licensing. Pro licensing is required for many of the features available in the Power BI Desktop tool. Just as what we did with Power BI Service, we will be sticking to just what can be done with the free licensing. The limitations are similar to what we saw in the Power BI Service tool. You are able to make reports for yourself; however, working collaboratively and publishing to others is not available. As we first enter the application, we are greeted with a splash screen that gives us the option of opening recent reports, as well as showing announcements about what is new in the tool. Once this splash screen is closed, we are brought into the main Power BI Desktop tool.

Immediately it is evident that this is the main creation tool for Power BI. While earlier we needed to navigate to the report builder, in Power BI Desktop, we start in the report builder screen as seen in Figure 12-26.

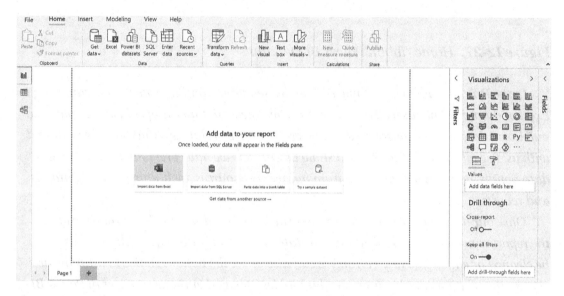

Figure 12-26. *Opening screen of Power BI Desktop*

Importing Data in Power BI Desktop

To the right, we see the same visualization options we had in the Power BI Service, with the addition of some important options. We are now about to add script visuals from both R and Python among others.

Of course, before we can choose visuals, we must first bring in data. In the main
canvas of our report builder, we can see four main options. We can paste data in, as we
did in Power BI Service, import Excel data, import from SQL Server, or test with sample
data. If we click the "Get data from another source" link below these options, we are
presented with a plethora of additional options. We can also bring in data using the first
section of the Power BI Desktop Home ribbon labeled Data as seen in Figure 12-27.

Figure 12-27. *Home ribbon Power BI Desktop*

*In the Data portion of the Home ribbon, we see some familiar options. We can bring in
Excel or data by hand, as well as SQL data. The Power BI datasets option will allow us to
pull down data we previously used in Power BI Service or datasets that have been shared
with us. Recent sources of course will show us datasets we have previously used. The Get
data option again allows us to pull from many more sources, including prebuilt datasets
and reports.*

*Once our data is in, we have some important options down the left-hand side of
the report canvas. We can look at the raw data. This is important if our data needs to
be cleaned or edited due to an error. We can also select the bottom choice to examine or
change the relationships between our data tables. Remember that the power of Power BI
is the relationships between our data. By relating our tables, we can delve even deeper into
what our data means.*

Power BI Desktop Ribbon

The ribbon in Power BI Desktop gives us a familiar look and feel to other Microsoft 365
products. We explored the Data portion of the Home ribbon already. The remainder
of the Home ribbon has four other sections. Refer to Figure 12-27 for a visual of the
remainder of this menu. The **Queries** section gives us two options. The first allows us to
transform our data. Here we can change data fields, alter our headers, slip our column,
or make other changes to clean our data. This ensures that our reports are showing
us the correct information. It also allows us to correct data that is giving us errors in

processing. We can also refresh our data, which is particularly important if we are pulling our data into Power BI from another source, be it Azure or another location. The **Insert** portion, as in Power BI Service, will allow us to insert new visuals, text boxes, and other elements to make our reports complete. There are many more options under the **Insert** tab in the ribbon, which we will discuss shortly. The **Calculations** area gives us an onscreen location to write out calculations similarly to what we would do in Excel. **Share** will allow us to publish our report to our own Power BI Service workspace. We are unable to publish to shared workspaces under the free licensing.

In the **Insert** ribbon option, in Figure 12-28, we have even more elements we can add to our report. We can add additional pages in order to make our report more organized and place visuals that are related on the same page. We are also able to add additional visuals. Clicking the **New visual** button puts a placeholder in our report until we choose which visual we would like from the right pane. We are also able to pull visuals from our computers as well as **AppSource**, which are published visuals. The **AI visuals** area consists of three options. The Q&A option puts a question box into our report where the user can ask questions in natural language, to be interpreted by artificial intelligence. The **Key influencers** and **Decomposition tree** options add these AI-powered visuals into our report. The **Power Apps** button within the **Power Platform** area allows us to place a PowerApp right into our report. We will be discussing Power Apps in Chapter 13. In addition to text boxes and shapes, the **Elements** section also allows us to now add images and buttons. These buttons can be extremely helpful as they can lead to other pages in our report.

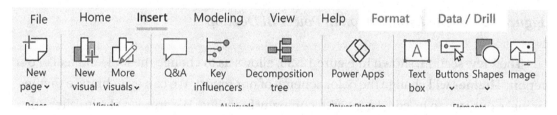

Figure 12-28. *Insert ribbon in Power BI Desktop*

The **Modeling ribbon,** shown in Figure 12-29, gives us some important tools. Here we can again manage the relationships between our data. This is an important aspect to Power BI as drilling through our data is only possible if that data is related. The **Calculations** area again allows us to type in formulas as we would in Excel as well as add new data to our report in the form of columns and entire tables. In **What if**, we can test what will happen before creating the entire visual. Want to see what will happen if you include the decimals in some data or just whole numbers? Head to What if and see what happens. The **Security** portion is particularly important if you are working with secure data or data that only some users should see. In the Security section, you can lock certain tables down to certain users. In this area, you define roles; these roles are linked to which tables they can view in our report. Once these are defined, we can link certain users with the role they need and allow them to only access certain parts of our report. In this way, we can build one report for all users while preserving some aspects to certain individuals. The **View as** allows us to test these roles by viewing our report as a specific user. The **Q&A setup** section refers back to the Q&A element we examined under the Insert tab. Here we can change how the Q&A element acts. We can teach Q&A to better understand the questions that are being asked as well as what language it will use.

Figure 12-29. *Modeling ribbon in Power BI Desktop*

The **View** section, shown in Figure 12-30, allows us to change the look and feel of our report. **Themes** will change the color scheme of our report. We can even browse themes or make our own to be consistent with company branding. We are also able to alter our page view as well as preview what our report would look like on a mobile device. Lastly, we can show or hide various panes to make more room for our report in the canvas.

Figure 12-30. *View ribbon in Power BI Desktop*

The **Help** portion gives as many options to learn about Power BI. The first section, labeled **Info**, gives us access to the About button. This button gives us the version of our install, as well as other information that would be useful should we need to contact support. The next section, labeled simply **Help**, gives us access to documentation to learn on our own, however we learn best. Whether we enjoy watching videos or reading documentation, the links are there to facilitate our learning. In the **Community** section, we have links to assist us learn with others. Finally in the **Resources** section, we can go through examples or finally contact consulting services to work with us.

Figure 12-31. Help ribbon in Power BI Desktop

Sample Report in Power BI Desktop

We will be utilizing sample data to create our report. Back on the Home tab in the ribbon, we can click "Try a sample dataset" to get started. Once there we have the option to launch a tutorial where Power BI will walk us through an example, or we can load some sample data. Let us load some sample data. Once our sample data is loaded, we can preview this data in the **Navigator** pane pictured in Figure 12-32. We must select, by checking the box next to the name, which dataset we would like to bring into our report. Once a dataset is selected, we can transform or change that data before it is brought into the report, as well as load the data. Let's load our data into our sample report.

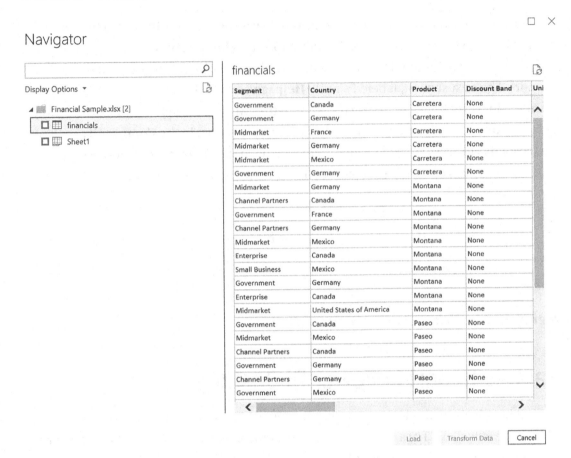

Figure 12-32. *Navigator pane*

Once as our data is loading, the tables will be brought in, and Power BI will attempt to automatically relate them. Unlike Power BI Service, Power BI Desktop will not automatically build us any visuals, instead allowing us to build our report from the ground up. We are able to select our desired visualization from the Visualizations column and then pick which data we would like represented by selecting our desired fields from the Fields column. In the example shown in Figure 12-33, we selected the stacked column chart as our visualization and had the Sales and Country fields used in that visual.

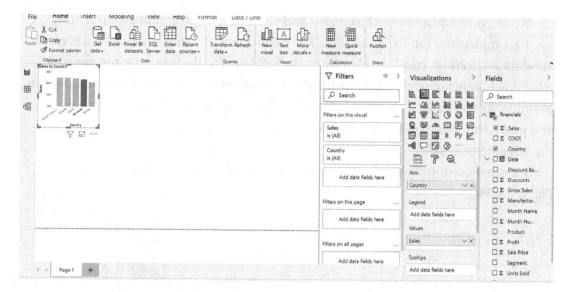

Figure 12-33. *Sample visual in Power BI Desktop*

Let's put a title on our report page by inserting a text box. We will need to select the **Insert** tab in the ribbon, the Text box option from the Elements section. For this example, we have left the font type the same but change the size to 42 as it is being used as a title. We can drag the element to anywhere we would like on the report by simply dragging and dropping. We can also move our one visual below our title by the same method. Notice in Figure 12-34 the red line helps us line our elements up with one another.

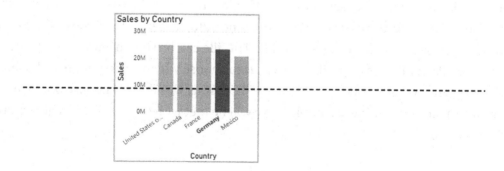

Figure 12-34. *Moving elements in Power BI Desktop*

We can now add additional elements and visualizations to complete our report.

To complete our report, let us add a Key influencers AI visual. This visual will read our data and look for trends to identify causation data. For these visuals, the more related fields are included, the more likely causation relationships will be found. For our example, we can include all of our sales-related data. We will include sales, gross sales, and profit. Our visual was able to find what caused sales to increase as well as our top three segments of sales.

We can move this new visual to line up with our title and other elements, shown in Figure 12-35.

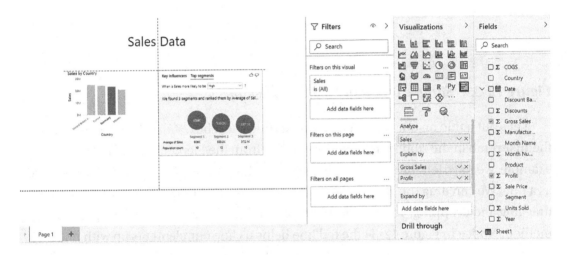

Figure 12-35. *Key influencer AI visual*

Now that our sample report is finished, we can publish our report, so we have access to it on Power BI Service as well as the Power BI mobile app. To do this, we will head back to the **Home** tab and select **Publish** from the end of the ribbon. Power BI Desktop will ask us if we would like to save our work if there are unsaved changes. It is of note that unlike other elements of Microsoft 365, there is no auto-save feature in Power BI. Power BI will have us save first locally as a .pbix file. This file can be shared with others to view your report. Power BI Desktop will then ask us to choose which workspace to publish our report. Since we are working with the free licensing, we can only choose our own workspace. Once publishing is complete, we will be met with a success message pictured in Figure 12-36.

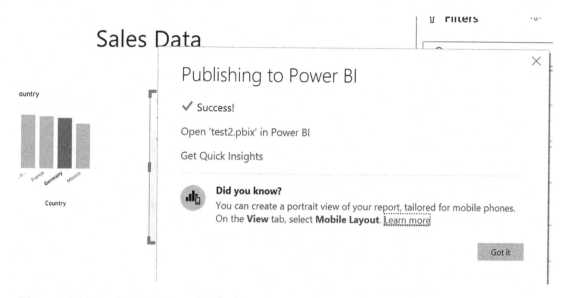

Figure 12-36. Power BI publish success message

Summary

In summary, Power BI is a powerful visualization tool. Its strength lies in examining related data, allowing the user to ask natural questions about their work to gain actionable insights.

CHAPTER 13

Power Apps

In the previous chapter, I discussed Power BI, Microsoft's data and reporting platform. In this chapter, I will be discussing Microsoft Power Apps, a new and innovative way to build solutions within Microsoft 365.

Like Power Automate and Power BI, Power Apps is the final application to make up the Power Platform. This platform allows for more advanced workflows, reporting, and now applications to make collaboration even more engaging. Power Apps is available in a wide variety of Microsoft 365 licenses, including E1, E3, and E5 Microsoft 365 plans.

Microsoft Power Apps allows you to create custom applications with connections to a wide variety of data sources. This application was designed to provide low- or no-code interfaces to users to begin to build applications. As your skills develop in Power Apps, you can then begin to build advanced Power Apps and have the ability to add code.

The goal of this chapter is to expose the reader to the basics of Microsoft Power Apps. For more information on using and creating great Microsoft Power Apps, please take a look at *Beginning Power Apps: The Non-Developer's Guide to Building Business Applications,* Second Edition, by Tim Leung.

Overview of the Power Apps Interface

Within Microsoft 365, click the app launcher in the upper-left corner and select Microsoft Power Apps, as shown in Figure 13-1.

Figure 13-1. *Launching the Microsoft Power Apps application*

© Ralph Mercurio and Brian Merrill 2021
R. Mercurio and B. Merrill, *Beginning Microsoft 365 Collaboration Apps,*
https://doi.org/10.1007/978-1-4842-6936-7_13

Once you click the application, you will be presented with the Power Apps dashboard (see Figure 13-2). The Power Apps dashboard includes links within the left-hand navigation (similar to the Power Automate interface), an area to access datasets, app wizards, trainings, and apps recently created by you.

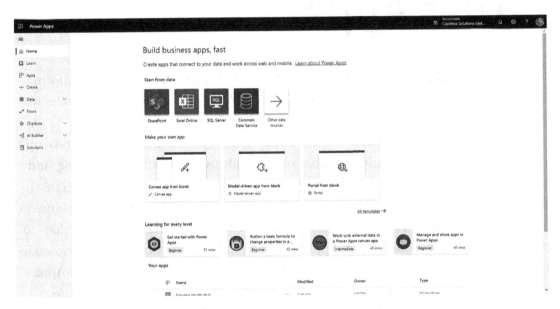

Figure 13-2. *Microsoft Power Apps interface*

Now that you know the layout, let's take a deeper dive and explore the options within Power Apps before we embark on our journey of Power Apps development. The left-hand navigation menu contains the following links:

- **Home:** Provides a link back to the home screen.

- **Learn**: Resources such as training, support, and documentation.

- **Apps**: Power Apps that have been developed by you along with the last time modified, owner, and Power Apps type.

- **+ Create:** Preconfigured Power Apps templates to use.

- **Data**: The Data menu contains Tables, Choices, Dataflows, Export to data lake, Connections, Custom Connectors, and Gateways. Tables are a way to structure and store data; Power Automate and Power Apps share tables. Connections will allow you to see all the connections that are used for your account, while Custom Connectors will list any custom connectors used. Gateways, which refer to data gateways, allow the cloud services to reach on-premises data.

- **Flows:** Shows flows that have been created on the Power Automate platform.

- **Chatbots:** Allows you to build chatbots to interact with users in a preprogrammed question/answer format we are used to.

- **AI Builder:** Allows you to add artificial intelligence to your applications. This functionality can be used to extract information, detect objects, or utilize predication.

- **Solutions:** Allows you to import prebuilt solutions from the marketplace or from software providers. These solutions can then be used within the Power Apps platform.

The Power Apps application contains four main areas, "Start from data," "Make you own app," "Learning for every level," and "Your apps":

- **Start from data:** Predefined connectors that allow you to connect to a wide variety of data sources including but not limited to Microsoft 365, SQL, Dropbox, Oracle, and so on.

- **Make your own app:** Default templates that allow you to create one of the three types of applications. We will explore each type more in the next section.

- **Learning for every level:** Provides training and documentation resources.

- **Your apps:** A list of applications that you have created.

Power Apps

Power Apps provides the ability to build three different types of applications from blank templates (see Figure 13-3.) Each one of these types has its own benefits and use. Let's take a look at each type and explore them in more detail.

Build business apps, fast

Create apps that connect to your data and work across web and mobile. Learn about Power Apps

Start from data

SharePoint   Excel Online   SQL Server   Common Data Service   Other data sources

Make your own app

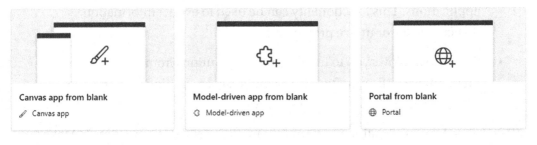

Canvas app from blank
🖌 Canvas app

Model-driven app from blank
♻ Model-driven app

Portal from blank
🌐 Portal

All templates →

Figure 13-3. *Types of blank Microsoft Power Apps templates*

Types of Power Apps

Start from Data

Power Apps gives you the option to begin development from a dataset. This dataset can be in Excel (as a table) or any of the other supported datasets. This is one of the fastest ways to build a PowerApp, and shortly we will walk through an example of creating a PowerApp from a dataset.

Canvas

Canvas apps are a type of PowerApp and are aimed at a zero-code development process. These apps allow the app builder full control over the interface and can connect to a wide variety of data sources. Canvas apps can be formatted to fit the tablet or phone devices.

Model Driven

Model-driven apps are a bit different than canvas apps in that they are based on the data source, not the user experience.

Portal

Portal apps are the third type of Power Apps that is available for use. These apps differ than the other apps in that they align with Dynamics 365. These apps are externally facing websites and allow for outside users to connect with a variety of authentication providers.

Overview of the Power Apps IDE

Left Navigation Menu

Once we choose the type of PowerApp we would like to create, we are brought to the canvas to build our application. The left-hand menu is replaced as seen in Figure 13-4.

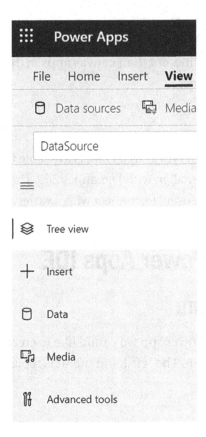

Figure 13-4. *Power Apps canvas left menu*

This menu allows us to control different elements of our PowerApp. We will describe each option in the following:

- **Tree view:** This option shows us the hierarchical view of the different screens that are part of our application. Each screen drop-down will show the different elements added to that screen in a list.

- **Insert:** This option allows us to add items to our current screen in our app. There are many options from buttons to user input. We will cover these options in more depth in a bit.

- **Data:** This option will allow us to see all of the data we are bringing into our app to use. We are also able to connect new data sources by clicking Add Data via this option.

- **Media:** Here we are able to see media, photos, videos, and audio files that we have access to in the app. We are also able to upload new items via this menu option.

- **Advanced tools:** We have two tools in this option: Monitor and Tests. Monitor allows us to see our app usage and the performance and monitor for possible bugs, presented in the app. Tests allows us to write tests to validate our app and ensure it does the correct actions depending on how our tests are written.

Create a PowerApp

Your First PowerApp

Now that we have a basic understanding of how to access Microsoft Power Apps, let's create one as seen in Figure 13-3. Our first PowerApp will be created from a data source (Excel). This will allow Power Apps to build out the majority of the entire application and with very little code.

The first step in creating this PowerApp from data is to create the data source in Excel. Open Excel, and enter the data (or similar) as seen in Figure 13-5.

Figure 13-5. *Creating the Excel data source*

Once the Excel data source is created, the next step is to format the cells and columns to be a table. By creating a table, Power Apps can ingest it and create the appropriate connectors to read and write to the file. To create the table, highlight the cells and choose "Format as Table" in the Excel ribbon, under the Home tab as seen in Figure 13-6.

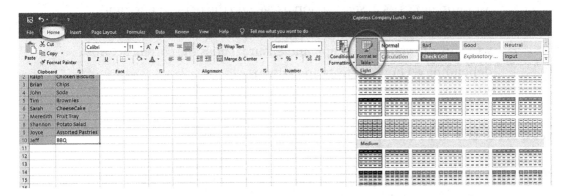

Figure 13-6. *Formatting the Excel as a table*

Pick a style and check the checkbox "My table has headers." When complete, it should look similar to Figure 13-7.

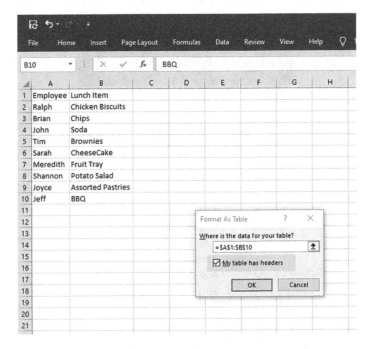

Figure 13-7. *Checking the checkbox "My table has headers"*

Now that the table has been completed and formatted, the final step is to rename the table, which can be done from the Design tab of the Excel ribbon. We are now ready to save the file to a location that Power Apps can access it. For this example, I will save the Excel document to my OneDrive. If you need a refresher on OneDrive, please refer to Chapter 3, which details the OneDrive application.

Once the file is saved to your OneDrive, we can then navigate back to Power Apps and create our first PowerApp. Navigate to Power Apps and choose "Other data sources" from the Start from data graphic as seen in Figure 13-3. Next, choose OneDrive for Business connection; if you do not see it, you may need to add the connection so Power Apps can access the file. Select the correct file as seen in Figure 13-8.

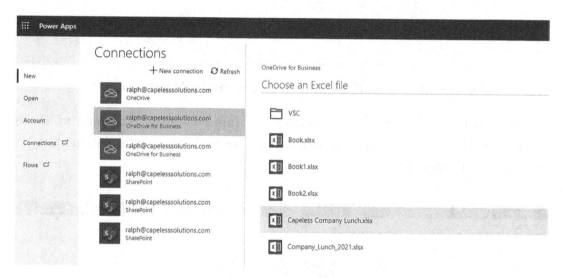

Figure 13-8. *Choosing the Excel file*

Once you select the file, Power Apps will ask for the table, select the correct table, and click "Connect" in the lower-right corner. This will initiate Power Apps and begin to build the data-driven application. The process takes a few seconds and after a few seconds will display the completed application as seen in Figure 13-9.

Note   The Excel file must be closed during this process as Power Apps creates connectors to read/write to the file. The file cannot be open while the application is in use as it will cause conflict errors.

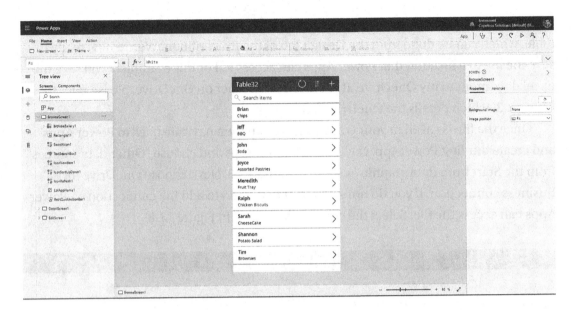

Figure 13-9. First version of the data-driven app created by Power Apps

When looking at the Power Apps interface, there are a few areas to be aware of. These areas include the Power Apps ribbon, Object panel, main design area, and Properties panel as seen in figure 13-10.

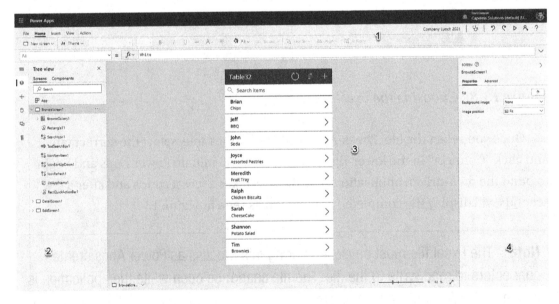

Figure 13-10. Power Apps IDE

The four areas pictured in the preceding are the following:

- **Power Apps ribbon (1)**: The Power Apps ribbon contains tabs that allow to insert controls, view objects of the PowerApp, and be able to set actions such as start a Power Automate. You will also be able to save the application and preview it.

- **Object panel (2)**: This panel shows the various components included in the PowerApp, as well as the ability to insert components similar to the Insert tab in the ribbon.

- **Main design area (3)**: This stage shows the PowerApp, and you are able to modify it as needed.

- **Properties panel (4)**: As you select an object in the Object panel, any associated properties will be displayed in this panel.

Now that we are familiar with the Power Apps IDE, let us take a look at the application and quickly change the table name to something that is meaningful. To change the table name (upper--left corner), left-click the "Table32"; once clicked, you then will be able to change the name by the property in the Properties panel. For reference, see Figure 13-11, which details the change.

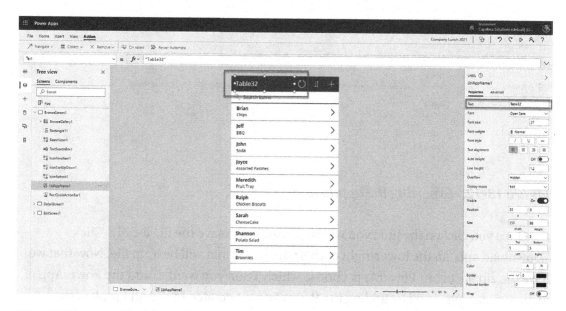

Figure 13-11. *Changing the name of the table text*

Let us preview our first PowerApp; to do so, click the play button in the upper-right corner. The application will render within the browser as a new tab, and the following functions will be available out of the box. These functions include sorting, adding an item, deleting an item, and refresh. To add a new item, click the plus sign in the upper corner of the application and enter an employee name and a lunch item. When entered, click the checkmark icon in the upper corner of the app to save your changes.

Like adding, deleting is very straightforward as well. To delete an item, select an item from the application and click the trash can icon in the upper corner. To edit an item, click the pencil to edit the item. Any changes within the application will be automatically saved back to the Excel spreadsheet.

Once we are satisfied with our application, let us add it to Microsoft Teams. To publish the app, click File in the Power Apps ribbon. Save the application, and then choose Share. In the Share window, select "Add to Teams" as seen in Figure 13-12.

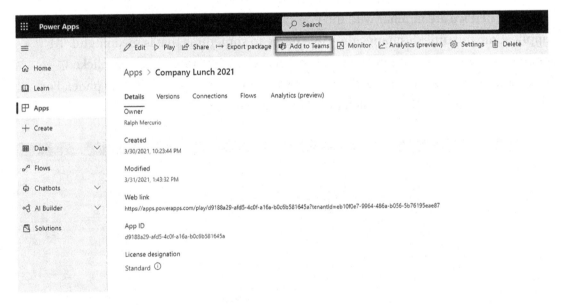

Figure 13-12. *Exporting the application*

Once you clicked the link, you will be promoted to save the file locally. Click "Download app," in the lower-right corner; the file format will be a zip file. Now that we have the zip file of our PowerApp, choose which Team you want to add the PowerApp to. In my example, I will be adding the PowerApp we created to the All Employees team. Within the General channel of the team, click the plus sign (Add a tab) and select Manage apps located in the lower-right corner as seen in Figure 13-13.

Figure 13-13. *Adding a custom app to Teams*

In the next screen, select "More apps" ➤ "Upload a custom app" and choose the file we saved from Power Apps earlier. In Figure 13-14, you can see that we embedded the PowerApp into Teams and in a new tab.

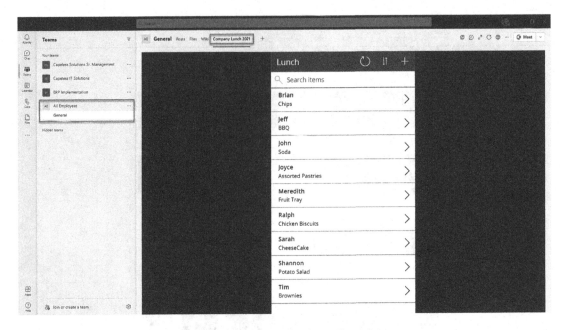

Figure 13-14. *The completed PowerApp deployed within a team*

This is a very simple PowerApp but shows the basic functionality that can be provided. As your skillset grows, you will be able to create more complex Power Apps.

Editing a SharePoint List Form with Power Apps

As we briefly mentioned in Chapter 2, we can edit the SharePoint list forms in Power Apps. For the IT users who are familiar with InfoPath, this is not a full replacement; however, it is getting closer. For new users, InfoPath, which has been deprecated from the Office product, was Microsoft's attempt at a user-friendly form product.

Editing a form in Power Apps only currently applies to lists and not libraries as well as some other restrictions. The first step in this project will be to create a SharePoint list and associated columns with the appropriate data type. Once completed, the list and form should look like Figure 13-15.

List name: Budget Details

Column: Title (single line of text)

Column: Amount (currency)

Column: New Request (yes/no)

Column: Vendor (single line of text)

Column: Renewal (yes/no)

Column: Contract Number (number)

Figure 13-15. *The configured SharePoint list and current form*

The next step is to edit the form in Power Apps. As discussed in Chapter 2, click Power Apps in the list and choose "Customize forms." This will open the form in Power Apps and allow us to begin to edit the form as seen in Figure 13-16.

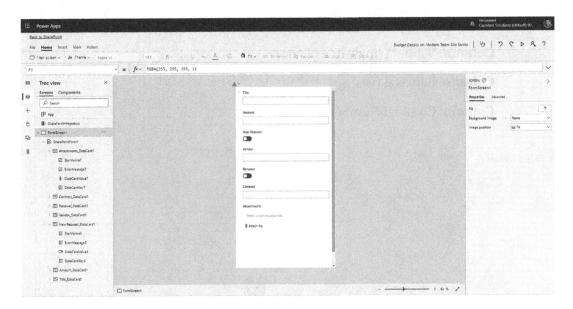

Figure 13-16. *Editing a SharePoint list form in Power Apps*

The first thing we are going to do is to remove the ability to add an attachment; to do so, simply delete the attachment field by highlighting the field and pressing the Delete key.

The next thing we are going to do is to set the visible property on the Vendor and Contract Number fields via conditional formatting. The idea is that if the user does not need to fill in those fields, we can leave them blank. In Power Apps this is very simple to accomplish; it starts with setting the visible property of the control to false via a formula. To do so, click the form to identify the control that will be used to hide the other fields as seen in Figure 13-17.

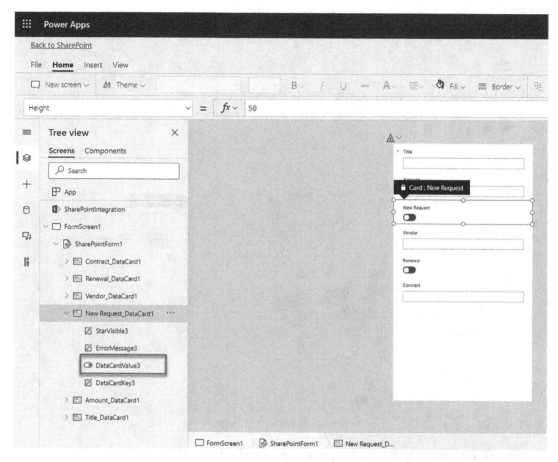

Figure 13-17. *Determine the control that will be used for hiding the other fields*

This toggle is identified as New Request_DataCard1, and the toggle control is called DataCardValue3 as highlighted in red in Figure 13-17. The correct formula for this example is "If(DataCardValue3.Value = true, true)," which will be used to hide the Vendor field. Other types of fields such as choice can be used for conditional formatting.

The next step is to select the Vendor field and set the visible property to "If(DataCardValue3.Value = true, true)," as seen in Figure 13-18. Repeat the process again by selecting the correct value for the Renewal toggle and setting the Contract Number field to hidden/shown based on the chosen value.

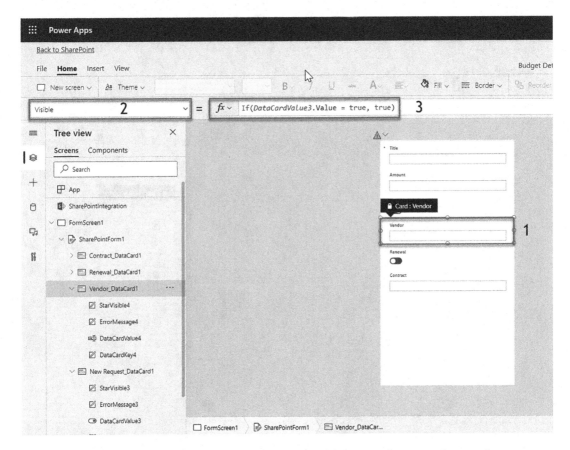

Figure 13-18. *Setting the visible property of a field based on conditional formatting*

Once completed, the form should look like Figure 13-19. To test functionality within the Power Apps IDE, hold down the Alt key and interact with the form. The fields should react to the chosen value for both New Request and Renewal toggle fields.

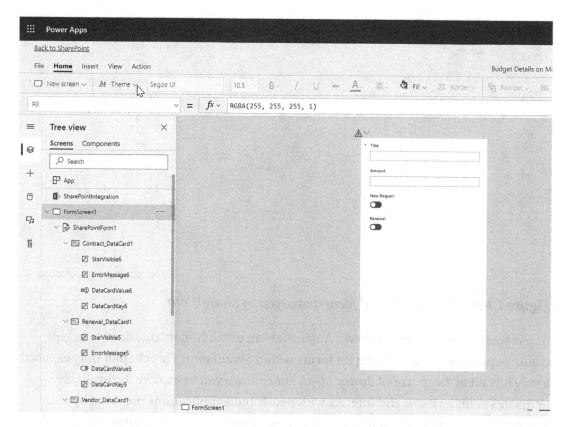

Figure 13-19. *The completed form edited in Microsoft Power Apps*

Once, you make the needed changes and are happy with the form, go to File ➤ Save. Once saved you will be able to publish back to the SharePoint list, by clicking "Publish to SharePoint." Once the form is published, navigate back to the SharePoint list, and click "New." The edited form will be displayed as seen in Figure 13-20.

Figure 13-20. *The completed form displayed in SharePoint*

As you can see, Microsoft Power Apps offers an extraordinary interface to begin crafting applications and editing list forms within SharePoint. This chapter only exposed a very tiny bit of the power of Power Apps. I encourage you to explore the available templates to understand and interact with nearly built applications provided by Microsoft. If you are interested in learning more about Power Apps, please take a look at *Beginning Power Apps: The Non-Developer's Guide to Building Business Applications,* Second Edition, by Tim Leung.

In the next chapter, we will summarize the key aspects of the applications and provide a very high-level plan to use them.

CHAPTER 14

Making Sense of It All

As you saw throughout this book, Microsoft 365 provides a comprehensive suite of apps to foster collaboration in the workplace. Collaboration is not just working on a document together but sharing information, working on a team, and managing aspects and artifacts in the workplace.

Microsoft 365 is Software as a Service (SaaS), for which a monthly license can be purchased. That license allows you to use the service. Because of this, Microsoft continually updates the applications and provides disaster recovery and continual uptime so that any downtime is mitigated.

Before I summarize each app and its intended use, remember that there is some overlap between the applications. Because of this, it can be challenging to choose the right application for the intended scenario, and at times it will feel like you made the wrong decision. Learning Microsoft 365 and using it are two different things, so my advice to you is to use Microsoft 365 as much as you can and just know that over time you will come to understand the nuances and be able to choose the right application.

SharePoint, OneDrive, Stream

This group of applications provide document, item, and video sharing and storage. These applications allow content to be easily shared with others, allow the ability to assign metadata, and allow for complex video sharing.

SharePoint is strongest when there is a need for structure and very organized data in a team environment. With SharePoint, a site can hold libraries, and those libraries can be defined with metadata columns. These columns in conjunction with document libraries and lists provide the structure that some teams require.

> **Best for: Structured sharing of documents/items in a team/ project setting**

© Ralph Mercurio and Brian Merrill 2021
R. Mercurio and B. Merrill, *Beginning Microsoft 365 Collaboration Apps*,
https://doi.org/10.1007/978-1-4842-6936-7_14

OneDrive, which is very similar in terms of function to SharePoint, is geared at personal storage of documents and sharing those items with people. In OneDrive, all content is stored in a single location and can be segmented via folders. Content in OneDrive can be shared with colleagues or external parties so that items can be part of a collaborative process.

Best for: Personal storage and sharing as needed with one or a few users

Microsoft Stream, which provides intelligent video storage in Microsoft 365, replaces the Microsoft 365 Video application. Videos can be organized into channels and shared throughout the enterprise or within specific groups. Stream introduces some new features generally absent from video platforms, such as facial recognition and video transcription in the premium license level. Facial recognition creates a People Map, which catalogs when a person's face is shown throughout the video. Transcription, while not perfect at all times, allows for the audio portion of the video to be transcribed into an editable transcript. These features happen automatically and do not require any intervention or execution from the uploader of the video.

Best for: Video management within the enterprise

Office

Microsoft Office, a cornerstone application of the work environment, is tightly integrated with Microsoft 365. With Microsoft 365, not only do you have access to the transitional Office install but you also have access to Office Online, which is the web-based version of Office. Office includes Outlook, Word, PowerPoint, Excel, OneNote, and Sway. These applications allow information workers to create and edit content.

Best for: Document creation and editing

Teams and Microsoft 365 Groups

Microsoft Teams provides a new and innovative way to work in the Microsoft suite. It is based on the concept of chat and does away with email. Members post to a channel and interact with other members via chat or video calls.

Best for: Group collaboration not centered on documents. Also allows for fluid communication (chat or video) with members.

Microsoft 365 Groups is an application mash-up of an Outlook inbox and calendar, SharePoint site, and OneNote notebook to provide a familiar toolset to its members. Microsoft 365 Groups is part of Outlook and currently only associable via Outlook.

Best for: Group collaboration centered on email and calendaring with the ability to store documents

Yammer

Yammer, an enterprise-level communication platform, allows news and updates to be posted to a single site for consumption. With Yammer, users can subscribe to Yammer groups, either public or private, and collaborate with them.

Best for: Social media–like tool to foster communication within an organization at any level

Planner and Forms

Microsoft Planner is a new way to assign and report on tasks. The application provides a central location for task management outside the typical task management apps (Outlook and SharePoint).

Best for: Assigning tasks and reporting on progress

Microsoft Forms allows for forms, quizzes, or surveys to be created to collect responses. Forms can be embedded within a SharePoint site, or a link to the form can be posted to be filled out.

Best for: Collecting data and tracking responses

Power Platform

The Power Platform consists of three applications: Power BI, Power Apps, and Power Automate. These applications are primarily used for data analysis and consumption, application development, and automation.

Power BI is used for data analysis and consumption. It has become the standard business intelligence tool and is very powerful as we discussed earlier.

Best for: Displaying business intelligence data and reports for end users to consume

Power Apps is an IDE (Interface Design Environment) where you create custom apps within Microsoft 365. These apps can be used to interact with users, connect data sources, and build Power Apps in a low-code manner.

Best for: Creating applications in a low-code environment for users to use and connect to data sources

Power Automate provides a workflow-like experience based on triggers and actions. Power Automate connects to a multitude of services, both Microsoft 365 and external third-party services.

Best for: Performing a repetitive task or getting approval based on a document or item

Conclusion

Thank you for both purchasing and reading the second edition of *Beginning Microsoft 365 Collaboration Apps*. I hope that it has answered many of your questions surrounding the collaboration applications and has provided a solid understanding of the Microsoft 365 platform. I also hope you feel confident with the platform and continue to explore the ever-changing Microsoft 365 platform.

Feel free to reach out to either Brian or myself on LinkedIn. We will try to respond as soon as we can. Good luck on your journey.

Index

P, Q, R

Printed in the United States
by Baker & Taylor Publisher Services